Studies in Language Variation:
semantics, syntax, phonology, pragmatics, social situations, ethnographic approaches

Ralph W. Fasold
Roger W. Shuy
Editors

Georgetown University Press, Washington, D.C. 20057

Library of Congress Cataloging in Publication Data

Colloquium on New Ways of Analyzing Variation,
    3d, Georgetown University, 1974.
    Studies in language variation.

    Papers from the Third Annual Colloquium on New
Ways of Analyzing Variation, held at Georgetown
University in Oct. 1974.
    Includes bibliographies.
    1. Language and languages--Variation--Congresses.
2. Pragmatics--Congresses. 3. Sociolinguistics--
Congresses. 4. Anthropological linguistics--
Congresses. I. Fasold, Ralph W. II. Shuy,
Roger W. III. Title.
P120.V37C6 1974   400   77-20689
ISBN 0-87840-209-8

International Standard Book Number: 0-87840-209-8

CONTENTS

VARIATION IN LANGUAGE PRAGMATICS

LANGUAGE VARIATION IN SOCIAL SITUATIONS

ETHNOGRAPHIC APPROACHES TO LANGUAGE VARIATION

INTRODUCTION

The articles in this volume were selected from papers presented
at the Third Annual Colloquium on New Ways of Analyzing Variation
(N-WAVE), held at Georgetown University School of Languages and
Linguistics in 1974. The N-WAVE colloquia provide a forum for
established and younger scholars to present their work on variation
in language. For the third colloquium, we were particularly interested in bringing together scholars who deal with variation from different perspectives. The result was a collection of papers in four areas.
Rather recently, many linguists have moved beyond the study of language isolated from its use and have examined the interaction of linguistic rules with the pragmatics of language in context. At the same
time, many scholars have taken a sociological approach to the structure of conversation and other communicative events. A number of
anthropologists are adding language variation to their traditional interest in language in relation to cultural phenomena. Linguists who work
in semantics, syntax, and phonology have also expanded their interests
to include language variation. We believe that the colloquium brought
together some of the best work in all four of these areas and that the
value of the conference can be extended to a wider audience by the
publication of this collection.

The emphases on language pragmatics, sociology, anthropology,
and more traditional linguistics provided a natural way to organize
the articles in this volume. The first section--on syntax, semantics,
and phonology--includes articles by Gregory Guy and Robert Berdan
on the theory of linguistic variation, by Mark Baltin and Donna Jo
Napoli on variation in syntax, and by James McCawley on language
acquisition. Two articles--one by Erica Garcia and Ricardo Otheguy,
and the other by David Zubin--apply William Diver's Form-Content
approach to linguistic variation. Martha Laferriere and Muriel
Saville attack the issue of variation in language change through time.

vii

In the section on language pragmatics, Ivan Sag and Jorge Hankamer explore the effect of pragmatics on anaphora and construct their arguments on the basis of some rather novel examples. Alice Davison and Bruce Fraser address the problem of how to account for indirect speech acts, a much-discussed issue in the study of language pragmatics. Gillian Michell's contribution deals with direct speech with respect to the analysis of sentence adverbs in explicit performative sentences. Alice Myers investigates the phenomenon of irony and Philip Tedeschi discusses the pragmatics of conditional sentences.

The section on language variation in social situations contains articles on the structure of conversation in observed speech events. Specific speech events are analyzed in Marilyn Merritt's article on service encounters and in the presentation by Lindsay Churchill and Susan Gray on auctions. The structure of speech events in which the investigator has exercised a certain amount of control are studied by Charlotte Linde and by Walt and Todd Wolfram.

Anthropological linguists have contributed a great deal to the understanding of language variation by applying the techniques of ethnography, and this emphasis is represented in the final section. Elinor Keenan examines variation in language use in Madagascar, while William Beeman looks at language variation in its cultural setting in Persian. Joel Sherzer has done the same in his study of the Cuna Indians of Panama. A fourth paper, by Paul Kay, presents an analysis of variation in English kinship semantics.

It is our hope that this volume, with its emphasis on variation in language as the object of study and on variation in disciplinary approach, will prove a valuable contribution to the understanding of language phenomena.

R. W. S.
R. W. F.

A NEW LOOK AT -t, -d DELETION

GREGORY R. GUY

University of Pennsylvania

In recent years one of the most studied variable phenomena in English phonology has been the rule deleting final stops from word-final consonant clusters. This is the rule which accounts for pronunciations such as bes' for best, and tol' for told. A very simple form of the final stop deletion rule is given in (1).

Final Stop-Deletion Rule
(1) $ → <∅>/C__##

This rule has been examined in many studies by Labov, Wolfram, Fasold, and others.[1] Most of these studies looked at Black English, where the rule is particularly prominent, but there is ample evidence that it is found in virtually every dialect of English. This paper reports the results of a new study of this phenomenon which was conducted as part of a research project supported by the National Science Foundation and directed by William Labov.[2]

If one considers rule (1) closely with regard to studying its application in natural speech, one finds that the vast majority of deletable stops falling under its scope are the apicals /t/ and /d/. Relatively few words in English have final consonant clusters ending in velar or labial stops. It is only the apical stops which can cluster with a full range of preceding consonants, including other stops. These distributional facts make it difficult to test the complete set of possible deletions implied by rule (1), since data are comparatively sparse on four of the stops thus characterized, namely /k, g, p, b/. Therefore, the present study was restricted to the examination of a rule of apical stop or -t, -d deletion, shown in simplified form in (2).

- $\underline{t}$, -$\underline{d}$ Deletion Rule

(2) $/\overline{t}, d/ \rightarrow \, <\emptyset>/C\_\_\#\#$

Rule (2), as it stands, of course incorporates none of what we know about the patterned variation in the application of this rule. The earlier studies mentioned have all demonstrated that it is conditioned by such factors as whether the cluster is mono- or bimorphemic, whether a following word begins with a vowel or a consonant, the nature of the consonant preceding the deletable segment, etc. To incorporate this information, we employ variable constraints on the rule, using the model and notation developed in Cedergren and Sankoff (1974).

This paper reports our results concerning only two main constraints on the rule, although there are several others which affect it. First, I am going to consider the morphemic status of the final stop. The affixation of a /t/ or /d/ signifying 'past tense' to verbs ending in consonants other than /t, d/ creates large numbers of clusters which are then subject to rule (2). Confirming the earlier studies already mentioned, we find that the resulting bimorphemic clusters, such as those in walked, fished, rained, are considerably more resistant to deletion than monomorphemic clusters such as those in act, best, or friend. A very plausible functional argument can be advanced here: these stops representing the -ed verb suffix are probably less subject to deletion because its effect would be to produce past tense forms of verbs which were everywhere indistinguishable from present tense forms (except in the third person singular). This finding can be expressed as a variable conditioning on the deletion rule according to the presence or absence of a morpheme boundary in the cluster, preceding the deletable stop.

However, a further complication is introduced by those irregular verbs which have both a stem vowel change and an alveolar stop suffix in the past tense, such as tell-told, keep-kept, leave-left, etc. The classification of these words as strong or weak verbs is ambiguous. They can be considered as having a derivational + boundary before the affixed -$\underline{t}$ or -$\underline{d}$, instead of the inflectional # boundary. [3]

These considerations give us a group of three conditioning factors according to what intervenes between the alveolar stop and the consonant preceding it. We have labelled them for computer analysis (and for mnemonic purposes) as M (monomorphemic), $\emptyset$ intervening; A (ambiguous), + boundary intervening; P (past tense), # boundary intervening. These three form a 'factor group' in Cedergren and Sankoff's terminology.

A second major constraint on this rule is the nature of the segment following the /t/ or /d/. All studies of this phenomenon have indicated that deletion is more likely to occur when a following word begins with a consonant than when it begins with a vowel. Thus more deletion is expected in phrases like best friend or told me than in best of all or told Alice. For this study we made a five-way distinction: consonants (coded K), liquids (U), glides (G), vowels (V), and pause--no following segment (Q). These also constituted a factor group for analysis with the Cedergren/Sankoff variable rule program.

A number of other constraints (all of lesser effect than the two just discussed) have been found significant for this rule: preceding segment, stress, speech style and tempo, etc. Although we did investigate several of these other constraints in our study, those results are not discussed here. This paper focuses primarily on two interesting findings, namely a dialectal difference between New Yorkers and Philadelphians in their treatment of following pause, and second, the existence of two discrete lects in the treatment of the ambiguous verbs.

The procedures for a study of this type are discussed in Cedergren and Sankoff (1974) and in Guy (1974). To those treatments I add only that in the present study, data were analyzed first individually for each speaker, and then subsequently in various groupings defined by extralinguistic facts such as geography, age, ethnic group, etc. Thus we were able to obtain and compare precisely quantified information on both individuals and social groups.[4]

The effect of following pause. One of the most interesting findings in our study concerns the effect of a following pause, which we labelled the Q factor. This constraint has been treated in several different ways in the previous studies. In Labov's early studies, only two following environments were distinguished: vowel and non-vowel. This approach grouped following pauses together with following consonants, indicating that both promoted deletion. Wolfram (1969), however, distinguished following environments of consonant and nonconsonant, thus grouping pauses together with vowels as conservative environments. Fasold (1972) considered the three categories separately, and reported that pause was similar in effect to consonant--both promoted deletion.

In the present study we tried to examine the fine structure of this constraint more closely. As noted earlier, we coded separately the five different factors: consonant, liquid, glide, vowel, and pause. From the results of previous studies, we expected that the four segmental factors would form a fairly tight ordering: consonants should promote deletion more than liquids, liquids more than glides, and glides more than vowels. This hierarchy can be neatly formalized using the distinctive feature notation shown in rule (3).

-t̪-d̪ Deletion Rule with variable constraints

$$(3) \quad /t, d/ \rightarrow \; <\emptyset>/C \left\langle \begin{matrix} \emptyset \\ + \\ \# \end{matrix} \right\rangle \underline{\quad} \#\# \left\langle \begin{matrix} [+cons] \\ [-voc] \end{matrix} \right\rangle$$

Using the Chomsky and Halle feature assignments for the four classes of segments (K = [+cons, -voc], U = [+cons, +voc], G = [-cons, -voc], V = [-cons, +voc]), this rule would correctly assign the expected ordering.

The following pause, however, has no obvious position in this constraint hierarchy. It is defined (if at all) by a totally separate feature ([-seg]), and it is impossible to say a priori where this constraint should be ordered. In fact, from a theoretical viewpoint, its constraint effect appears rather arbitrary. This becomes important in the light of some suggestions about variation by Kiparsky (1972). Kiparsky prefers not to treat processes such as -t̪-d̪ deletion as 'rules of grammar' at all, but rather as the result of 'general functional conditions impinging on speech performance'. The effect of such an approach would of course be to make it unnecessary to investigate variation of this type. For the K-U-G-V hierarchy, and for the M-P ordering discussed elsewhere in this paper, such 'general, functional' explanations may be possible. But it is not clear how the Q factor would fit into such a system.

The group results on nineteen Philadelphians and four New Yorkers in our study for the following environment factor group are presented in Table 1.

TABLE 1. Group values for New Yorkers and Philadelphians.

	K	U	G	V	Q	No. of tokens
19 Philadelphians	1.00	.77	.59	.40	.19	2886
4 New Yorkers	.82	1.00	.74	.47	.76	529

These figures represent the probabilistic contribution to rule application which each factor makes when it appears in the rule environment. A value of 1.00 most favors deletion, but does not imply categorical deletion, since other factors will also impinge on the rule and all the relevant factor values will be multiplied together to obtain an overall probability of rule application in a specified environment.[5]

In Table 1 the ordering of the values for the four segmental factors, K, U, G, and V, are as expected and are the same for both groups. (The one exception is the high U value for the New Yorkers. This deviation is probably due to insufficient data--there are only 17 instances of following liquid in the New Yorkers' data set, or about 3 percent. My studies have indicated that to obtain reliable results, a factor value should be based on 30 or more instances of the factor in question (Guy 1974).) However, the Q values for the two groups are quite different. The New Yorkers have a very high Q value, higher than both their G and V values. But for the Philadelphians, Q is the lowest value of the five. In short, Table 1 makes a case for a dialect difference between our two populations as regards their treatments of a following pause: for Philadelphians it inhibits -t̲, -d̲ deletion, while for New Yorkers it promotes it.

These relationships that are apparent for the group figures presented in Table 1 also hold for all the individuals who make up these groups, as Table 2 demonstrates.

TABLE 2. Pairwise comparison of constraints on -t̲, -d̲ deletion for 19 Philadelphians and 4 New Yorkers.

K				
12-1-4				
2-0-2	U			
15-1-3	11-1-5			
2-0-2	2-0-2	G		
16-1-2	14-0-3	14-0-5		
4-0-0	3-0-1	3-0-1	V	
19-0-0	15-0-2	17-0-1	18-0-1	
2-0-2	2-0-2	2-0-2	0-0-4	Q

Each group of three numbers shows respectively the number of individuals who had the first factor greater than, equal to, and less than the second factor for that cell. In each cell, the top line represents Philadelphians, and the bottom line represents New Yorkers.

The sets of three numbers in this table show, for each comparison of a pair of factors, the number of individuals in a group who had the first factor respectively greater than, equal to, or less than the second factor. In each cell the first row of figures represents the Philadelphians and the second row the New Yorkers. Examining the lower right cell in the table, one finds that 18 of 19 Philadelphians had a Q value lower than their V value, while all four New Yorkers had a Q value higher than their V value. Turning to the cell which compares K and V, in the lower left corner, one notes that all nineteen Philadelphians have Q less than K, while 2 New Yorkers have a Q value greater than K, indicating that for them, following pause promotes the rule more than any other following environment. It seems clear that there is a dialectal difference between Philadelphians and New Yorkers concerning the treatment of this variable constraint.

Finding such a dialectal difference makes it clearly impossible to explain this constraint by 'general functional conditions' such as Kiparsky has proposed. If the effect of a following pause on the -t, -d deletion rule is arbitrarily defined for a given dialect, it must be learned by children acquiring the dialect and it must be accounted for in a grammar of the dialect. And what is arbitrary and learned is clearly not attributable to any universal condition. Thus it will be impossible to write 'descriptively adequate' grammars which do not pay attention to at least some of the facts of variation.

It has been pointed out to me by Ralph Fasold that the discovery of this dialect difference between New Yorkers and Philadelphians suggests an explanation for one puzzling fact about previous studies of this phenomenon reported in the literature. As was noted earlier, Wolfram in his Detroit study classed following pause together with following vowel as being maximally conservative in affecting the -t, -d deletion rule. This is the only treatment of any Black English dialect which suggests that Q is a conservative environment. All other studies of Black English have indicated that it is generally a high-Q dialect--following pause promotes deletion, just as it does for the white New Yorkers in the present study. Perhaps Wolfram's treatment was influenced by the fact that he is a white Philadelphian, and presumably a low Q speaker, and therefore his phonological intuitions would readily suggest to him an analysis indicating that pause is a conservative environment.

The high-A lects. Let us now consider the 'morphemic status' factor group, M-A-P. Here one also finds two discrete lects in the treatment of one of the factors, namely the A factor, the ambiguous verbs. Such a two-lect pattern for this factor is first suggested in Labov (1975) by data from four speakers. These lects are not geographically characterizable. However, as we shall see, they may be definable along other dimensions. One of these lects is exemplified by a group of people who have an A value falling between their M and P values. Functionally speaking, we may say they have recognized the 'ambiguity' of these verbs, retaining the -ts, -ds more often than those in monomorphemic words, since they do represent here the -ed suffix, but deleting them more often than those in regular past tense verb forms since the past tense morpheme is also encoded elsewhere in the A words, namely in the vowel change. More formally one could say that the + boundary has only part of the inhibitory effect on the rule that the # boundary has.

However, there is another group of speakers who consistently have a very high A value, indicating that for these speakers A promotes the rule as much as or more than M does. These people have apparently begun to obscure this separate class of irregular verbs, throwing its contents in with the ordinary strong or ablauting verbs. Thus it appears that this group is beginning to identify tell, sleep, keep, etc. as vowel changing verbs with past tense forms toll, slep, kep, just like feed-fed or swim-swam. The result of this is that these words have final /t, d/ deleted as often as or more often than monomorphemic words. This shows up in our variable rule program analyses as an A value equal to or greater than M.

The evidence for these two lects can be found in the distribution of individual A factor values shown in Figure 1. This figure shows, for the twenty Philadelphians and New Yorkers from whom any A words were obtained, the number of individuals whose A values fall within the given ranges. It is a clearly bimodal distribution--one set of speakers clusters around .70, while the other puts A at 1.00, indicating that for them it favors deletion as much as or more than any other factor in its factor group. Data quantity does not affect this pattern at all, nor does geographical origin of speaker. Our four New Yorkers, for example, are evenly divided between the two modes. These data exactly parallel the bimodal distribution suggested in Labov (1975), which reports two speakers with A values of 1.00, while the remaining two have values of .68 and .65, respectively.

FIGURE 1. Distribution of A values.

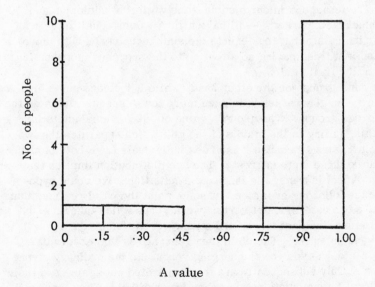

A value

When the speakers with the higher A values are considered as a group, an interesting pattern emerges. The tendency to delete /t, d/ preferentially appears to be typical of the children in our sample.

This can be seen from the figures given in Table 3, which compares the group values for four children (from King of Prussia, a Philadelphia suburb) with values for teenage and adult speakers.

TABLE 3. Comparison of morphemic status factor values.

	M	A	P
Four children (King of Prussia, Pa.) Ages 8-12	.96	1.00	.35
Franny P. (Philadelphia) Age 14	1.00	1.00	(0.0)
Three teenagers (New York City) All Age 15	1.00	1.00	.30
Nine adults (Philadelphia) Ages 21-58	1.00	.82	.39

For our youngest speakers, ages 8-12, A is the highest value in this factor group, indicating that these /t, d/s either undergo deletion preferentially, or aren't present in underlying form to begin with. The teenagers in our sample--one white Philadelphian and three black New Yorkers[6]--all have high A values equal to their M values, indicating that they equate the ambiguous verbs with monomorphemic words, paying no attention to the supposed morphemic status of the final /t, d/.

The adult group, on the other hand, while it includes some high A speakers, [7] in general tends to have more low A speakers than do the younger age groups. The group A value of .82 for nine adults indicates this, falling in the middle of the gulf which separates the two modes in Figure 1 because it includes individuals from both modes.

What do these facts suggest? The age distribution implies that the high A lect is a stage in language acquisition. We could hypothesize the following evolution: at some point the child realizes that there are two categories of verbs: weak verbs which take an -ed suffix to form the past tense, and strong verbs which take a vowel change and no suffix. The child then generalizes this observation, putting all the A-type vowel-changing verbs into the ordinary strong category. Only subsequently are they separated out again, and their exceptional intermediate nature taken into account. The teenagers' data suggests that the exceptional A alternants are at first learned holistically, without a morphemic boundary separating the dental stop from the root. Therefore they undergo the -t, -d deletion rule at exactly the same rate as other monomorphemic words. In this hypothesis the identification of the final stop in A words with the -ed suffix would be the final step in the development within the idiolect of this exceptional category. Those low A speakers who arrive at such an analysis are making a discrete adjustment to their grammar. The sharp bimodality of Figure 1 clearly demonstrates this. The fact that virtually no one has an A value falling in the interval .75-.90 between the two modes is a strong argument in favor of the existence of a quantum modification in the grammars of the low A speakers: a 'rule' to account for this class of 'exceptions'.

But what does a speaker gain by adding this rule? Not much, it would appear. It is a very limited rule applying only to a small class of high frequency items. Apparently this rule addition is functionally and practically equivalent to the alternative treatment which the high A speakers use: simply learning each irregular A type past tense individually--which probably has to be done for all strong verbs anyway. The roughly equal distribution of the two lects in the adult population suggests that they are roughly equal in terms of efficiency, compactness of representation, or whatever evaluative metric the mental grammar uses. 8

Conclusion. The foregoing raises a number of issues which are too large in scope to be fully treated in this paper. I hope, however, to have demonstrated the following points. First, I have documented a case where phonological variation cannot be accounted for by the sort of 'general functional conditions' suggested by Kiparsky, but rather probably must be considered a 'rule of grammar'. Second, I have described a situation where two distinct linguistic strategies regarding morphemic analysis produce two discrete, observable lects. Finally, I have tried to show the utility--indeed, the necessity--of the quantitative study of speech for advances in the understanding of linguistic structure. Quantitative study will lead us not only to the observation of new linguistic facts like (dia-)lectal differences, but also to new conclusions about the nature of the mental grammar and even the strategies used in its construction.

NOTES

1. The major treatments of final stop deletion are: Fasold (1972), Labov, Cohen, Robins, and Lewis (1968), Wolfram (1969, 1971), and Guy (1974). Several articles by Labov, Summerlin's dissertation, and Griffin, Guy, and Sag (1973) all deal with the issue too, but in more limited contexts.

2. The research reported here was supported by National Science Foundation grant GS-36382X, 'The Quantitative Study of Linguistic

Change in Progress'. I would like to thank William Labov, Peg Griffin, Sharon Snyder, John Baugh, Carolyn Fuller, Bruce Johnson, Arvilla Payne, and Ralph Fasold for their suggestions, ideas, assistance, and support. I am sure the positive influence of William Labov is evident throughout this study.

3. Chomsky and Halle use the terms 'Formant Boundary' (+) and 'Word Boundary' (#). Ralph Fasold has called our 'Ambiguous' verbs (with the + boundary) 'Semi-weak' verbs.

4. The separate examination of individuals in variation studies, the necessity of which was first demonstrated very effectively by Bickerton (1971, 1973a, 1973b), is essential for the discovery of (dia-)lectal differences such as those to be discussed here.

5. For a detailed discussion of variable rule theory and notation, see Cedergren and Sankoff (1974).

6. These three New York teenagers are black Harlem peer-group members, recently added to my sample and not included in the figures for New Yorkers mentioned elsewhere in this paper.

7. The distribution of the two A lects among adult speakers may exhibit social class stratification, with the high A lect being more typical of working-class speakers. At present I do not have the data to demonstrate this, however, so it must remain a tentative conjecture.

8. Many of the ideas in this section were developed in discussions with Tony Kroch, for whose assistance I would like to express my profound appreciation.

REFERENCES

Bailey, Charles-James N. and Roger W. Shuy, eds. 1973. New ways of analyzing variation in English. Washington, D.C., Georgetown University Press.

Bickerton, Derek. 1971. Inherent variability and variable rules. Foundations of Language 7.457-492.

Bickerton, Derek. 1973a. Quantitative vs. dynamic paradigms: The case of Montreal que. In: Bailey and Shuy. 23-43.

Bickerton, Derek. 1973b. On the nature of a creole continuum. Lg. 49.3.

Cedergren, Henrietta J. and David Sankoff. 1974. Variable rules: Performance as a statistical reflection of competence. Lg. 50. 333-55.

Fasold, Ralph. 1972. Tense marking in Black English. Arlington, Va., Center for Applied Linguistics.

Griffin, Peg, Gregory Guy, and Ivan Sag. 1973. Variable analysis of variable data. In: Language in the context of space, time and society. University of Michigan Papers in Linguistics 1.2.

Guy, Gregory R. 1974. Variation in the group and the individual:
The case of final stop deletion. Pennsylvania Working Papers on
Linguistic Change and Variation 1.4.

Guy, Gregory R. 1975. Use and applications of the Cedergren/
Sankoff variable rule program. In: Analyzing variation in language. Edited by Ralph W. Fasold and Roger W. Shuy. Washington, D. C., Georgetown University Press. 59-69.

Kiparsky, Paul. 1972. Explanation in phonology. In: Goals of
linguistic theory. Edited by S. Peters. Englewood Cliffs, N. J.,
Prentice-Hall.

Labov, William. 1967. Some sources of reading problems for Negro
speakers of non-standard English. In: New directions in elementary English. Edited by A. Frazier. Champaign, Ill.,
National Council of Teachers of English. 140-167.

Labov, William. 1969. Contraction, deletion, and inherent variability of the English copula. Lg. 45.715-762.

Labov, William. 1975. The quantitative study of linguistic structure. In: The Nordic languages and modern linguistics 2. Edited
by K. H. Dahlstedt. Stockholm: Almqvist and Wiksell International.

Labov, William, Paul Cohen, Clarence Robins, and John Lewis.
1968. A study of the non-standard English of Negro and Puerto
Rican speakers in New York City. Cooperative Research Report
3288. Vols. 1 and 2. New York, Columbia University.

Summerlin, NanJo C. 1972. A dialect study: Affective parameters
in the deletion and substitution of consonants in the deep South.
Unpublished Florida State University dissertation.

Wolfram, Walt. 1969. A sociolinguistic description of Detroit
Negro speech. Washington, D. C., Center for Applied Linguistics.

Wolfram, Walt. 1971. Overlapping influence in the English of
second generation Puerto Rican teenagers in Harlem. Final
report on OE grant 3-70-0033(508). Washington, D. C., Center
for Applied Linguistics.

POLYLECTAL COMPREHENSION AND
THE POLYLECTAL GRAMMAR

ROBERT BERDAN

SWRL Educational Research and Development

In theory, generative grammar makes no claims to being either a
grammar of production or a grammar of comprehension. It is conceived of as neutral with respect to speaker or hearer. In practice,
argumentation tends to be analogized to the speaker and to production.
Data on comprehension have played a minimal role in our understanding of grammar. Thus it is not surprising to find, even among linguists, inferences based on comprehension that are highly problematic.

In this paper two claims from comprehension are discussed. The
first is a claim made by certain educationalists and psychologists,
notably Hall and Turner (1974). They reason that because children
from ethnic minorities can hear a Standard English sentence, translate it, and repeat back the appropriate dialectal equivalent, educational problems of the children cannot be accounted for by language
differences. Obviously, if the children can repeat the semantic
equivalent, they comprehend the language of instruction. The second
claim is most explicitly articulated by Bailey (1973:17, 23-24). He
argues that speakers exposed to more than one lect have polylectal
comprehension, and therefore necessarily polylectal grammars.

It will be convenient for the present to define comprehension rather
casually as the hearer's act of associating a semantic structure with
a phonetic string. A communication is successful if the semantic
structure of the hearer is equivalent to that of the speaker. If it is
not, it can be said that they have miscommunicated, or that the hearer
has miscomprehended the speaker.

In the real world, comprehension is a complex event. In comprehending statements, persons draw not just on their linguistic knowledge but on all of their knowledge of the real world. Further, as linguists know, but seem at times to forget, linguistic knowledge is highly complex, including semantic relations, syntactic rules, phonological rules, and a knowledge of possible lexical items. The combination of linguistic knowledge and real world knowledge frequently introduces redundancy into the message of any particular sentence. Comprehending a sentence does not necessarily imply comprehending all of the intricacies of its syntax. To comprehend a particular sentence it may be sufficient, in real world contexts, to understand the meaning of the lexical items without comprehending any of the implicit rules of syntax. In some limited contexts, a message is so culturally constrained that it is not necessary to have any linguistic understanding of the utterance to make an appropriate response.

Communication between persons necessarily involves a discontinuity. The formal attributes of the grammar of the speaker are not accessible to the hearer. The hearer knows only what can be inferred from the sentences he hears. The speaker and the hearer may or may not share identical grammars and they have no direct way of determining this. At best they can attempt to assess whether or not they have comprehended each other.

Consider for the moment the minimal case of one speaker, one hearer, and the utterance of one sentence. The speaker may or may not share the grammar of the hearer. The hearer may or may not comprehend the speaker. There are thus four logically possible communication situations, as shown in the 2 x 2 table in Figure 1. While all the combinations are logically possible, it remains to be shown that they are linguistically plausible.

FIGURE 1. Possible relations between comprehension and grammars.

Grammars of speaker and hearer

		Same	Different
Comprehension	Yes	Situation 1	Situation 2
	No	Situation 4	Situation 3

The first situation is perhaps what would be considered the unmarked case; the grammars of the speaker and the hearer, or at least the relevant portions, are identical, and comprehension takes

place. The second situation may be somewhat less obvious, but
would be predicted if there exist weakly equivalent grammars, i. e.
grammars generating the same set of strings but assigning them
different derivational histories. Such grammars could differ without
impeding comprehension.

One example is got as a verb of possession. For many speakers
got is understood as possessive only with auxiliary have, as in (1a, b):

(1a) My friend h̸a̸s got a new car.
(1b) My friends h̸a̸ve got a new car.

Many of the speakers who produce the sentences of (1) allow for
deletion of contracted have (2b), but not of contracted has (2a)
(McDavid 1967:10):

(2a) *My friend h̸a̸s̸ got a new car.
(2b)   My friends h̸a̸v̸e̸ got a new car.

The use of possessive got for many other speakers, particularly
black Americans, is quite different. For these speakers, it is a
regular main verb (Berdan 1973) which negates with do (3) and questions with do (4).

(3) My friends don't got a new car.
(4) Do my friends got a new car?

For some of these speakers who use agreement markers in the
present tense, got can be inflected:

(5) My friend gots a new car.

The speaker who utters (2b), using a grammar where have-deletion
operates, will be comprehended perfectly by a hearer whose grammar only has got as a regular main verb, giving (6):[1]

(6) My friends d̸o̸ got a new car.

This would then be a case where the grammars are different, but
comprehension exists.

The situation in cross-dialect communication is not always as
fortuitous as the one just described. Differences in grammars may
also result in differences in comprehension, Situation 3. Sentence
(6) is phonetically indistinguishable from (2b). It is also indistinguishable from (7):

(7) My friend h̷a̷s got a new car.   (=1a)

In this environment, as in most, contracted <u>has</u> is not perceptibly
different from the plural morpheme (Palmer 1968:32). The sentence
is ambiguous across dialects. Thus (7) uttered by a <u>have-got</u> speaker
may be understood by a main-verb <u>got</u> hearer to be an utterance of
(6). In this case miscomprehension occurs. The nature of the miscomprehension is made apparent by the tag questions in (8), which
provide disambiguation.

(8a) My friend h̷a̷s got a new car, $\begin{Bmatrix} \text{hasn't} \\ \text{doesn't} \end{Bmatrix}$ he?

(8b) My friends d̷o̷ got a new car, don't they?

The nature of the miscommunication would be, in most cases, trivial,
and the parties may never become aware of its existence. At some
subsequent point, however, it may become apparent that a miscommunication has occurred. For example, the hearer, comprehending
plural (6) rather than the speaker's singular (7), might ask a question
like (9a). The response from the speaker of (7) is likely to be a very
confused (9b):

(9a) Which one gets it on Saturday nights?
(9b) Which one what?

As far as the speaker is concerned, no plural exists in the conversation, and (9a) has no possible referent. By this point the source of
the miscommunication could be totally obscured.

The fourth possible situation in Figure 1 seems to be not at all
infrequent in actual communication: speaker and hearer share the
same grammar, but they fail to comprehend each other. There is
another sentence that is phonetically indistinguishable from (2b), (6),
and (7). This is sentence (10) where <u>got</u> is the regular past tense of
<u>get,</u> meaning <u>obtained</u>.

(10) My friends got a new car (didn't they)

The grammar of the speaker of (7) also generates (10); thus both
readings are possible within a single lect. Potential for this type of
situation occurs whenever a single string has more than one possible
derivational history associated with it within a single grammar.

Given the linguistic possibility of all four situations, it is apparent
that from many cases of comprehension, or lack of it, there can be
no direct arguments for similarity or difference of grammars.

In all the examples discussed thus far, it has been assumed that comprehension is necessarily consistent with the syntactic cues of a surface string. There may be several different ways of comprehending a sentence, but the possible semantic structures are those predicted by the syntactic and lexical form of the sentence. However, in the actual process of comprehending, the hearer must integrate many cues besides those provided by the syntax. In particular, the semantic cues of one portion of a sentence may override syntactic cues in another portion, thus influencing comprehension. This point can be illustrated with experimental data.

It is possible to determine how a hearer comprehends a particular sentence by observing the tag question he constructs for it. At least it is possible to determine what the hearer comprehends to be the number, person, and gender of the subject, and what he comprehends to be the tense and aspect of the verb. The readings of the potentially ambiguous got sentences are uniquely disambiguated by their tag questions, as (8a, b) and (10). The pronominalized equivalent of the sentential subject is explicitly marked for number; if third singular, it is also marked for gender. Further, the carrier of tense and aspect marking is much more immune from phonological deletions in the tag than it is in the full sentence. [2]

The following data derive from a study in which four classes of undergraduates at California State University, Long Beach, listened to 60 potentially ambiguous sentences and constructed tag questions for them. [3] Two classes were of students enrolled in the Educational Opportunities Program. All of these students identified themselves as black. Two other English composition classes were largely Anglo and only students who identified themselves as Anglo are included here. The sentences were sequenced in two random orders and read by the author. Each order was heard by one class of blacks and one class of Anglos. Students made their responses by checking one of twelve possible verb alternatives and one of six possible pronouns for each item.

Like contracted has, contracted is is often phonetically indistinguishable from the plural morpheme. Thus the sequence [frɛnz] in (11a) with contracted is is indistinguishable from the plural [frɛnz] in (11b).

(11a) Her best friend ís playing jump rope.
(11b) Her best friends are playing jump rope.

There is, of course, no sentential ambiguity because of the plural copula are in (11b). But not everybody says (11b). There are many speakers who use instead the semantically equivalent (12), with deleted copula.

(12) Her best friends a̶r̶e̶ playing jump rope.

Sentence (12) with plural subject is phonetically identical to (11a). Tag questions again function to disambiguate in (13a, b):

(13a) Her best friend i̶s playing jump rope, isn't she.
(13b) Her best friends a̶r̶e̶ playing jump rope, aren't they.

On hearing sentence (11a) or (12), speakers of a dialect that does not allow copula deletion could understand them both only as (13a). Speakers of a dialect that optionally deletes the copula would find the sentence ambiguous, with either (13a) or (13b) as possible interpretations.

For the sentence, <u>Her best [frɛnz] playing jump rope</u>, all 25 of the Anglo students provided <u>isn't she</u> or <u>isn't he</u> as a tag, showing that they understood the sentence as (11a). So did all but two of the 26 black students. Such a difference is not significant. This suggests either that the copula-deleting dialect is not well represented in the sample, or that this item is simply skewed toward a singular reading. It appears to be possible to change semantic and contextual cues in an ambiguous sentence to make one reading more plausible than another without making either reading ungrammatical. For example, super-latives like <u>best</u> seem to facilitate a singular reading, but still allow plurals, as in (14).

(14) They are my best friends.

Also, the singular possessive pronoun <u>her</u> would seem to facilitate a singular reading, while a plural pronoun like <u>their</u> would increase the possibility of a plural reading.

In order to explore the effects of contextual cues, the four sentences of (15) were included among the test items.

(15a) Her best friend's playing jump rope.
(15b) Her friend's playing jump rope.
(15c) Their best friend's playing jump rope.
(15d) Their friend's playing jump rope.

It was predicted that order of magnitude of influencing a singular reading would be in the sequence of (15a) to (15d). The possessive pronoun with overt number would exert a stronger influence than the superlative adjective, with its weak implication of singularity.

Table 1 gives the percent of singular responses for each sentence in each classroom. The prediction of order of effect was confirmed in all four classrooms. In each class the singular possessive pronoun facilitated a singular understanding of the sentence. So to a lesser extent did the superlative adjective.

TABLE 1. Percent of singular interpretations of four auxiliary be sentences.

	Anglo 1 N=12	Anglo 2 N=13	Black 1 N=12	Black 2 N=14
(a) Her best friend[z]	100	100	100	85
(b) Her friend[z]	100	92	83	64
(c) Their best friend[z]	58	77	36	21
(d) Their friend[z]	33	54	25	7

It had been predicted that this would be found in the black classes, but not in the Anglo classes. The people who were expected to be susceptible to this kind of contextual conditioning were only those people for whom the sentences would be ambiguous: persons who could delete auxiliary is and are. What was not expected was the large number of plural readings, particularly for sentence (d), from a population not known to allow this deletion.

It appears that the relationship between comprehension and grammar is less direct than might have been anticipated. For some informants, contextual cues, such as the plurality of a possessive pronoun, are sufficient to override syntactic cues such as the absence of a plural copula. Compounding of contextual cues increases the effect. The magnitude of the conditioning effect is smaller in the Anglo classrooms than in the black classrooms. It appears that the influence of contextual cues is stronger when they do not conflict with syntactic cues than when they do conflict.

The pattern found for groups obtains for individuals as well. The hierarchy of contextual weighting predicts that individuals will use one of the five patterns shown in the columns of Figure 2. Some individuals will understand all of the sentences as singular, some will understand all as plural, and the rest will use one of the three other patterns out of the remaining fourteen logically possible patterns.

FIGURE 2. Patterns of interpretations of four auxiliary be sentences.

Sentence	Pattern 1	2	3	4	5
(a) Her best friend[z]	Sing.	Sing.	Sing.	Sing.	Plural
(b) Her friend[z]	Sing.	Sing.	Sing.	Plural	Plural
(c) Their best friend[z]	Sing.	Sing.	Plural	Plural	Plural
(d) Their friend[z]	Sing.	Plural	Plural	Plural	Plural

Most of the individuals do conform to these predictions; 83 percent of the blacks and 92 percent of the Anglos evidenced one of the five patterns in Figure 2. The percentage of the population in each ethnic group using each of the five patterns is shown in Figure 3. Other individuals are randomly distributed across the nonpredicted patterns.

FIGURE 3. Percent of individuals of each ethnicity showing each pattern.

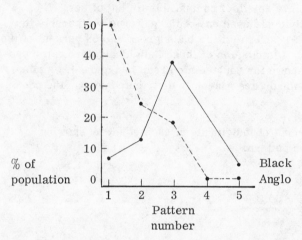

This patterning of contextual influence is not an isolated phenomenon in these data. The test included four more sentences.

(16a) His favorite horse[ɨz] got long legs.
(16b) His horse[ɨz] got long legs.
(16c) Their favorite horse[ɨz] got long legs.
(16d) Their horse[ɨz] got long legs.

Here the ambiguity rests on the possibility of using got as a possessive verb without auxiliary has or have. For some speakers got is a regular main verb that requires no have auxiliary. Other speakers who use have got can delete have, apparently by phonological processes. Speakers who, for one reason or another, can use got without auxiliary can interpret the [Z] morpheme as a syllabic plural marker on horse; other speakers who require an auxiliary with possessive got will interpret the [z] morpheme as the contracted form of has. The two interpretations result in the tags (17a) and (17b), respectively.

(17a) His favorite horse[ɨz] got long legs, don't they?

(17b) His favorite horse[ɨz] got long legs, hasn't/doesn't he?

As with the deleted copula case, the perception of singularity for the four sentences conformed to the predicted hierarchy in all four classrooms: in each group, more individuals understood (16a) as singular, than did (16b), than did (16c), than (16d). The effect of the singular or plural possessive pronoun is the same as was previously observed; the adjective <u>favorite</u>, though not morphologically a superlative, appears to have an effect comparable to that of <u>best</u>.

Again, most individuals used one of the patterns comparable to those in Figure 1: 91 percent of the black group and 88 percent of the Anglo group did so. Distribution of these individuals across the predicted patterns is shown for each ethnic group in Figure 4. Again, the remaining individuals are randomly distributed across the nonpredicted patterns.

FIGURE 4. Percent of individuals of each ethnicity showing each pattern.

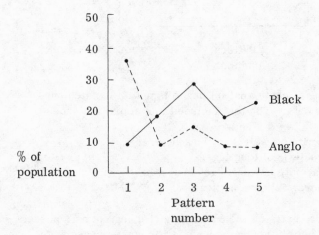

The populations are clearly distinct in one respect. Most of the Anglos show no sensitivity to these conditioning factors, but most of the blacks do. Almost half of the Anglos understood all of the sentences to be singular, but only about 8% of the black listeners did. For the <u>be</u> sentences that difference was greater than for the <u>have</u> sentences. Given that many Anglos delete <u>have</u> in production, but few delete <u>are</u> and <u>is</u> (cf. Wolfram 1974), this is not surprising.

There are many other sources of potential ambiguities and miscomprehensions across dialects. For example, there is a set of verbs in English that has the same form in the present tense and in the past tense, e.g. cut, hit, put. However, a sentence like (18a) is unambiguously past tense for many speakers; if it were present tense they would use an agreement morpheme as in (18b).

(18a) Everyday the teacher put up new pictures.
(18b) Everyday the teacher puts up new pictures.

Many speakers in the black community, however, do not require the use of that agreement morpheme in the present tense. For them (18a) is ambiguous, and can be disambiguated as either (19a) or (19b).

(19a) Everyday the teacher put up a new picture, didn't she.
(19b) Everyday the teacher put up a new picture,
$\begin{Bmatrix} \text{doesn't} \\ \text{don't} \end{Bmatrix}$ she.

The tag question task included five sentences of this type. Each of the sentences was weighted toward present tense with devices such as adverbial every day. Figure 5 shows the distribution of past tense comprehensions in each of the ethnic groups. About half of the black students understood none of the five sentences as past tense. On the other hand, almost half of the Anglo students understood all five sentences to be past tense. Among the individual sentences there were no notable differences in the proportions of past tense tags.

FIGURE 5. Percent of individuals of each ethnicity by number of past tense responses for unmarked verbs.

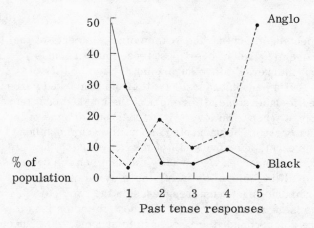

A similar situation can be created when the past tense marker is masked by assimilation with a following dental. Speakers who do not require the agreement morpheme could thus use either (20a) or (20b); speakers who do require the agreement morpheme would only use (20a).

    (20a) My sister always walked to school, didn't she.
    (20b) My sister always walk to school, {don't / doesn't} she.

The percent of each ethnic group giving 0 to 5 past tense responses for the five masked past tense items is shown in Figure 6. The differentiation across ethnic groups is comparable to that shown in Figure 5.

FIGURE 6. Percent of individuals of each ethnicity by number of past tense responses in masking environments.

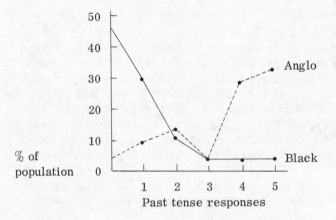

This could be expected, given that the grammatical elements of the ambiguity are the same: lack of overt past tense markers and present agreement markers. More surprising is the stability of individual scores. If a person understood all of the unmarked verbs as past, he tended to understand all or most of the masked past tense constructions as past tense. However, if he understood some of the unmarked pasts as present, he understood about the same number of masked pasts as present. For over half of the individuals, the number of past tense responses was exactly the same on the two sets of sentences. For all but four of the rest, there was a difference of only one in the number of past tense responses on the two sets.

    The inferences being made here from tag question indications of how sentences are comprehended are not hard to support. Extraneous responses to these sentences were minimal, despite the large number of possible tags available to students. In other words, virtually all

responses are amenable to linguistic explanation. Where the ambiguity involved singular and plural differences, there are attested
grammars with and without copula deletion. Where the ambiguity
involved tense, it could be predicted from the known existence of
grammars that do and do not employ an agreement morpheme.

More interesting, however, is the support of inferences between
the comprehension of ambiguous sentences and the grammars for the
individuals involved. As has been shown, there is no absolute relationship in all cases between comprehension and grammars. However, in the past tense sentences there is very strong evidence of a
direct relationship. Formation of the tag question is itself an act of
language production. Of particular interest here is the possibility
that present tense singular tags may or may not be marked for agreement. Thus in (19b) and (20b) there is the possibility of either don't
she or doesn't she as a tag. Summing across all 60 test items,
three-fourths of the black students and one-fourth of the Anglo students gave at least one present tense singular tag without agreement.
Each of these students who constructed tags without agreement also
gave tags that indicate a comprehension of present tense without
agreement. They are not randomly distributed with respect to
present tense comprehensions; they are exclusively in the half of the
population that perceived most of the sentences as present tense:
the left-most columns of Figures 5 and 6. There seems to be a
direct relationship in this instance between production and comprehension.

I return now to the two claims mentioned initially. The peda-
gogical claim is summarized by Hall and Turner (1974). They
introduce their review of research by asking rhetorically, 'Does the
black child have a difficult time comprehending the SE speaking
teacher or vice versa?' (1974:70). They conclude that there is no
language difference sufficient to cause comprehension problems:

In general, no acceptable, replicated research has found that
the dialect spoken by black children presents them with unique
problems in comprehending SE. If there are problems, they
occur in relatively rare cases (e.g., possessive sentences).
What really seems to occur is that speakers of NNE automatically translate the SE into their dialect. It is this
translation which is given in imitation studies (1974:79).

Linguists, in general, do not endorse this conclusion by psychologists
and educationalists that language differences are insufficient to cause
educational problems. Linguists do, however, seem tacitly to endorse
a fundamental premise of the argument: imitation of this type implies
comprehension. Butters, for example, in discussing material from

the Natalicio and Williams (1971) study of sentence repetition, mentions the situation in which a child hears (21a) and responds with (21b):

(21a) Mother helps Gloria.
(21b) Mother help Gloria.

Butters concludes that 'obviously the respondent understands the utterance, even though he can repeat it exactly only with difficulty (if at all)' (1972:31).

Given the possible relationships between utterances and comprehension, nothing is obvious in this instance. A child who could respond to (21a) with (21b) could use the latter equally well as a repetition of (22).

(22) Mother helped Gloria.

One could argue equally well that there has been a compounding of miscomprehension: the child misunderstood the tense of the original sentence, and the linguist misunderstood the intent of the child. Such sentence repetition tasks simply have very little to say about comprehension.

Hall and Turner do, in fact, recognize this. In another study (Hall, Turner, and Russell 1973) they devised a modification of the Osser, Wang, and Zaid (1969) task to test imitation and comprehension independently. The child is given a sentence to imitate and then chooses from among a set of pictures the one which best exemplifies the sentence. The sentences are constructed to have potential ambiguities, with three pictures matching possible readings of each sentence. They used four sentences to test imitation and comprehension of past tense (23a–d).

(23a) The man chopped the oak logs.
(23b) The boy jumped over the puddle.
(23c) The woman washed the dirty clothes.
(23d) The boy kicked the big ball.

Consider first the imitation task. All four of the verbs end in nondental consonants and the past tense morpheme is thus represented by a single consonant. In three of the four test sentences, the past tense morpheme is followed by the definite article. There is a phonological process of assimilation operating across this word boundary, making perception of the past tense marker phonetically impossible in most cases. This is true particularly for speakers of a dialect in which the initial phoneme of the article may be a stop,

affricate, or fricative ([dIs, ddIs, dIs] respectively). In three of the
sentences, the child would not be able to hear the past tense marker;
the experimenter could not hear its repetition.

As would be expected, the mean number of sentence imitations
containing past tense markers is about 1. 0 (range 1. 0-1. 8) for the
lower-class black and lower-class white children. It is somewhat
more surprising that for the suburban, middle-class white fourth
graders, the average number of past tense responses was 2. 7, in
spite of the fact that each child has only one sentence in which the
presence of the past tense morpheme can be ascertained reliably.
It would seem that there is, in fact, an act of comprehension involved in sentence repetition tasks. That act is the experimenter's
comprehension of the child's response. In this instance comprehension appears to be based on sociological cues as much as or more
than it is based on linguistic cues.

What is being comprehended by the child in the three sentences is
not presence of the past tense marker, but the absence of any present
tense agreement marker. The published pictures are somewhat
obscure. Not surprisingly, mean rates of comprehension for the
groups of children on the four sentences ranged from 0. 8 to 1. 4,
suggesting that many of the children may be performing randomly.

The task includes another set of sentences which are supposed to
measure comprehension of the agreement morpheme (24a-d).

(24a) The sheep eats all the hay.
(24b) The girl slides down the hill.
(24c) The deer runs across the road.
(24d) The boy climbs up the ladder.

Two of the sentences (24b, d) are described as double cue sentences,
being marked both by the absence of a plural marker and by the
presence of the agreement morpheme on the verb. The other sentences with sheep and deer are marked only on the verb. But that is
a strictly ethnocentric view of language. For many children, particularly black children, the plural of sheep is sheeps, and the plural of
deer is deers. For such children there should be no difference among
the four sentences.

That is exactly what the study found. Means for the Anglo children
are about twice as high on the boy and girl sentences as on the sheep
and deer sentences; for the black children the difference is negligible.
Apparently, the children are responding to perceived plural cues, or
their absence, on the nouns, rather than to verb markers. Not surprisingly, no significant differences were found among the groups of
children in their comprehension of these sentences. There is no

reason to believe that deletion of plural markers plays a major factor in distinguishing among ethnic dialects.

A third set of sentences in Hall et al. (1973) tests the imitation and comprehension of the possessive marker (25a–d):

(25a) The girl wears the clown's hat.
(25b) The boy carries the cowboy's boots.
(25c) The girl paints the dog's house.
(25d) The boy takes the baby's doll.

The results are exactly what can be predicted from knowledge of the dialects involved. In imitation, black children repeat the possessive marker less often than do the white children, but in comprehension no significant differences are observed among groups. It appears that the possessive marker is understood, but is deleted in production, black children giving responses like (26):

(26) The girl wears the clown's hat.

Unfortunately, the task tests the wrong question. The interesting question is, what does the Anglo experimenter comprehend when he hears the black child utter (26)? Does he comprehend the child's intended possessive construction, or does he comprehend only the noun phrase construction that his own grammar allows? The potential for ambiguity is only in the sentences with no overt possessive marker, not in the sentences with the marker.

The fourth set of sentences used in this task contain what are termed 'critical phrase markers'. These contain subordinating conjunctions in constructions that have never been shown to be dialectally differentiated (27a–d):

(27a) Mother puts the cake where he can reach.
(27b) Father throws it so they can catch.
(27c) The boy sees that the girl runs.
(27d) The girl swings before the boy slides.

Again, not surprisingly, no significant differences are noted either in imitation or comprehension among ethnic groups.

From another study, beset with comparable linguistic problems, Hall and Turner (1971:1749) conclude that

if the superior comprehension performance of the [white lower class] sample reflected a true difference in that group's ability to comprehend the sentences, it was probably due to

a difference between the two groups in reasoning ability
rather than in linguistic competence.

Comprehension is very difficult to test, and testing comprehension of particular linguistic structures is even more difficult. Testing comprehension across dialects requires extraordinary caution to
ensure that all relevant aspects of the grammars involved are being
considered. Demonstration of comprehension problems across dialects is not a socially negative finding. Rather it is a demonstration
of the linguistic basis for a situation that is known tacitly to exist.
The fact that black students responded differently than Anglo students
did on the tag question task does not demonstrate a failure to comprehend. The black students did comprehend these ambiguous sentences,
but not in the same way that Anglo students did. The cross-dialect
communication problem is in many cases not failure of comprehension, as seen by the parties to the communication. The problem is
rather that the expectations based on those asymmetrical comprehensions are not shared by both parties to the communication.
The second claim mentioned initially relates to the concept of the
polylectal grammar. Under the heading 'Justification of polylectal
grammars', Bailey makes the following statement:

Since it is known that women are about a generation ahead of
men in some changes, the language of one's mother will be
different from that of one's father, even if their age and
class traits are similar. Each of the interlocutors encountered by a child has a multitude of styles which he or
she must competently deal with (1973:24).

The form of the argument is that the child comprehends different
lects. Therefore, receptively at least, he must have a polylectal
grammar. Setting aside any objections to the rather dubious universal generalization that women lead men by a generation in language change, is there any evidence for the argument, and what
characteristics would the evidence have to possess?
Suppose, for whatever reason, mother and father employ different
lects, different grammars. From that fact, and the observation that
the child makes the socially appropriate responses, what can be inferred about the child's receptive grammar is very little indeed. It
may be Situation 1 (Figure 1) with identical grammars; it may be
Situation 2, with unlike grammars but comprehension. In most instances it will be difficult to determine if the child's comprehension
results from particular syntactic cues, or from constraints placed on
the possible meanings by real world contexts. Even if the child does
comprehend both sets of syntactic cues, it does not follow that this

must represent polylectal comprehension. The production may involve different grammars for mother and father, but the child's
comprehension may well be a variable process integrated into one
grammar. In order to demonstrate the need for a polylectal grammar from comprehension data it is necessary not only to show that
the different sets of linguistic cues are in fact part of comprehension,
but also that they are comprehended to be parts of different linguistic
systems. In many cases that will be difficult to do.

For example, Politzer and Hoover (1972) had children listen to
sentences in what they termed 'standard Black English' and 'non-
standard Black English'. The children were asked to identify the
sentences as 'school talk' or 'dialect'. From their results it can be
determined that most second grade children and many fourth grade
children reliably make distinctions. Even then it is not clear what
cues the children use to make distinctions, or that they comprehend
the semantic import of those cues.

The polylectal grammar undoubtedly exists. It can be observed
that there are persons who switch in their production. That the polylectal grammar exists in comprehension for persons who do not also
have it in production, however, is based on unsubstantiated inferences,
not on experimental data. The complexity of comprehension is such
that those inferences are not well supported by available data. Grammars of polylectal comprehension may well exist. However, documented cases of comprehension across lects fail to provide sufficient
evidence for the polylectal grammar.

Responses to the tag question task show that comprehension is
conditioned, though not absolutely determined, by grammar. It is
also conditioned by contextual cues that may or may not produce comprehension consistent with the syntactic cues of the sentence. Showing that a black child comprehends a certain Standard English sentence
does not show that he comprehends all of Standard English. To the
contrary, there appear to be systematic differences in grammars that
lead to major differences in comprehension for certain kinds of sentences.

NOTES

1. For the present argument it is irrelevant whether do is present
in underlying structures and deleted or is inserted by a do-Support
Rule.

2. Depending on how one wishes to analyze tags (see, for example,
Stockwell et al. 1973:620ff.), this may be related to the nonreduction
of stress before deletion sites (Baker 1971).

3. Arrangements for the testing were made with the kind assistance
of Professors Steven Ross and Edward Twum-Akwaboah.

REFERENCES

Bailey, C.-J. N. 1973. Variation and linguistic theory. Washington, D.C., Center for Applied Linguistics.

Baker, C. L. 1971. Stress level and auxiliary behavior in English. Linguistic Inquiry, 2(2). 167-181.

Berdan, R. 1973. Have/got in the speech of Anglo and Black children. Professional Paper No. 22. Los Alamitos, Calif. SWRL Educational Research and Development.

Butters, R. R. 1972. Competence, performance, and variable rules. Language Sciences, No. 20, 29-32.

Hall, V. C. and R. R. Turner. 1971. Comparison of imitation and comprehension scores between two lower-class groups and the effects of two warm-up conditions on imitations of the same groups. Child Development, Vol. 42, 1735-1750.

Hall, V. C. and R. R. Turner. 1974. The validity of the 'different language explanation' for poor scholastic performance by black students. Review of Educational Research, 4. 69-81.

Hall, V. C., R. R. Turner, and W. Russell. 1973. Ability of children from four subcultures and two grade levels to imitate and comprehend crucial aspects of Standard English: A test of the different language explanation. Journal of Educational Psychology, 64. 147-158.

McDavid, R. I. 1967. A checklist of significant features for discriminating social dialects. In: Dimensions of dialect. Edited by E. Evertts. Champaign, Ill., NCTE. 7-10.

Natalicio, D. and F. Williams. 1971. Repetition as an oral language assessment technique. Austin, Center for Communications Research, School of Communications, University of Texas.

Osser, H., M. D. Wang, and F. Zaid. 1969. The young child's ability to imitate and comprehend speech: A comparison of two subcultural groups. Child Development, Vol. 4, 1063-1075.

Palmer, F. R. 1968. A linguistic study of the English verb. Coral Gables, Fla., University of Miami Press.

Politzer, R. L. and M. R. Hoover. 1972. The development of awareness of the black standard/nonstandard dialect contrast among primary school children: A pilot study. R&D Memorandum No. 83. Stanford Center for Research and Development in Teaching.

Stockwell, R. P., P. Schachter, and B. H. Partee. 1973. The major syntactic structures of English. New York, Holt, Rinehart and Winston.

Wolfram, W. 1974. The relationship of white Southern speech to Vernacular Black English. Lg. 50. 498-527.

QUANTIFIER-NEGATIVE INTERACTION

MARK BALTIN

University of Pennsylvania

In the study of syntactic variation within a generative framework, perhaps the most explicit case for the usefulness of variation data in choosing among competing analyses has been made by Guy Carden in a number of publications (1970a, 1970b, 1973). The case which Carden has studied most intensively, and which has been followed up most (Heringer 1970; Labov, Hindle, and Baltin forthcoming) is that of the quantifier-dialects, based on the interpretation of sentences like (1).

(1) All the boys didn't leave.

Some speakers (Neg-V speakers) construe the negative with the verb, and interpret (1) as a paraphrase of (2).

(2) None of the boys left.

Other speakers (Neg-Q speakers) interpret the negative as being associated with the quantifier, and see (1) as meaning:

(3) Not all the boys left.

A third group (AMB speakers) see both readings. Thus, we have three dialects without geographical or social correlates. Carden then goes on to show how his analysis of quantifiers as higher predicates predicts three different grammaticality patterns for these three dialects based on the interaction of his rule of quantifier-lowering with various independently motivated syntactic rules and constraints.

30

I will not concern myself with these arguments here (see Carden 1970b). Instead, I will show what seems to be the relevant principle in determining the relative scope of quantifiers and negation in sentences like (1), indicate what machinery would be necessary in a theory of grammar which incorporated this principle directly, and suggest a way in which this principle could be explained by more general aspects of cognition.

Now let us get down to cases. It is interesting to note that there is an entailment relation between the two readings of (1), so that if it is the case that none of the boys left, it follows that (3) is true. However, (3) could be true, and (2) false. Therefore, we would say that Neg-V entails Neg-Q, and the following principle suggests itself:

A. When there exists an ambiguity with a relationship of logical entailment between the readings, speakers <u>can</u> use this relationship to interpret the sentence.

Notice the emphasis on <u>can</u>, in order to cover the case of Carden's AMB speakers. The discerning reader will note that in postulating Principle A, I have simply described Carden's data, for Principle A is consistent with the data but not motivated by it. There is, however, another ambiguity with an entailment relationship between the readings. This is the ambiguity of prenominal modifiers (Bach 1968):

(4) The philosophical Greeks liked to talk.

which can mean either

(5) The Greeks, who are philosophical, liked to talk.
    (nonrestrictive)

or

(6) The Greeks who are philosophical liked to talk.
    (restrictive)

Notice that a speaker who asserts (5) is also committing himself or herself to the truth of (6), which is the limiting case. Therefore, we would say that a nonrestrictive relative entails the corresponding restrictive reading.

We are now in a position either to motivate or to refute Principle A as the correct parameter for variation between speakers. If Principle A is correct, then Neg-Q speakers should also prefer restrictive relative paraphrases of prenominal modifiers, since both are the entailed readings in ambiguities; those who prefer the entailing

reading on the quantifiers (Neg-V) should also prefer the entailing
reading on the modifiers, the nonrestrictive or appositive paraphrase;
finally, those who are AMB speakers on the quantifiers should also
switch readings on the modifiers.

We now have a testable hypothesis. A few remarks on methodology
used in ascertaining its correctness would be relevant here. Anybody
who works with informants knows that the ability of speakers to focus
upon their internalized grammars is by no means an infallible one
(see Labov 1972:191-203, for an illustration of the pitfalls involved
in using intuitive data alone). Therefore, it seemed that a way of
avoiding this problem would be to force speakers to use their knowledge of the language in order to perform a task. In this way, one
could infer certain facts about linguistic knowledge, such as the
interpretation of a sentence, from the way the task was performed.

Another point about trying to determine preferred readings of an
ambiguous construction was considered, and this point is that belief
systems interact crucially with grammar. To show this obvious
point, I am sure that most speakers would agree that

(7) All men aren't 20 feet tall.

forces a Neg-V reading, while

(8) All men aren't 6 feet tall.

forces a Neg-Q reading.

The following paradigm was thus developed to test Principle A,
which circumvented both the problem of intuitions and the problem of
belief systems. Speakers were presented with thirty sentences each,
comprised of five quantifier-negative sentences, five sentences with
pronominal modifiers, ten sentences with an ambiguity of pronominal
referent, and ten unambiguous sentences. Subjects were told that
they were participating in a test of short-term memory, and were
presented with the sentences as captions to pictures. In order to
control for belief systems, nonsense syllables were used in place of
the nouns, since I assumed that most people do not have predisposi-
tions about wugs and zoks. Their interpretation of the sentence was
determined by asking them a question which was ostensibly designed
to test their recall of the sentence, but which was actually framed
so as to disambiguate. After presentation of the stimulus sentence,
and before presentation of the disambiguating question, subjects were
asked to perform a simple arithmetic task, such as counting by twos
until told to stop. Thus, a sample task was the following:

(9) All the binks aren't hungry? (Task) Question: Jom is
     a bink, so can he be hungry?

A 'yes' answer was scored as Neg-Q, a 'no' answer as Neg-V.
One might note that a 'yes' answer is indeterminate in actuality,
since the 'yes' might indicate either a Neg-Q reading or else that
the subject saw both readings. In order to control for this flaw in
the procedure, the subject was asked to paraphrase the sentence
All the boys didn't leave after the test. In only three cases out of
sixty-one did the post-test questioning reveal results at variance with
the experimental data. Thus, some intuitive data was necessary, but
was strengthened by the results of experimentation.

The subjects were thirty-one introductory psychology students at
the University of California, Irvine campus, and thirty students who
happened to be in the student union at the University of Pennsylvania
at the right time of day. The pattern was replicated, with $p < .005$
both times, so I show the results for both groups in Tables 1 and 2.
I should mention my scoring procedure here. For a speaker to be
classed as 'Neg-Q', he had to exhibit a Neg-Q response on all five
quantifier-negative sentences. A similar criterion was used to
classify speakers as 'Restrictive' or 'Nonrestrictive'. Anybody who
exhibited less than five consistent responses for one of these sentence
types was put into the switch cell for that sentence type. The results
are as follows, with Table 1 showing the observed cell frequencies
and Table 2 showing the predicted cell frequencies under the null
hypothesis, which is that Neg-Q preference is independent of restrictive preference, etc. (I am indebted here to Steve Herman and
Don Hindle, who did the statistical analysis.)

TABLE 1. Observed cell frequencies.

	Neg-Q	Neg-V	AMB
Restrictive	13	2	2
Nonrestrictive	2	10	4
Switch-Mod	6	1	21

TABLE 2. Predicted frequencies under null hypothesis.

	Neg-Q	Neg-V	AMB
Restrictive	5.85	3.62	7.52
Nonrestrictive	5.51	3.41	7.08
Switch-Mod	9.69	5.97	12.39

With a chi-square of 41.32 with four degrees of freedom, $p < .005$,
so that the null hypothesis is refuted, Principle A is supported, and

entailment between possible readings is a principal determinant of quantifier-negative scope.

Now that we have isolated this determinant of quantifier-negative scope, we should try to see where it fits into our present conceptions about grammar. If Principle A were to be stuck into grammars, it would have to be transderivational, since it would always have to look at two different semantic representations to determine its applicability. Also, Principle A would have to wait until the surface to apply, since it would first have to determine the string's ambiguity.

It is beyond the scope of this paper to argue for the existence or nonexistence of transderivational constraints (see Hankamer 1973; G. Lakoff 1973). I happen to believe that at our present stage of knowledge, much of the discussion as to whether or not perceptual strategies interact with grammar, or are part of grammar but functionally motivated, is terminological. If a functionalist wants to explain away transderivational constraints as being purely perceptual and not grammatical, it is certainly incumbent upon that functionalist to provide the perceptual motivation for the constraint. However, once this is done, given that some aspects of grammar (Bever and Langendoen 1972) seem to be perceptually determined, the transderivationalist can point to this fact and simply say that Transderivational Constraint X is a functionally motivated part of grammar. Of course, the last word in this hypothetical dialogue might end with the functionalist saying to the transderivationalist, 'Aha. I can explain every case of transderivational constraints by a non ad hoc, well motivated theory of perception. In so doing, I also reduce the expressive power of the grammar, and the number of descriptive devices available. Therefore, my description is preferable to yours.' As of now, we are a long way from this scenario becoming a reality.

In the case of Principle A, however, there may be a cognitive explanation, and I am pursuing this possibility with Steve Herman. Harris Savin and Ross Quillian independently have suggested to me that Principle A might be a particular instance of a more general phenomenon known as category width. Category width (Bruner, Goodnow, and Austin 1956; Pettigrew 1970; Tajfel, Richardson, and Everstine 1970) is a phenomenon which divides members of the population into those who perceive the domain of a category very widely and those who perceive category boundaries very narrowly over a wide variety of perceptual tasks. Given that wide categories include narrow categories, just as an entailing proposition includes the truth conditions for an entailed proposition, one might try to correlate speakers who prefer the entailing reading with wide categorizers and speakers who prefer the entailed reading with narrow categorizers. This correlation, if established, would have obvious implications for cognitive psychology.

In any event, the perceptual explanation for Principle A is made more testable by the fact that it is based on variation. There is always a possible objection to most functional explanations of linguistic facts. If the argument runs that human beings do X and also do Y, then it is to be inferred that Y is the reason for X. This is obviously not a tight argument, since one could then argue that since most humans have five fingers and also have two eyes, one fact might be the basis for the other. However, if one were to observe that not all humans had five fingers, and that those who had less also had only one eye, this would certainly be an interesting fact which a comparative anatomist would have to explain. The same is true of the correlation mentioned in the foregoing paragraph, since a systematic covariance would certainly strengthen the inference. It remains to be seen whether category width interacts crucially with Principle A. In any event, by isolating the reality of Principle A, I bring it to the attention of other investigators.

NOTE

This paper was inspired by work done in 1971-1972 under NSF Grant GS-3287 with William Labov as principal investigator. I am indebted to William Labov for much encouragement and the opportunity to see a great methodologist in action. I am indebted also to many friends and teachers who have discussed this material with me: Peter Culicover, Ken Wexler, W. C. Watt, Don Hindle, Steve Herman, and Harris Savin. The standard exculpations hold for them.

REFERENCES

Bach, Emmon. 1968. Nouns and noun phrases. In: Universals in linguistic theory. Edited by E. Bach and R. T. Harms. New York, Holt, Rinehart and Winston. 91-124.

Bever, Thomas, and Terence Langendoen. 1972. The interaction of speech perception and grammatical structure in the evolution of language. In: Linguistic change and generative theory. Edited by R. Stockwell and R. Macaulay. Bloomington, Indiana University Press. 32-95.

Carden, Guy. 1970a. Logical predicates and idiolectal variation in English. Unpublished doctoral dissertation, Harvard University.

Carden, Guy. 1970b. A note on conflicting ideolects. Linguistic Inquiry 1.

Carden, Guy. 1973. Disambiguation, favored readings and variable rules. In: New ways of analyzing variation in English. Edited by C.-J.N. Bailey and R. W. Shuy. Washington, D.C., Georgetown University Press. 71-182.

Hankamer, Jorge. 1972. Unacceptable ambiguity. Linguistic Inquiry 4.17–68.
Labov, William. 1972. Sociolinguistic patterns. Philadelphia, University of Pennsylvania Press.
Labov, William, Donald Hindle, and Mark Baltin. To appear. For an end to the uncontrolled use of intuitions in linguistic analysis.
Lakoff, George. 1973. Some thoughts on transderivational constraints. In: Papers in linguistics in honor of Henry and Renee Kahane. Edited by B. Kachru et al. Champaign, University of Illinois Press.

VARIATIONS ON RELATIVE CLAUSES IN ITALIAN

DONNA JO NAPOLI

Georgetown University

1.0. Introduction. All speakers of Italian produce at least two
types of relative clauses, those introduced by a relative pronoun and
those introduced by che 'that' with no pronoun coreferential with the
head NP (call it Pro$_{rel}$) present. Many speakers also produce relatives introduced by che with Pro$_{rel}$ present. For these speakers
there is a deletion rule (call it DEL) which deletes Pro$_{rel}$ in certain
syntactic configurations.[1] DEL cannot apply, optionally applies, or
must apply, depending on two factors which are shown to form a
squish on the application of DEL.

I propose that for those speakers who never have Pro$_{rel}$ present
in the surface, DEL is an obligatory rule. Thus all relatives introduced by che are produced in the same way by all speakers. The
fact that some speakers allow che relatives with Pro$_{rel}$ and others
do not is due to the sensitivity to syntactic structure of DEL for the
first set of speakers but the obligatoriness of DEL (regardless of the
structural configuration) for the second set of speakers.

2.0. The data. In the examples in this section we find relatives
introduced by che with and without Pro$_{rel}$. We find that the two
factors affecting the appearance of Pro$_{rel}$ in the surface are the
structure in which the relative clause appears[2] and the role Pro$_{rel}$
plays in the relative clause. The data presented here are not new.
Keenan (1972) has found similar data for many languages.

Four distinctive roles for Pro$_{rel}$ are examined: subject, accusative object, nonaccusative cliticizable object,[3] and noncliticizable
object.[4] We see these roles exemplified here in five different
structures.[5]

2.1. S_1. The lowest S dominating Pro_{rel} is S_1:

(1)
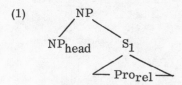

(2a) Subject:
Ecco il ragazzo che (*lui) studia legge.
'Here's the boy that (*he) studies law.'
(2b) Accusative object:
Ecco il ragazzo che Maria (*lo) conosce.
'Here's the boy that Mary knows (*him).'
(2c) Nonaccusative cliticizable object:
Ecco il ragazzo che gli parlavo.
'Here's the boy that I was talking to him.'
(2d) Noncliticizable object:
*Ecco il ragazzo che litigavo con (lui).
'Here's the boy that I was arguing with (him).'

In (2c) gli is optional for some speakers.

2.2. S_2. Pro_{rel} appears in an S embedded in S_1:

(3)
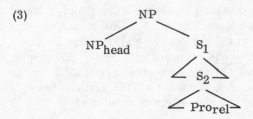

Now more roles exhibit a Pro_{rel} in the surface.

(4a) Subject:
Ecco il ragazzo che so bene che (??lui) studia legge.
'Here's the boy that I know well that (??he) studies law.'
(4b) Accusative object:
Ecco il ragazzo che so bene che Maria (lo) conosce.
'Here's the boy that I know well that Mary knows him.'
(4c) Nonaccusative cliticizable object:
Ecco il ragazzo che so bene che ne parlavi.
'Here's the boy that I know well that you were talking about him.'

(4d) Noncliticizable object:
   Ecco il ragazzo che so bene che litigavi con lui.
   'Here's the boy that I know well that you were arguing
   with him.'

Example (4d) is ungrammatical for some speakers.

2.3. Embedded Q. Pro$_{rel}$ is in an embedded question:

(5)
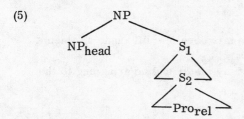

where S$_2$ is a question. Now Pro$_{rel}$ must appear in all roles except
subject, where it is optional:

(6) Ecco il ragazzo che non capisco perchè (lui) studia legge.
   'Here's the boy that I don't understand why (he) studies law.'

Another structure which behaves exactly as embedded questions do
is an adverbial of the type demonstrated in (7).

(7) Ecco il biscotto che tu gridavi a me mentre lo facevo.
   'Here's the cookie that you were yelling at me while I
   made it.'

2.4. CNP. Pro$_{rel}$ is in a Complex Noun Phrase.

(8)
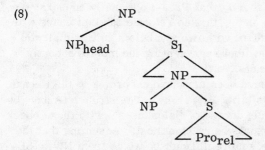

Pro$_{rel}$ must appear in this structure in the surface regardless of its
role.

(9a) Ecco il ragazzo che conosco la maestra che lui odia.
      'Here's the boy that I know the teacher that he hates.'
(9b) Ecco il ragazzo che il fatto che lui odia la maestra
      è ovvio.
      'Here's the boy that the fact that he hates the teacher
      is obvious.'

2.5. CS. When the relative clause is formed in a Coordinate
Structure, Pro_{rel} must appear in the surface regardless of its role. [6]

(10a) NP and NP
(10b) Ecco il ragazzo che mia sorella e lui vanno al cinema
       domani.
       'Here's the boy that my sister and he are going to the
       movies tomorrow.'

(11a) NP and   NP
                  Pro_{rel}

(11b) Ecco il ragazzo che ho raccomandato Maria e la
       signora che lui ha sposato per il posto.
       'Here's the boy that I recommended Mary and the
       woman that he married for the job.'

Note that in (11b) Pro_{rel} is not only in a CS, it is also in a CNP.

3.0. The Relative Squish. If we arrange the two factors, role
and structure, in a matrix with structure heading each column and
role heading each row, and if we then fill in each square with information about whether or not Pro_{rel} appears in the surface, we find
the squish shown in Table 1. [7] In this table x signifies that Pro_{rel}
cannot appear in the surface; 0, that Pro_{rel} optionally appears; +,
that Pro_{rel} must appear; and -, that no relative can be formed with
che in this context. A square with two symbols signifies dialectal
variation, with the first symbol representing the most frequently
found data for my informants.
    The roles in Table 1 have been arranged according to the Keenan
and Comrie (1972) Accessibility Hierarchy. The structures have been
arranged according to their degree of 'islandness', with those observing Ross's (1967) constraints being rightmost. Assuming that the
positions get progressively more difficult as we go from NW to SE
on the matrix, we see that Pro_{rel} does not appear in easy contexts,
optionally appears in more difficult contexts, and must appear in the
most difficult contexts. [8]

TABLE 1. Squish on the appearance of Pro_{rel}.

	S_1	S_2	em Q	CNP	CS
subject	x	x	0	+	+
acc. object	x	0	+	+	+
nonacc. clit. object	+, 0	+	+	+	+
nonclit. object	–	+, –	+	+	+

4.0. The Deletion Rule DEL. The squish in Table 1 is written as a squish on the appearance of Pro_{rel} in the surface. I argue here that there is a rule DEL which deletes Pro_{rel} and that DEL cannot apply, optionally applies, or obligatorily applies, depending upon the difficulty of the context. If it were possible to motivate such a rule, Table 1 would offer support for Lakoff's (1972) claim that 'rules of grammar do not simply apply or fail to apply; rather they apply to a degree'.[9]

One kind of evidence which would support the proposal of DEL would be something which would make us posit an underlying level for (2b), for example, in which Pro_{rel} was present.

(2b) Ecco il ragazzo che Maria (*lo) conosce.

Such evidence exists. Consider (12). Pensare a NP 'think about NP' is unusual in Italian, in that if a NP is replaced by a clitic we get an accusative clitic (having the same gender and number as the NP) but never a dative clitic. A NP in other predicates, however, is replaced by a dative clitic if the NP is animate.[10]

(12a) Penso a mia madre.
       'I'm thinking about my mother.'
(12b) *Penso mia madre.
       'I'm thinking my mother.'
(12c) *Le (dative) penso.
       'I'm thinking about her.'
(12d) La penso.
       'I'm thinking about her.'

In a relative clause with pensare a NP we find that Pro_{rel} cannot appear. All speakers of Italian, as far as I know, accept (13a):

(13a) La signora che pensavi entra adesso.
       'The woman that you were thinking about is entering now.'

(13b) *La signora che la (accusative) pensavi entra adesso.
'The woman that you were thinking about her is entering now.'

(13c) *La signora che le (dative) pensavi entra adesso.
'The woman that you were thinking about her is
entering now.'

Had the relative clause in (13a) been formed directly on an underlying
full dative NP as in (14),

(14) [la signora [(tu) pensavi alla signora] entra adesso]

we would expect a dative clitic to appear in the surface obligatorily
for most speakers and at least optionally for many others, since
dative objects are nonaccusative cliticizable objects (see row 3 of
Table 1). Yet no such clitic may appear, as (13c) shows. If, instead, the dative object in (13a) went through a pronominal stage
first, it would become an accusative clitic, as (12d) shows. Then
this clitic would be deleted by DEL, since accusative Pro_{rel} does
not show up in a structure like that in (13) (see the first column of
Table 1). And, in fact, no clitic appears.

Thus the positing of a pronominal stage in the history of (13a)
explains the absence of a clitic in the che relative there. Note that
if we formed a relative clause with a relative pronoun in the same
environment, the relative pronoun would appear after the dative
marker a and not as an accusative object. [11]

(15a) La signora alla quale/a cui pensavi entra adesso.
'The woman to whom you were talking is entering now.'

(15b) *La signora la quale pensavi entra adesso.
'The woman who you were thinking is entering now.'

Example (15) shows that (13a) must be derived from a stage in which
an accusative clitic was present and not from a stage in which a relative pronoun was present. [12]

Another argument in favor of proposing DEL depends on dialectal
variation. The relative clauses given in Sections 2.1 through 2.5 are
grammatical for a large number of speakers. Many other speakers
reject many of the examples in Sections 2.1-2.5. All speakers,
however, accept relative clauses introduced by che of the following
types.

(16a) La ragazza che canta bene è Maria.
'The girl that sings well is Mary.'

(16b) La ragazza che so che canta bene è Maria.
      'The girl that I know sings well is Mary.'
(16c) La ragazza che mi domando perchè piange è Maria.
      'The girl that I wonder why she's crying is Mary.'
(16d) La ragazza che conosco bene è Maria.
      'The girl that I know well is Mary.'
(16e) La ragazza che so che tu conosci bene è Maria.
      'The girl that I know that you know well is Mary.'

These examples are of the type given in row 1 of columns 1, 2, and 3, and row 2 of columns 1 and 2 of the squish seen in Table 1.

Assuming DEL exists, the fact that (16) is accepted by all speakers of Italian, while the other types of relative clauses given in Sections 2.1-2.5 are accepted only by some, can be explained if we propose that DEL is an obligatory rule for the speakers who accept relatives with che only of the types seen in (16). To see this, look back at the squish in Table 1. Italian observes Ross's (1967) constraints on deletion and movement out of CNP and CS. If DEL is obligatory for a given speaker, then the speaker must delete Pro_{rel} in the environments in columns 4 and 5. But the CNP Constraint and the CS Constraint block this deletion. Since an obligatory rule is blocked from applying, such a speaker cannot produce the types of relative clauses found in columns 4 and 5.

Likewise for these same speakers, DEL must delete Pro_{rel} in row 4, yielding sentences such as:

(17a) *La ragazza che parlavi con è Maria.
      'The girl that you were talking with is Mary.'
(17b) *La ragazza che so che parlavi con è Maria.
      'The girl that I know you were talking with is Mary.'
(17c) *La ragazza che mi domando perchè parlavi con è Maria.
      'The girl that I wonder why you were talking with is Mary.'

However, there is a constraint against stranding prepositions in Italian.[13] Since the application of DEL to sentences like those in (17) would result in a stranded preposition (con 'with'), such sentences are ungrammatical.

For the speakers with obligatory DEL the impossible grids left to be accounted for in Table 1 then, are those shown in (18).

(18)

	S_1	S_2	embed Q
accusative object			✓
nonaccusative clit. object	✓	✓	✓

Note that all the speakers who produce the che relatives of columns 2 and 3 of (18) keep Pro_{rel} in the surface. That is, for these speakers the contexts represented in columns 2 and 3 of (18) are of a level of difficulty that requires the presence of Pro_{rel}. Thus there is some kind of constraint that blocks DEL from applying in these contexts. If this same constraint operates in the grammars of those speakers who have obligatory DEL, an obligatory rule is blocked from applying in these contexts and the relatives of columns 2 and 3 of (18) cannot be produced.

The only grid left to be accounted for is the nonaccusative cliticizable object in S_1. Most speakers who produce che relatives in this context keep Pro_{rel} in the surface. Thus there is a constraint blocking DEL here for them. However, there are also speakers for whom DEL optionally applies in this context. Thus we expect that for most speakers who produce (16) but not the other types of relatives exemplified in Sections 2.1-2.5, (19) should be out.[14]

(19) Il gesto che sono capace è sputare in faccia al maestro.
'The act that I am capable (of) is spitting in the face of the teacher.'

Example (19) is out for these speakers because DEL is obligatory but at the same time it is blocked by a 'difficulty' constraint. However, there should be speakers who produce (16) and (19) but not the rest of the sentence types in Sections 2.1-2.5. That is, there should be speakers with obligatory DEL who do not consider the context in (19) difficult enough to block deletion, just as there are speakers with structure-sensitive DEL who do not consider the context in (19) difficult enough to block DEL. I have found no such speakers, and if they, in fact, do not exist, my explanations are greatly weakened. However, my sampling of speakers is small, so the possibility that such speakers exist remains.

Without a rule such as DEL, there must be a third relative clause strategy in Italian. This strategy would introduce relative clauses by che and leave no Pro_{rel}. Compare the two resulting che relative clause strategies. One has che plus Pro_{rel}. The other has che with no Pro_{rel}. If both strategies exist and are independent of one another, we would expect to find speakers with only the first of the two strategies as well as speakers with only the second of the two strategies. But, in fact, there are no speakers who produce che relatives with Pro_{rel} who cannot also produce che relatives without Pro_{rel} (of the type seen in (16)). Also, if the two strategies are independent, the fact that they are in complementary distribution (with only three exceptions) is unexplained.

4.1. Actual usage. While many speakers accept relative pronouns in relatives of the types seen in columns 1 through 3 of the
squish in Table 1, [15] in actual usage relative pronouns are found in
such structures usually only in the roles seen in rows 3 and 4. That
is, il quale, the relative pronoun, rarely occurs as the subject or
accusative object of its clause. In fact, many speakers do not even
accept il quale as an accusative object. [16] For rows 3 and 4, the
roles in which the NP coreferential with the head is in a prepositional phrase at some point in the derivation, the relative pronoun
relative is more common than the che relative, but the preferred
choice of relative pronoun is not il quale, but rather cui. Thus
(20a) is more frequently used than (20b):

(20a) La ragazza con cui parlavi è Maria.
(20b) La ragazza con la quale parlavi è Maria.
       'The girl with whom you were speaking is Mary.'

The preference for che and cui relatives, as opposed to il quale
relatives, may be related to the fact that che and cui are invariant
forms whereas il quale has different forms, depending on the number
and gender of the referent. I think there is a general tendency in
colloquial Italian to use invariant forms whenever one has a choice,
witness the preference of (21a) to (21b):

(21a) Noi donne siamo meglio (unmarked) degli uomini.
(21b) Noi donne siamo migliori (feminine plural) degli uomini.
       'We women are better than men.'

5.0. Conclusion. All relative clauses introduced by che in Italian
are produced by the same relative clause strategy by all speakers.
The fact that some speakers exhibit relatives with Pro_{rel} in the surface while others do not is directly due to the fact that DEL is
structure-sensitive for the first group of speakers but obligatory,
regardless of structure, for the second group.

NOTES

I would like to thank Judith Aissen, Nick Clements, Susumu Kuno,
and Bob Rodman for suggestions and criticisms of various stages of
this work; Dwight Bolinger, for some tantalizing questions and suggestions; my informants, especially Claudio Moser, Marina Nespor,
and Bartolo Vattuone, for many hours and comments; and, above all,
Pasquale Tatò, for his generous giving of time and incisive comments, the effects of which are apparent throughout this paper. A

preliminary version of this paper was presented at the summer, 1974, LSA meeting.

1. Emonds (1970:169ff.) assumes for English that all relative clauses are introduced by that and go through a stage in which the NP coreferential with the head is pronominalized or deleted. In the case of pronominalization, wh-fronting applies, optionally pulling along a preceding preposition and replacing that in the COMP with the relative pronoun. In the case of deletion, that introduces the surface relative. (That may be deleted in certain instances.)

Chomsky (1973), alternatively, proposes that relative pronouns may delete and that then that may be inserted in COMP.

Both linguists see relative clauses introduced by wh forms and that as being produced by one basic strategy, with deletion (either of a pronoun within the relative clause or of a fronted wh pronoun) resulting in that appearing in the surface. If che relatives and wh relatives in Italian were the result of one basic strategy, then wh-fronting would apply to Pro$_{rel}$ before Clitic Placement or else be inapplicable to clitics (because of sentences such as (14a) in the text) and wh-fronting would be obligatory for some speakers in certain contexts but optional for others in the same contexts. Of course, there are some contexts (such as Complex NP's or Coordinate Structures) in which wh-fronting could not apply. If wh-fronting did not apply, Clitic Placement would apply where applicable and then DEL would apply. Determining whether or not this is the proper characterization of relativization in general in Italian is beyond the scope of this paper. In particular, the interaction of wh-fronting and Clitic Placement must be explored.

2. Many linguists have noted that the structure in which the relative clause appears may affect whether or not a Pro$_{rel}$ appears. See Ross (1967), Neubauer (1970), and Givon (1973), among others.

3. Possessive NP's behave the same as nonaccusative cliticizable objects.

4. In Italian, unemphatic pronominal forms appear as clitics on the verb unless they are the object of a preposition that cannot be stranded or they are a possessive NP or they cannot be moved because of some other constraint (for example, a pronoun that was a conjunct of a Coordinate Structure could not be cliticized).

5. I have not included relativization in Sentential Subjects because the resulting sentences may well be ruled out for independent reasons. Thus, in (i)

(i) ?*Ecco il ragazzo che che (lui) ama Maria è ovvio.
     'Here's the boy that that (he) loves Mary is obvious.'

the sequence <u>che che</u> is what most speakers say they object to. As in English, relativization into extraposed SS's is possible:

(ii) Ecco il ragazzo che non mi piace che lui sposi mia figlia.
'Here's the boy that it doesn't please me that he should marry my daughter.'

Regardless of role, Pro_{rel} must appear in relatives formed in extraposed SS's.

6. For some Italians (11) is better than (10). Grosu (1973), because of similar data in English, has proposed that the CS Constraint is not unitary but rather consists of two separate constraints, the Conjunct Constraint (which is relevant to (10)) and the Element Constraint (which is relevant to (11)). Neeld (1973) points out further distinctions between the two constraints. Neubauer (1972) has noted that SuperEqui distinguishes between the two constraints.

7. For discussions of squishes, see Ross (1972) and Lakoff (1972), among others.

8. Keenan (1972) argues that 'the more a syntactic process, such as relative clause formation, preserves logical structure, the greater the variety of contexts in which it applies and the more "difficult" the positions it applies to.' Assuming that a relative clause with a Pro_{rel} in the surface is closer to the 'logical' structure than a relative clause with a relative pronoun in clause initial position, the squish in Table 1 bears out Keenan's claim. Relative clauses introduced by relative pronouns cannot even be formed for columns 4 and 5, since Italian observes Ross's (1967) constraints on movement out of CNP and CS.

Relatives with relative pronouns also cannot be formed for the bottom square in column 3. I do not know why.

9. For another approach to the same kind of problem, see Neeld (1973), among others.

10. <u>A NP</u> of <u>pensare a NP</u> may also be replaced by the locative clitic <u>ci</u>, as in:

(i) Ci penso.
'I'm thinking about it.'

The major point in this example in the text is the contrast between a predicate like <u>parlare a NP</u> 'speak to NP' and <u>pensare a NP</u>. In the first, <u>a NP</u> is replaced by a dative clitic,

(ii) Gli parlo. (dative)
'I'm speaking to him.'

whereas in the second it is replaced by an accusative.

Also, I found a speaker from Padova who accepted (12b). For such speakers the following argument in the text is vitiated, since the NP coreferential with the head could have been an underlying accusative object, regardless of any pronominal stage.

11. Many speakers do not allow the relative pronoun to be used as the accusative object of its clause. (For a discussion of similar facts in French, see Kayne 1976.) However, even those speakers who do use the relative pronoun for accusative objects reject (15b).

12. There are some relative clauses introduced by che for which the positing of an underlying stage with Pro_{rel} present amounts to positing an underlying ungrammatical stage. For example, in (i)

(i) La ragazza che dicevo ieri è Carla.
     'The girl I was talking about yesterday is Carla.'

since no Pro_{rel} can appear in the surface, we would posit an underlying accusative clitic. Thus the relative clause in (i) would derive from the ungrammatical (ii),

(ii) *La dicevo ieri.
      'I was talking about her yesterday.'

The problem is that dire with the sense of 'refer to' or 'talk about' (rather than its usual meaning of 'assert') does not appear other than in relative clauses of the type seen in (i). Thus one cannot say:

(iii) *Dicevo Carlo quando tu sei entrato.
       'I was talking of Carlo when you entered.'
(iv) *Dicevo di Carlo quando tu sei entrato.
 (v) *Il ragazzo il quale dicevo è Carlo.
      'The boy who I was talking about is Carlo.'
(vi) *Il ragazzo di cui dicevo è Carlo.
      'The boy of whom I was talking is Carlo.'

Examples such as (i) are not evidence against the existence of DEL, however. Rather, since (iii)-(vi) are also bad, they are problems for any analysis of these relative clauses, regardless of the positing of a pronominal stage.

13. So-called prepositions like dietro 'behind', attorno 'around', davanti 'before', etc., which can be stranded, are really adverbs. See Napoli (1974) for evidence.

14. The version of (19) with Pro_{rel} present has ne.

(i) Il gesto che ne sono capace è sputare in faccia al maestro.

15. Relative pronouns cannot be used in columns 4 and 5 because of Ross's constraints.
16. See note 11.

REFERENCES

Chomsky, Noam. 1973. Conditions on transformations.
Festschrift for Morris Halle. New York, Holt, Rinehart and Winston, Inc.
Emonds, Joseph. 1970. Root and structure-preserving transformations. Unpublished doctoral dissertation, MIT.
Givon, Talmy. 1973. Complex NP's, word order and resumptive pronouns in Hebrew. You take the high node and I'll take the low node. Comparative Syntax Festival. Chicago, Chicago Linguistic Society.
Grosu, Alexander. 1973. On the non-unitary nature of the Coordinate Structure Constraint. Linguistic Inquiry 4.188-192.
Kayne, Richard. 1976. French relative que. In: Current studies in Romance linguistics. Edited by Marta Luján and Fritz Hensey. Washington, D.C., Georgetown University Press. 255-299.
Keenan, Edward. 1972. The logical status of deep structures. To be published in the proceedings of the 11th International Congress of Linguists at Bologna, Italy.
Keenan, Edward and Bernard Comrie. 1972. Noun phrase accessibility and universal grammar. Unpublished mimeo of the King's College Research Centre in Cambridge, England.
Lakoff, George. 1972. Hedges: A study in meaning criteria and the logic of fuzzy concepts. Papers from the Eighth Regional Meeting. Chicago, Chicago Linguistic Society.
Napoli, Donna Jo. 1974. Reflexivization across S boundaries in Italian. Paper presented at the winter meeting of the Linguistic Society of America.
Neeld, Ronald. 1973. On the variable strength of island constraints. Papers from the Ninth Regional Meeting. Chicago, Chicago Linguistic Society.
Neubauer, Paul. 1970. On the notion 'chopping rule'. Papers from the Sixth Regional Meeting. Chicago, Chicago Linguistic Society.
Neubauer, Paul. 1972. SuperEqui revisited. Papers from the Eighth Regional Meeting. Chicago, Chicago Linguistic Society.
Ross, John. 1967. Constraints on variables in syntax. Unpublished doctoral dissertation, MIT.

Ross, John. 1972. The category squish: Endstation hauptwort.
Papers from the Ninth Regional Meeting. Chicago, Chicago
Linguistic Society.

ACQUISITION MODELS
AS MODELS OF ACQUISITION

JAMES D. McCAWLEY

University of Chicago

Chomsky's discussions of language acquisition in <u>Aspects</u> and other works involve a number of eminently reasonable premises, for example, that children are innately equipped to acquire a native language, that the innate language-acquisition mechanisms define the set of possible grammars of human languages, and that what grammar a child learns depends on the interaction between his faculty for language acquisition and the linguistic data that he is exposed to.

This paper consists mainly of an attack on some not so reasonable conclusions which Chomsky appears to draw from these assumptions but which are in fact non sequiturs, specifically, (i) the conclusion that what grammar the child learns is predictable from the set of data that he is exposed to, and (ii) the conclusion that when more than one grammar is consistent with the data that the child has been exposed to, his choice among alternative grammars is made on the basis of an 'evaluation measure' (EM), which associates to each grammar a numerical measure of complexity, with a 'less complex' (= 'more highly valued') grammar to be preferred to a more complex one, and the further step to the conclusion (iii) that the evaluation measure is of the general type assumed in Chomsky and Halle (1968, henceforth, SPE), in which there is a fixed notational scheme for grammars and the complexity of a grammar can be measured by counting the number of symbol tokens in the grammar as formulated in the standard notation (cf. Chomsky 1965:31). I will argue that those conclusions, while conceivably true, would be fairly surprising results, and, if true, would not imply anything in particular about language acquisition. I will attribute the popularity of these nonsequiturs to something that has obscured the issues, namely, Chomsky's 'idealization' of treating

acquisition as if it were instantaneous (Chomsky 1965:202), which I
will argue, idealizes away the subject matter of a theory of language
acquisition.

Conclusion (i) is embodied in the diagram which Chomsky (1966)
gives for an idealized scheme of language acquisition:[1]

FIGURE 1.

primary
linguistic ——▶ AD ——▶ grammar
data

Let us for the moment suppose that conclusion (i) is true and that, as
Chomsky holds, the 'acquisition device' (AD) involves an evaluation
measure, which is to serve as the basis on which the child picks a
grammar that fits the given facts.

Let us first consider how an evaluation measure could function as
part of a method of finding a grammar that is consistent with a given
set of data. Suppose that there is an algorithm whereby for any given
grammar of the given type and any fact of the type that is taken into
consideration, one can determine whether the grammar is consistent
with that fact. (The nature of the facts can be left open for the
moment; they might be confined to facts of the form 'x is grammatical' and 'x is ungrammatical', as has generally been tacitly
assumed, or they might be allowed to take other forms such as 'x
allows the interpretation y' or 'x is inappropriate in contexts meeting
condition z'. Chomsky's description of 'primary linguistic data' is
as follows (1965:25): 'This must include examples of linguistic performance that are taken to be well-formed sentences, and may include
also examples designated as non-sentences, and no doubt much other
information of the sort that is required for language learning'). If
you can determine whether a given grammar conforms to any given
fact, then you can do the same for any finite set of facts: you simply
check each fact in the set to determine whether the grammar is consistent with it. An evaluation measure provides a way of enumerating
grammars: one can arrange the infinite set of possible grammars
into a sequence by listing first the grammars of cost 1 (if any), then
the grammars of cost 2 (if any), then those of cost 3, . . . For the
type of evaluation measures that have been considered in the literature, the 'cost' which the evaluation measure associates to a grammar is a positive integer and there are only finitely many grammars
of any particular cost; thus any grammar will turn up in this enumeration after some finite number of steps. One can find a grammar
consistent with a given set of facts by going through the enumeration
and checking each grammar in turn until one is found that is consistent with the given set of facts. That grammar will, in fact, be

the 'least costly' grammar consistent with those facts, [2] relative to
the given evaluation measure, since all less costly grammars will
have been shown not to be consistent with those facts. If it can be
shown that for every consistent set of facts of the type under consideration there is a grammar of the given type that is consistent
with those facts, then this procedure will be 'effective' in the technical sense that for any consistent set of facts it will provide a
mechanical way of finding a grammar consistent with those facts.
It should be noted that with this algorithm the 'optimality' of the result comes for nothing: one finds a grammar at all by starting one's
search with the simplest grammars and stopping when one finds a
grammar that works, which will necessarily be the 'simplest' one
that works, since the simpler ones do not work. I must emphasize
that the central issue of a theory of language acquisition is that of
how the child finds a grammar at all, and 'optimality' comes into the
picture only to the extent that one can justify a theory according to
which considerations of 'optimality' guide the child in his search for
a grammar.

The above algorithm is the most simple-minded 'acquisition device'
that is consistent with Figure 1. Less simple-minded variants of it
could be obtained by supplementing it with principles which narrow
down the search (i. e. which for a given set of facts will eliminate
certain grammars from consideration altogether) while keeping the
same order of 'accessibility' for the grammars that remain in the
running. I take Chomsky's principal substantive claim embodied in
Figure 1 to be that the relative accessibility of alternate grammars
to the language learner is determined by an evaluation measure of
the type that Chomsky envisions, regardless of what additional constraints might be imposed on the class of 'accessible' grammars to
make some version of the above algorithm more 'effective', not in
the technical sense but in the popular sense of 'efficacious'.

I have already mentioned the 'idealization' involved in Figure 1:
acquisition is treated as if it goes in one fell swoop from tabula rasa
to adult linguistic competence. Chomsky does not indicate how this
idealization could be undone, i. e. how the model could be revised so
as to take into account the hundreds of intermediate stages that the
child goes through in the course of his linguistic development. First,
Chomsky does not make clear whether he thinks that all stages in the
child's development conform to Figure 1, i. e. whether every time the
child changes his internalized grammar he adopts the simplest grammar (relative to the given EM) which conforms to the set of facts
that he has processed so far, or whether the sequence of grammars
that the child goes through is only supposed to 'converge' on an
optimal grammar. If the latter is the case, then Chomsky's scheme
gives no clue as to what stages the child goes through in acquisition.

But in that case, the role of the EM in acquisition becomes minor: whatever principles determine the choice of the intermediate stages would determine the final grammar (if there ever really is such a thing as a 'final' grammar), and the fact that the final grammar was 'optimal' relative to a certain EM, while of some interest, would not imply that the EM was part of the innate linguistic capacity of the child. I will thus restrict my attention to the interpretation which makes Chomsky's proposal a real theory of acquisition: that in which all stages of acquisition are to conform to Figure 1.

Here I must digress for a minute and discuss the matter of what 'facts' are relevant to the child's acquisition of his language. It is an error to speak of the input to the acquisition device as being 'facts that the child is exposed to'. The mere fact that a child has heard a certain sentence uttered does not mean that the grammaticality of that sentence (or its semantic interpretation or appropriateness to the context) is a 'fact' that he must make his grammar conform to. The child has to succeed in making an analysis (even a wrong analysis) of the sentence before it can play any role in his language acquisition, and it is that analysis rather than his sensory input that serves as the basis for his construction of a grammar. The child's wrong analyses play just as much of a role as do his right analyses (indeed, they play exactly the same role) in his language acquisition; of course, he will ultimately be disabused of most of his wrong analyses as he encounters further facts that conflict with them.

The role of the child's own analyses in determining the input to his AD makes less mysterious the fact (much stressed by Chomsky) that the child acquires 'normal' language despite being exposed to large quantities of 'degenerate' data, involving speech errors, false starts, etc. Most of the speech errors simply will not be perceived accurately: the child generally will either perceive something which is appropriate to the situation and conforms to his grammar or not arrive at any analysis at all; the same, of course, is true of his perception of error-free speech. Either way, the error would not turn up in the input to his AD. In addition, the editing out of false starts and hesitations is probably accomplished by mechanisms that are not specific to language: the same mechanisms are undoubtedly involved in the perception of music and in one's interpretation of what he sees when he watches a person operating a machine. [3] I should add that there is a major gap in the sketch of language acquisition that I am giving, namely, any indication of what determines whether a child will correctly perceive something that does not conform to his grammar and thus acquire a fact that might trigger revision of his grammar. To fill that gap, it would probably be necessary to get into the area (studied in much detail by Montessori in connection with other domains of learning; see, e.g. Standing 1957:Chapter 7) of differences

among the various stages of a child's development as regards what
kind of learning he is most receptive to. I note in this connection
that the widely quoted example of a child's immunity to correction
(McNeill 1966:69), in which the mother's ten repetitions of the correction resulted in nine repetitions by the child of his original 'error',
followed by an instance of a new error, does not show that children
are in general immune to correction (or to less blatant types of
'negative data', such as the failure of an attempt to communicate
something); such occurrences are consistent with the hypothesis that
at any given point in the child's linguistic development, only certain
parts of his linguistic competence will be open to change, and only
corrections within those areas will even be perceived correctly, let
alone trigger changes in the child's competence and/or performance.

I now turn to a second respect in which it is unclear how Chomsky's
'idealization' could be undone. At any stage of the child's development,
his grammar is supposed to be the least costly one that conforms to
the total set of facts that he has processed up to then, and his next
grammar is supposed to be the simplest one conforming to the
(slightly larger) set of facts that he has processed up to that slightly
later point in time. 4 However, except for extremely early stages of
development, the child will never carry around with him the entire
set of facts that he has processed and will not be able to distinguish
reliably between those linguistic facts which are in his past experience and those which are not. And even if a child could remember
the entire corpus of data that he has processed, it would not do him
any good, since that entire corpus would not be internally consistent.
At each stage of his acquisition he perceives utterances in terms of
the grammar that he has available at that moment, and I conjecture
that the system in terms of which he perceives utterances at an early
stage of his development will lack entirely certain morphemes which
play a role in his later grammars, e.g. articles. A child will have
done an awful lot of language acquisition before he can perceive all
the morphemes in The boys have been pulling the cat's tail, and until
he achieves that level, he will treat various of the adult morphemes
as being at most features of an adult accent without morphemic status,
and thus will treat as not merely grammatical but indeed as 'primary
data' such sentences as Cookie allgone. To the extent that that conjecture is correct, the total set of linguistic data that the child processes not only is not available to serve as input to his acquisition
device but would indeed yield a grossly wrong output if it yielded any
output at all, were it used as the basis for constructing a grammar:
a combination of morphemes that is grammatical or even 'primary
data' at one stage of the child's development will often be ungrammatical at a later stage, and the data that the child has perceived at
age 18 months in terms of his grammar of that stage will have no

direct bearing on how he gets from his grammar of age 36 months to his grammar of age 37 months. His early acquisition has left him not with a corpus of data that he can refer back to in later years but with a system of rules that are modified and supplemented in the course of his subsequent development, and it is only data that the child perceives in the framework of his current system of rules that have a bearing on how those rules can be further altered to give his next stage of linguistic development.

This last remark gives the main reason why I doubt that an EM is involved in language acquisition. An EM is supposed to determine the relative accessibility to the child of alternative grammars that he might adopt. However, it pays no attention to what grammar the child at present has, and if a grammar significantly different from the child's present grammar happens to be 'less costly' than one only slightly different from his present grammar, [5] the former will be preferred to the latter if both are consistent with the set of facts that is to be the input to the AD. But the input to the AD cannot be just a set of facts, since the child does not have available to him a set of facts such as could be the basis of a choice of a grammar. His current internalized grammar is his only link to most of the facts that he has processed, and all that he has available to him besides that grammar is a fragmentary corpus of facts that he has perceived in terms of that grammar, some of which are consistent with that grammar and some of which are not. The choice of the next grammar must thus be made on the basis of a grammar plus a small corpus of facts, rather than on just a huge corpus of facts.

The child's current grammar has worked reasonably well as a tool of communication, deception, bullying, and whatever other uses he puts language to, and there is no reason why he would change it in respects other than those where it has been found deficient. He isn't going to stop complaining to his mother about the food or heaping verbal abuse on his sister for territorial encroachments on him while he goes back to the drawing boards to find the optimum way of incorporating John is easy to please or Nobody said anything into his grammar. Linguistic business as usual must continue while his linguistic place of business is under renovation. I accordingly conjecture that at any stage of the child's development, the 'most accessible' grammars are those which differ least from his present grammar.

This conjecture would make language acquisition accord with the general property of living things that Simpson (1949) expressed in his aphorism 'Evolution is opportunistic'. Simpson intended this as an improvement on the older slogan 'Survival of the fittest': whether a variety of life survives depends not on how 'fit' it is in an absolute sense but on whether it can find an ecological niche that it is fit for, and a 'new' variety of life can displace an 'old' variety from an ecological niche only if the 'new' variety is better able to exploit that niche.

The closest analogue to an EM that could be expected to play a role in this revised theory of language acquisition would be a metric expressing distance between grammars. The acquisition device would contain such a metric, and alternative grammars would be accessible in inverse proportion to their distance from the current grammar. Figure 1 would then have to be replaced by Figure 2, where the AD device is now to contain a measure of distance between grammars.[6]

FIGURE 2.

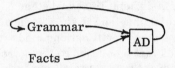

There is, of course, no reason to expect that the sequence of outputs from such an acquisition device would be 'optimal' relative to any evaluation measure: acquisition would be proceeding according to a principle of least effort (i.e. it is less of an effort to make a minor change in the grammar than a major change), but principles of least effort can give rise to 'nonoptimal' results, as in the case of the meandering of rivers, which is known to result from a principle of least effort.

While this revised scheme for acquisition is more realistic than Chomsky's, it shares with Chomsky's scheme a property which I have come to have serious doubts about, namely, that it is deterministic, i.e. its input (or sequence of inputs) determines its output uniquely. I will proceed now to indicate why the assumption of deterministic language acquisition may serve only to create spurious problems.

One area of linguistic analysis that has not been put on a solid footing in transformational grammar is that of morphemic identity. Are two and tw- of twice the same morpheme? Or break and the first syllable of breakfast? Or brother and the frater of fraternal? Or does brother perhaps involve the word broth plus a derivational suffix? Such questions have been given only fragmentary answers, and not many even of those. It is occasionally suggested that questions of this type can be answered on the basis of the generality of the rules involved, which would amount to an invocation of the notion of evaluation measure: which would cost more--a grammar containing the rules that would be needed to relate the various items or a grammar in which they simply had independent dictionary entries?

The suggested recourse to an evaluation measure can be taken in either of two ways: either it refers to the generality of all the rules that would be involved--rules not just to account for the phonological forms of the various words but also to account for their meanings--or it refers to the generality only of the phonological rules. Either way, however, the proposal yields different morphemic identifications than have generally been assumed by generative phonologists. Rules that would relate the meanings and forms of <u>instrument</u> and <u>instrumental</u> (SPE:117) or <u>right</u> and <u>righteous</u> (SPE:233) do not appear to be particularly general (e.g. there is no semantic/phonological parallel with a pair such as <u>slight/*slighteous</u>), certainly less general than rules relating pairs such as <u>brother/fraternal</u> which are generally treated as not synchronically related. Generality of semantic relationships has played so little overt role in generative phonological argumentation that it is difficult to say whether anyone subscribes to the first horn of the dilemma, and if so, whether an adherent of it would accept the morpheme identifications made in SPE. In any event, it is not obvious that a solution to the morpheme identity problem on the basis of the generality of semantic and phonological rules can be made to yield reasonable results.

However, the other horn of the dilemma is even less attractive. If it is only the generality of the relevant phonological rules that determines morphemic identity, then it would be hard to justify relating <u>prestige</u> to <u>prestigious</u> (since no other pair of words exhibits that ž/ǰ alternation), though it would be much easier to justify relating such pairs as

moth	broth	cough	boss	mock	rot	blob
mother	brother	cover	buzzer	mugger	rudder	blubber

rob	bog
rubber	bugger

as well as (assuming that the vowel-raising rule, supposedly exemplified by the above pairs, applies also to front vowels and before other derivational suffixes)

stomp	romp	wrap	cap	nap	tank	laugh
stumble	rumble	ribbon	kibitz	nibble	tingle	liver

gas	lass	quaff	mat	fat	rat	mass[7]
gizzard	lizard	quiver	midden	fiddle	riddle	misery

Even just assuming the rules of SPE, there is nothing to prevent the <u>gen-</u> of <u>genitive</u> from being identified with <u>gene</u> (by analogy with <u>declare/declarative</u>) or even with the name <u>Jean</u>, or to prevent <u>sign</u> from being related to <u>cynic</u>.[8]

I submit that formal analysis of distributional and/or semantic data cannot suffice to determine the morphemic segmentation and morphemic identities that are psychologically real for a given speaker. Rather, a speaker's morpheme identifications depend on details of his language acquisition that are influenced by many random factors. Learning a new word presents the learner with opportunities for dividing it into morphemes and identifying those morphemes with others that he has already identified. However, which particular segmentations and identifications he makes is not obviously pre-dictable, and the best that linguistic theory may be able to do is to identify the factors that influence the likelihood of the learner making a particular analysis. Learning a word involves learning its meaning (or rather, assigning a meaning to it, which need not be the same meaning that was intended by the speakers from whom one learned the word), and the learner has the opportunity to associate consti-tuents of that meaning with portions of the phonological form. If a constituent of the meaning of the new word coincides with the mean-ing of a morpheme that the learner has already identified; if a stretch of the new word has the same phonological shape as that morpheme or a phonological shape that could be related to it by 'plausible' phono-logical rules (especially by rules that the learner already knows); and if the identification of that stretch of the new word with the old morpheme yields a segmentation of the word that agrees with the learner's knowledge of possible morpheme arrangements in the lan-guage (especially if the residue can be identified with morphemes that the learner has already identified, appearing in the type of combination in which he has already identified them); then the learner will be likely to identify that part of the new word with the already identified morpheme. However, he is not going to go out of his way to find a morphemic analysis. If these factors make some analysis obvious to him, he will adopt that analysis, but there is no reason for him to do anything if he does not see an obvious analysis.

The factors mentioned in the last paragraph come in degrees (e.g. the phonological alternation can be irregular or unnatural to varying degrees; the segmentation can conform to varying degrees to the learner's conception of word structure in his language; and the 'residues' can involve more or less regular extensions of the use of previously identified morphemes), and there is no reason to suppose that there is a uniform threshold for these variables. Whether the learner will segment a new word can be expected to depend on what morphemes he has previously identified, and later learning can be expected generally not to lead to his imposing a segmentation on a word that he had learned as a unit: provided that he has learned the meaning of that word (and any inflectional irregularities) correctly, his existing knowledge 'works' and is thus not in need of 'correction'. [9]

Whether he sees a particular morphemic relation as he learns a new
word may also depend on really ephemeral factors, such as what
areas of vocabulary happen at that time to be foremost in his mind,
as a result of what he happens to have been doing or talking about.

The learning of phonological rules may also be nondeterministic
to a significant extent. When the learner identifies part of a new
word with a phonetically nonidentical morpheme that he already
knows, he must either treat the alternation as irregular (i. e. learn
separate allomorphs) or bring it under some old or new generalization. What exactly he does may simply depend on whether he
happens to notice a parallelism between the new morpheme and other
morphemes that he has already identified, and that could depend on
the ephemeral factors just noted. Nondeterministic learning of
phonological rules would agree with standard generative phonology to
the extent that the more morphemes a learner had identified in which
a particular alternation occurred, the greater the likelihood that he
would have learned a general rule to cover the alternation: the more
chances you have to learn a rule, the greater the likelihood that you
will learn it. However, there would be no fixed number of alternating morphemes that the learner would have to learn in order to
learn the general rule, and there would be large variation, even
among speakers who have essentially identical vocabularies, as to
what morpheme identifications they make. There appears, in fact,
to be quite a lot of such variation. For example, there are certain
speakers of English who identify the first syllable of hierarchy with
the adjective high; the fact that I am such a speaker has been brought
forcibly to my attention on a number of occasions when I have caught
myself writing higherarchy. [10]

Finally, I wish to observe that the learning of morphemic analyses
of derived and compound words is radically different from much of
the rest of acquisition, in that regardless of what morphemic analysis
one makes (if any), the resulting grammar works. While a child may
be forced to learn an extraposition rule, since otherwise he would
have no way of understanding many things that he hears nor of expressing many things that there is otherwise no acceptable way of
expressing without circumlocution, a child is never forced to divide
righteous into right plus a suffix: he can speak and understand speech
perfectly well regardless of whether he makes that division or not.
What plausibility Chomsky's acquisition model has is the plausibility
of the idea that when a child has to revise his grammar, he examines
the various possible new grammars in order of increasing 'cost'.
Within that domain, acquisition could conform to Chomsky's model
without there ever being any mental events in which the child compares alternative grammars for 'simplicity': the child would simply
be testing individual grammars against the facts until he found one

that worked. However, for the learning of morpheme boundaries and morpheme identities to conform to the fragmentary sketch of acquisition that Chomsky has provided, it would be necessary that the child compare an already available grammar that works (namely, that in which he does not divide the newly learned word into morphemes) with alternative grammars that may differ in many details from what he has so far learned (namely, grammars involving morpheme divisions not only in the newly learned word but also in previously learned words that he had not hitherto divided into morphemes), and at least sometimes reject the current grammar for a 'less costly' one that involves significant differences in the lexicon. I submit that in this case a nondeterministic acquisition scheme is far more plausible than one involving an evaluation measure: if the child sees a plausible morphemic analysis as he learns a new word, he makes the analysis, and if he does not see one, he does not make any; but either way, he has a grammar that works, [11] and the work of searching for a less costly alternative (if any) to the resulting grammar, or even of evaluating the relative costs of the grammar with the morphemic analysis that he 'sees' and the grammar without any breakup of the new word, would be wasted.

My exploration of possible schemes of language acquisition has been based largely on conjecture, and it will take much observation and experiment to determine how close to the truth the acquisition model sketched here is. However, I have at least established that there are plausible approaches to language acquisition within generative grammar that do not involve directly or indirectly any measure of complexity of grammars. This shows that the popular argument for an evaluation measure on the grounds that an evaluation measure is a necessary part of an explanation of language acquisition is fallacious.

This then leaves the notion of evaluation measure highly suspect. Indeed, I know of no good argument for incorporating any notion of evaluation measure into linguistic theory. The popularity of the notion of evaluation measure can be attributed to several factors: it has had a good press; it can serve as the basis for mildly interesting and easily gradable homework problems; and, most importantly, it provides a rationalization for scientific isolationism, that is, it helps perpetuate the comforting belief that linguistic questions can be answered without going beyond linguistic data. I think that my discussion above establishes that one cannot determine whether <u>high</u> is a morphemic constituent of <u>hierarchy</u> in speaker X's idiolect (or even whether <u>broth</u> is a morphemic constituent of <u>brother</u>) without looking at data that are psychological rather than linguistic. To the extent that a belief in an evaluation measure has left linguists unconcerned about the factual basis of morphemic identity, its effect has been pernicious.

NOTES

1. It is doubtful that the input data can be restricted to being both 'primary' and 'linguistic'. A restriction that the input to the AD be 'linguistic data' is plausible only if 'linguistic data' is taken to include propositions concerning what various utterances mean and the conditions under which they can be used. But those data are not 'primary': they are the result of inferences that the child has made from really 'primary' data about the circumstances under which various utterances have been produced and what has ensued after they have been produced. I find a restriction that the input of the AD be 'linguistic data' far more plausible than a restriction that it be 'primary data'.

2. There may, of course, be more than one 'least costly grammar' consistent with given facts. This will be the case, for example, in a theory involving ordered rules whenever there are rules that can be arranged in different orders without affecting the set of facts that the grammar is consistent with.

3. I am grateful to William Labov (conversation, December, 1966) for making me aware of this point.

4. Thus, according to this version of Chomsky's acquisition model, each step in language acquisition will yield a grammar of complexity greater than or equal to the grammar of the previous stage: the set of facts F_2 at the later stage properly includes the set of facts F_1 at the earlier stage, and thus every grammar consistent with F_2 is consistent with F_1, though generally not vice versa. Thus, the simplest grammar consistent with F_2, being one of the grammars consistent with F_1, has to be at least as complicated as the simplest grammar consistent with F_1. This, of course, would provide a way of narrowing down the search for the next grammar: all grammars of lower cost than the present one could be eliminated from consideration.

5. Given the EM of standard generative phonology, such situations should be quite common. The justification of a phonological rule is whether it allows enough of a 'savings' in the lexicon to pay its 'cost'. Thus, if a certain rule becomes a bargain when it is applicable to five morphemes, the learning of a fifth such morpheme should trigger not only the addition of the rule but also the revision of the dictionary entries of the four morphemes previously learned.

6. It probably matters little whether the 'facts' in the input are just 'new' facts which the current grammar does not conform to, or the whole set of facts, old or new, that the child happens to remember:

if the revised grammar should conflict with some of the facts that the
earlier grammar was supposed to cover, the revised version will be
subject to further revision. Perhaps the appropriate way to insure
an eventual revision that is an improvement over the original grammar is to take all revisions 'on option': the child is allowed to test-
speak a new grammar for a day or two before deciding whether to
trade his old one in on it. If one revision of the grammar does not
work, then it is discarded and a new revision tried, until one is found
that works, in the sense of both conforming to the 'new' facts that
were the occasion for revising the earlier grammar and functioning
adequately in the situations where that grammar worked.

7. Words such as bother and gather are not counterexamples to
the putative vowel-raising rule, since the rule might be sensitive to
morpheme boundary or even to the specific 'suffixes' and would thus
be applicable to /broθ + er/ while not applying to /boθer/. It should
be noted that if these rules were accepted, then the relationship of
prestige to prestigious could perhaps be justified on the basis of
parallelism to smash/smidgeon and posh/pudgy.

8. The objection that this would conflict with the relationship between sign and signature begs the question. Under the given
hypothesis, there is no reason to prefer a relationship between sign
and signature to one between sign and cynic. Indeed, the latter would
be easier to justify, since there are so many cases of vowel-shift
and laxing, but so few cases of the supposed g→y rule that is to apply
in sign.

9. This does not rule out the possibility that he might independently learn a productive rule of word formation that covers a
word that he had learned as a unit. One case where it would be
reasonable to expect a child to impose a morphemic analysis on an
item that he had hitherto taken as an unanalyzed whole is the case in
which the item would conflict with a newly acquired syntactic generalization unless it were segmented, e.g. the child has just learned that
English has obligatory inflection of verbs for tense and must somehow
fit a tense inflection into his hitherto unanalyzed unit go-potty.

10. Kostas Kazazis suggests that a similar folk etymology is
responsible for the standard Greek spelling of Jerusalem, which is
written with the 'hard breathing' sign even though it never had an
initial [h]. According to Kazazis, its first two syllables were simply
identified with hiero- 'sacred', even though the remainder could not
plausibly be identified with any Greek morphemes.

11. This statement is an exaggeration, in that a 'wrong' analysis
may lead the child to produce wrong spellings, as in the example of
higherarchy. However, by the time that such spellings manifest
themselves, it may be too late to change the child's analysis of the
words in question.

REFERENCES

Chomsky, Noam A. 1965. Aspects of the theory of syntax. Cambridge, Mass., MIT Press.

Chomsky, Noam A. 1966. Topics in the theory of generative grammar. In: Current trends in linguistics, Vol. 3. Edited by T. Sebeok. 1-60.

Chomsky, Noam A. and Morris Halle. 1968. The sound pattern of English. New York, Holt, Rinehart, and Winston.

McNeill, David. 1966. Developmental psycholinguistics. In: The genesis of language. Edited by F. Smith and G. Miller. Cambridge, Mass., MIT Press. 15-84.

Simpson, George Gaylord. 1949. The meaning of evolution. New Haven, Yale University Press.

Standing, E. M. 1957. Maria Montessori: Her life and work. London, Hollis and Carter. Reprinted 1962, New York, Mentor.

DIALECT VARIATION IN LEISMO:
A SEMANTIC APPROACH

ERICA C. GARCIA AND RICARDO OTHEGUY

City University of New York

1. A widely discussed problem in Spanish dialectology during the past century, and one which has received no satisfactory solution, is the question of dialectal differences with respect to leísmo, or the use of the form le where lo would be expected (Bello and Cuervo 1847, Kany 1945, Carfora 1968, Zlotchew 1969, Angeles 1970). This paper details the findings of a year-long study[1] on the use of le and lo involving over 200 informants from six different areas of the Spanish-speaking world. We show that previous studies of the use of these forms in the different dialects--and indeed the very notion of leísmo--have rested, (1) on a syntactically based analysis which fails in all dialects and is therefore a poor basis for comparisons between them; (2) on the implicit assumption that the use of these forms in the environments where they alternate can be understood without reference to their use in those environments where no alternation is possible; and (3) on the related assumption that le and lo are equivalent in the alternating environments and that their distribution should therefore be random with respect to any contextual factor.

In contrast, our view of the use of these forms in the different dialects rests, first, on a semantic analysis; second, on the validated claim that the use of le and lo in the environments where either can occur will yield to the same explanation as their use in the environments where only one can occur; and third, on the related claim that le and lo are as different in the alternating environments as they are in the invariant ones, so that predictions can be made in terms of contextual factors as to choice of one form over the other in the alternating environments. On this basis, we are able to show that dialect differences in the use of le and lo are due to differences in the relative strength of inferential strategies as well as to differences in their ranking from one dialect to another.

This paper is in four parts. In Section 2 we explain leísmo and the hypothesis about the use of le and lo on which it rests; in Section 3 we outline the alternative hypothesis on which our investigation was based; in Section 4 we present our findings.

2. The expectation concerning the use of le and lo which serves as the basis for leísmo is rooted in a syntactic analysis of these forms as Dative and Accusative respectively, whose function is to express Indirect (le) versus Direct Object (lo) (Bello and Cuervo 1847:297ff.; Gili y Gaya 1961:232ff.; Hadlich 1971:71-80, 232-233). According to this analysis, then, leísmo is the anomalous use of Dative le as a Direct Object. Such an obvious lack of fit between hypothesis and actual language use might well be regarded as evidence that the hypothesis is wrong. But instead of being seen as a clear counterexample to the analysis in terms of syntactic function, leísmo has been regarded as an anomaly or an error in the usage of the pronouns, and the analysis has been left unchanged. Dialectologists, accepting the grammarians' point of view, have considered it their task to determine in what dialects this anomaly does or does not exist and to what degree it is found. In other words, what is assumed to differ from dialect to dialect is simply the frequency of the 'error' or the 'anomaly'.

Clearly, this approach to dialect differences in the use of le and lo is doomed to failure since it will at best tell us only to what extent the hypothesis about the syntactic function of these forms is disconfirmed in each particular dialect. We have instead based our study on a hypothesis about the meanings of these forms which has been validated (García to appear:chapter 7) for Buenos Aires Spanish and has also been found to work for Cuban Spanish. It is outlined in the following section.

3. Our meanings of le and lo are taken from the analysis of the Spanish pronoun system found in García (to appear), which was undertaken within the Form-Content approach. A detailed account of this analysis and of the linguistic theory on which it rests is beyond the scope of this paper. Nevertheless, we will present both in summary form here, in order to facilitate understanding and assessment of the findings which are the subject matter of this paper. The interested reader should consult, in addition to García (to appear), such works as Diver (1969), Kirsner (1969), Klein (1973), Reid (1974), and Zubin (1972, 1974).

The Form-Content approach rests on two orienting principles, which are assumed to be self-evident: (1) that language is a device of communication and (2) that language is a particular instance of human behavior. Because language is a device of communication, we expect languages to convey meanings by means of signals. It is the task of the linguist, then, to formulate hypotheses about what the signals in a language are, and about what meaning each one of them conveys. It should be noted that meaning is a technical term, used here to refer only to that which is communicated by signals, also a technical term. From utterances which can be analyzed as sequences of meaning-carrying signals, the speaker, through a process which it is also the task of the linguist to elucidate, infers particular messages. In the case that concerns us here, the signals <u>le</u>, <u>lo</u>, and <u>la</u> have been analyzed to have the meanings outlined in (1).

(1) le = LESS ACTIVE PARTICIPANT
     lo = LEAST ACTIVE PARTICIPANT: NONFEMININE
     la = LEAST ACTIVE PARTICIPANT, FEMININE

That is, <u>lo</u> is a signal which always and only--that is, invariably--conveys the meaning LEAST ACTIVE, NONFEMININE; <u>le</u> always and only conveys LESS ACTIVE, without specification of gender. The subject--expressed by the verb ending--is understood to be the most active participant in the event described by the verb. The three forms <u>le</u>, <u>lo</u>, and <u>la</u> also distinguish number, but we can ignore this opposition since it does not help to differentiate among <u>le</u> and <u>lo/la</u>.

There are, then, two differences between <u>le</u> and <u>lo/la</u>. One is a difference in gender: <u>le</u> is neutral, nonspecific as to gender, whereas <u>lo</u> and <u>la</u> specify the gender of their referent; the other is a difference of degree of participation or activeness in the event described by the verb. Here the Form-Content analysis differs profoundly from the traditional one: whereas Dative and Accusative are morphological labels motivated by syntactic functions, we see in <u>le</u> and <u>lo</u> the signals of meanings, the terms of a semantic opposition whose substance is the relative degree of activeness of an object in the event named by the verb. In a three-participant situation this system is exploited to the maximum degree, so that in an utterance such as

(2) Yo le hice comerla 'I made him/her eat it'

where the presence of three entities forces a maximum differentiation of participant roles, we find that the subject (referred to by the verb ending) is most active, <u>le</u> refers to a participant who is less active than the subject but more active than <u>la</u>, and <u>la</u> refers to the participant

which is least active of all. We wish to emphasize that what these
forms categorize are relative, not absolute degrees of activeness in
an event. In other words, le and lo/la serve to rank different participants in a scale of decreasing activity. This appears most clearly in
constructions with infinitives, as in (2), where the participant in the
middle--le--is less active than the object of the infinitive. Similar
situations arise in other three-participant situations, such as

(3) Le di el libro 'I gave him/her the book'

where the book is the least active participant in the act of giving
described by the verb, the giver--verb ending--is the most active
and the recipient--le--is less active than the giver but more active
than the book.

In a three-participant situation, then, there are no alternations
between le and lo/la. In this type of environment there is a perfect
fit between the number of entities participating in the event and the
number of forms in the language that signal participation. The forms
lo/la are thus always used for the least active participant and the
form le for the participant whose degree of activeness is more than
lo/la but less than the verb ending. This state of affairs, of course,
precludes the possibility of alternations. The meaning hypothesis
about these pronouns is thus able to explain a fact that has escaped
notice under the syntactic function hypothesis, namely, that leísmo
is avoided in three-participant situations, where all speakers from
all dialects, constrained by the demands made on a three-member
system by the presence of three entities, use the language in an
invariant way in the manner we have outlined.

What happens, however, in a two-participant situation? In order
to answer this question, we must first consider the following. The
difference in meaning between le and lo/la, which is crucial for their
use in three-participant situations, is of the sort that does not pre-
clude either form from appearing in two-participant situations, since
all that must be signalled in such cases is that the participant referred to by the pronoun is at a lower point than the most active
subject in the participation scale. This point can be the farthest one
from the subject (lo) or a relatively closer one (le), so that the
English utterance 'I saw him' can be rendered in Spanish as either

(4) Lo vi.

or

(5) Le vi.

Now, it must be understood that, as demonstrated in García (1975), it is not the case that the le and the lo of (4) and (5) are different forms from those in (2), nor is it the case that the meaning difference between them is temporarily suspended or neutralized in two-participant situations. Rather it is the case that these forms are always the same and always have the same meaning. The difference between two-participant situations, as in (4) and (5), and three-participant situations, as in (2), is that in a two-participant situation the speaker has more forms available than he needs in order to convey the message, since in a two-participant situation there is (in addition to the subject) only one entity involved. That is, the Spanish system offers two forms whose meaning makes them appropriate to refer to entities that are lower than the subject in the participation scale. Thus the speaker has two forms available where only one would suffice. In every two-participant situation, then, the language presents the speaker with a choice that he does not have to make in three-participant situations. And it is precisely this fact that explains leísmo. That is, the alternation between le and lo/la in two-participant situations is a direct result of the meanings of these forms, and of the fact that both meanings are adequate for the task of signalling a degree of activity that is lower than that of the most active participant. This, the reader will recall, is quite different from the situation that obtains in cases with three participants, where the range of activeness below that of the subject must be parceled out specifically between less and least active participants.

In our view, then, the meaning hypothesis explains why the invariant environment is the three-participant one and the environment where alternations occur, the traditional environment of leísmo, is the two-participant one. From the semantic point of view, leísmo, far from being an anomaly, is the expected state of affairs when, as in this case, the available morphology exceeds, strictly speaking, the communicative needs of the speaker. It is the main concern of this paper to deal with alternating environments (two-participant situations) while leaving aside the nonalternating environment (three-participant situations). But it should be kept in mind, we emphasize and repeat, that the meaning relationship that explains the use of these forms in the latter will also account for the use, including the alternation, in the former.

How is it, then, that the meaning relationship of these forms accounts for the alternation in two-participant situations? The meaning relationship, outlined in (1) and given again in diagram form in (6), places le not only in a higher position than lo/la in the participation scale but also in a position closer to that of the most active subject.

(6) most active = Vb ending
     less active = le
     least active = lo/la

That is, the meaning of le defines a smaller difference in activeness between le and the subject, as indicated graphically in (6). One
might say that le places its referent nearer to the subject in terms
of activeness: le is closer to the subject, more subject-like than lo/
la. In our view, it is this characteristic of le which accounts for its
invariant use in three-participant situations, which also accounts for
its use in the alternating, two-participant environment. Those objects which--for whatever reason--are 'close' to the subject will rate
le, while those objects which--again for whatever reason--are distant
from the subject will rate lo/la. The choice of le or lo/la in two-
participant situations is thus fundamentally the same as the one
operating in three-participant situations: le is used always for the
same reason, regardless of the number of participants, and that
reason is its meaning LESS as opposed to LEAST ACTIVE.

It should be noted, furthermore, that the syntactic function
hypothesis is rendered untenable by the existence of numerous minimal pairs involving only two participants, such as (7) and (8), in
which the use of either le or lo/la for the object with the same verb
radically alters the message.

(7) María le llora 'Mary complains to him'
(8) María lo llora 'Mary mourns him'

Such minimal pairs are of course to be expected if one adopts the
Form-Content approach, since meaning differences such as that between le and lo/la are normally used to distinguish messages, and
the Form-Content approach rests on the fact that language is a device
of communication. In other words, the speakers of the language are
using le vs lo/la in (7) and (8) in order to suggest different messages,
i.e. they are exploiting the meaning difference that is constant between the two forms. Since the meaning difference between le and
lo/la is as clear here as it is in three-participant situations, we have
no reason to believe that it is absent in cases such as (4) and (5),
where the English glosses fail to reflect it. The difference in meaning may be expected to emerge, however, when sentences like (4)
and (5) are considered in context.

In order to make clear the claim that le is used in two-participant
situations when the object is closer to the subject, we have to provide an answer to the question: what is it, in fact, that brings an
object 'closer' to the subject?

Since we are concerned, fundamentally, with judgments as to relative degree of activeness, it follows that the relative position of the object vis à vis the subject may be influenced by properties of the object or by properties of the subject. Thus, an unusually active or potent object will rise in importance, resemble the subject in being more subject-like, and deserve le, while a weak or inactive object will be quite unsubject-like and be appropriately referred to with lo. Similarly, an unusually inactive or weak subject will make the object look more active in comparison and consequently evoke le for it. A more extensive discussion of this problem, as well as numerous examples, are given in García (to appear). Two minimal pairs will provide sufficient material for our explanation here. Let us first consider (7) and (8), where choice of le vs lo for the object of Mary's crying correlates strongly with degree of activeness: the man is alive when he is referred to as le and Mary's crying is motivated by the expectation that he will respond to it (hence the gloss 'she complains to him' or, perhaps, 'she nags him'), but he is totally inert when referred to as lo; in this case Mary's crying is addressed to somebody incapable of response: she beweeps him.

Consider now another pair, illustrating the effect on choice of le vs lo of properties of the subject:

(9) No haga ruido, niño, que le molesta a su padre.
    'Don't make noise, child, because it annoys your father' (le)
(10) No haga ruido, niño, que lo molesta a su padre.
    'Don't make noise, child, because you'll annoy your
       father' (lo)

Here we find that choice of le vs lo for the object of the annoyance suggests different subject for the event: in (9), referring to the father as le prompts the inference that the subject of annoy is an inanimate activity--the noise--while reference to the father with lo correlates with the inference that the subject of will annoy is a person, inherently more active--the child. It should be stressed that these judgments concern the relative activeness of the parties in the event; they are, furthermore, judgments based on common sense appreciations such as, in this case, the fact that a person is held to be more active and potent than a thing. It is, in fact, necessary to appeal to common sense in outlining the way in which the hypothesized meanings are exploited in the language, given that the equivalent manipulations that characterize the actual use of language must be carried out by ordinary men using language in ordinary circumstances.

We have now seen the use of le and lo in three different environments and discussed two of them. First, in three-participant situations such as (2) and (3) we find that le and lo are used invariantly due to the perfect match between entities in the world and forms in the system. Second, we have seen in (7), (8) and (9), (10) the use of these forms in two-participant situations in order to convey different messages. Here le and lo/la are also invariant inasmuch as selection of one over the other depends on the intended message, yet the rationale for the choice of le vs lo is the same in the two- as in the three-participant situation, in that le is chosen for the entity that is closer to the subject. Third, we have cases such as (4) and (5) where le and lo, despite their meaning difference, are both appropriate and therefore alternate; yet, we expect the difference in meanings to explain why le is chosen where it is. These cases of--only apparent--free variation form the subject matter of our dialect study.

While this division of the use of le and lo/la into three different environments is somewhat oversimplified (factors such as context and the meaning of the verb add a degree of complexity that we have no space to discuss here) it serves to highlight the importance of the shared rationales that allow speakers to utilize the forms in varied but regular ways. These rationales can be regarded as 'strategies' for the exploitation of the meaning of a form, i. e. different reasons for which the meaning of, say, le is more appropriate than that of lo/la under different circumstances. In cases such as (2) and (3) and (7) through (10) the strength of the strategies is such that one form is almost always preferred over the other and, furthermore, the operation of the strategy can be demonstrated, as in the case of the child and the noise above, even when the utterances appear out of context. What happens, however, in cases such as (4) and (5) where both le and lo/la can be used without radically altering the message? In these situations the speaker still uses the forms in terms of specific strategies, but here the strategies that suggest choice of one form over the other are of such strength as to produce less sharp skewings in favor of one or the other form and, furthermore, they are dependent on factors that become apparent only in context and thus make it impossible to demonstrate the operation of the strategy in utterances in isolation.

For instance, if the referent of the pronoun in such a situation is an animate, both le and lo/la are appropriate since both meanings can be used to signal a lesser degree of participation than that of the subject and neither meaning specifies whether the referent is animate or inanimate. But one would expect that the meaning of le, that is, its position in the participant scale, would lead users of the language to prefer le for animates. This is, in fact, the case, as has been noticed, but never explained, in the literature on the Spanish pronouns. In other words, the utilization of le and lo/la takes place in terms of strategies motivated by the meaning of the forms even in those cases

where both le and lo/la can be used without a striking difference in the
resulting message.

It should be noticed, incidentally, that if the meanings of le and lo/
la were neutralized in the alternating environment, that is, if they
truly were in free variation, one would expect their distribution to be
random and would not expect any correlation between contextual
factors and the use of one or the other form. The fact that on the
basis of the hypothesized meanings one can predict statistical skewings in favor of one or the other form in the alternating, two-
participant situations, is strong confirmation not only of the correctness of the meanings, but also of the claim that they always are the
same in all environments.

If the use of le and lo/la in the alternating environment, as in all
others, is the result of meaning-based inferential strategies that are
sensitive to contextual factors, then it would seem that a useful research procedure would be to study dialectal differences in terms of
these strategies. (The reader will recall that it is in the third,
alternating environment where dialect differences are most striking.)
This is, in fact, what we have done. The key to our research has
been the manipulation of a sufficiently specific but still controlled
context in such a way as to bring out sharply the relevance of inferential strategies that are almost inaccessible to study from isolated sentences and also difficult to pin down and compare with one
another in the flux of actual language use.

4. From our point of view, then, three possibilities suggested
themselves as reasons for the dialectal differences in the use of the
pronouns. They are given in (11).

(11a) All dialects of Spanish may or may not have the same
meanings for le and lo/la (the meanings in (1)).

(11b) The strategies whereby the le vs lo/la opposition is
exploited may or may not be the same for all dialects.
That is, dialectal differences may consist of a difference in strategies for the exploitation of the same
meanings, rather than of a difference in meaning.

(11c) If the strategies of exploitation are indeed the same,
dialects may differ in the relative strength of these
strategies. That is, dialectal differences may consist simply of a different weighting of the same,
common strategies, of different sensitivity to the
same contextual factors.

To determine to what extent these possibilities actually account
for dialectal differences, a questionnaire was given to 210 informants

from seven different areas. The informants were, in six of the
seven cases, residents of New York City but had all lived in their
country of origin at least through the completion of secondary school.
The countries involved were: Argentina, Colombia, Cuba, Ecuador,
Mexico, and Spain. They were chosen because they are generally
regarded as belonging to different dialect areas. In addition to the
thirty New York Cubans, we also obtained questionnaires from thirty
Cubans currently living in Puerto Rico. They make up the seventh
group in our sample. The informants were asked to fill in blanks
with either le or lo/la in thirty-nine sentences where context was
manipulated along seven different variables. The informants were
also given the option of leaving the space blank if they thought that
none of the forms was appropriate. The questionnaire appears in
the Appendix. The seven variables that we controlled were the
following:

(a) The gender of the object is known or unknown.
(b) The gender of a known object is male or female.
(c) Known male objects are/are not double-mentioned in
    a coreferential a-phrase.
(d) The subject is inanimate or it is an animate unknown
    third person.
(e) The subject is first person or it is an animate unknown
    third person.
(f) A third person subject appears before or after the verb.
(g) A third person subject postposed to the verb is definite
    or indefinite.

The choice of variables was based on our assumption that the
analysis of le and lo/la as signals for the meanings given in (1)
would allow us to predict which factors, when made known to the
informant by placing them in the context of the test sentence, would
favor the use of one or the other form. That is, we predicted that
factors which speakers could perceive as enhancing an object's
degree of participation in an event should result in a statistical
skewing in favor of le in all dialects in which the meanings of the
forms are as in (1). Further, in the case of variable (a), we predicted that the lack of gender marking would increase the proportion
of le. To these predictions we now turn. Due to limitations of space,
we will discuss variables (a), (b), and (d) in detail and will make
more general remarks about the rest of them.

First prediction (variable (a)): If the gender of the object is unknown, le should be favored more than when the gender of the object
is known. In other words, the percentage of le with objects of unknown gender should be higher than the percentage of le with objects

of known gender. The reason in this case is not directly connected with the place of le in the participation scale but is rather due to the fact that le is neutral in gender, and thus allows the informant to avoid the issue of gender and to escape committing himself to one gender or the other--as he is forced to do if he is to pick a form meaning LEAST ACTIVE. The items in the questionnaire that contained an object of unknown gender were numbers 1, 7, 13, and 19. All other items contained objects whose gender was known.

Second prediction (variable (b)): If the object is a male, le should be more frequent than if the object is a female. The rationale is as follows: a male is generally viewed as stronger, more active, and socially higher than a female. He is thus at least potentially more active than a woman would be. We therefore expect that the percentage of le found with male objects should be greater than the percentage of le found with female objects. The items in the questionnaire where the object is a female are numbers 2, 15, 18, and 26. The items where the object is a male are numbers 8, 16, 24, and 31.

Third prediction (variable (d)): If the subject is inanimate, le should be more frequent than when the subject is animate. An inanimate subject can be expected to be inherently weaker, less active, than an animate subject. In comparison with what is perceived as a weak subject, the object will appear as relatively more active. Consequently, le will be used for the object more often when the subject is inanimate than when it is animate. The items in the questionnaire where the subject is inanimate are numbers 9, 14, and 33. In all other items where the subject is known, it is animate.

Let us now see to what extent our predictions have been confirmed.

First, in all dialects, the percentage of le for objects of unknown gender is indeed higher than the percentage of le when the gender is known. In Figure 1 we show this graphically, by means of bars for the actual percentage of le given by the informants under the two contextual conditions. Under each pair of bars (in addition to a figure indicating the level of confidence for the difference between the two bars) we list the ratio between the two conditions, gender unknown and gender known, that is, the proportion between le responses for gender unknown object and le responses for gender known objects. Thus, in Argentinian Spanish informants used le 15 percent of the time when the gender of the object was unknown, but only 9 percent of the time when the gender was known. This means that le was used 1.67 times more when the gender was unknown than when it was known, reflected in the fact that for Argentina the gender unknown column is almost twice as high as the gender known column. It should be clear that a ratio larger than 1 constitutes a confirmation of our prediction and that the ratios express the graphically obvious relation holding between the two contextual factors for each dialect. The advantage of

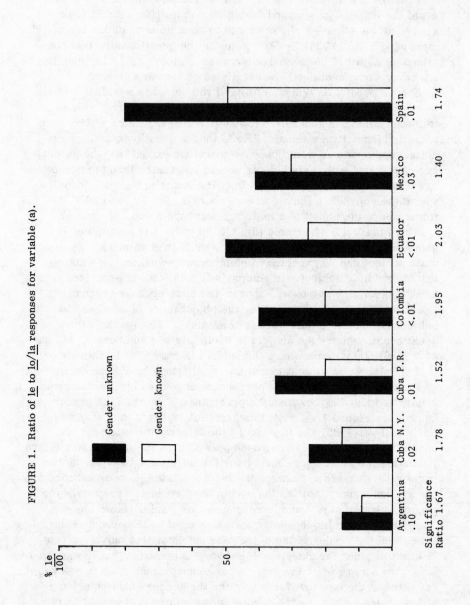

FIGURE 1. Ratio of le to lo/la responses for variable (a).

expressing the relation by means of ratios is that it allows us to eliminate the difference in absolute percentage of le between different dialects.

Second, in all dialects, le is more frequent with male objects than with female objects; the bars and the corresponding ratios are given in Figure 2. Note, for this pair of factors, the extremely high ratio of male le responses to female le responses in Spain. It is apparent that this factor is much more powerful in Spain than in the remaining dialects, though it is clearly operative in all. Note also that the country with the highest ratio of male to female le's after Spain is Argentina, despite the very low absolute percentage of le's in this dialect. We see, then, that attention to absolute percentages may obscure very significant differences and similarities. Mexico is closest to Spain in absolute percentage of le for males, but in terms of the exploitation of the meanings of the language, Mexico is least like Spain (it has the lowest ratio) in that in Mexico females as well as males are given le rather freely, while Argentina, with the lowest absolute percentage of le for males, is most like Spain, in that the pattern of polarization by sex of the object is most similar.

Third, in all dialects, le is more frequent with inanimate subjects than with animate ones. In Figure 3 we show the bars and ratios for the different dialects. Note that Spain has a particularly low ratio for Inanimate/Animate subject, only 1.06. This should not be interpreted as proving that this factor is inoperative in Spain. Rather, the smallness of the ratio is due to the fact that all questions testing the subject variables contained a male object. Consequently, since Spain is heavily influenced by the sex of the object, the percentage of le prompted by a male object will be so high that the effect of the subject will hardly be noticeable. It is therefore perfectly possible that with a female object the animacy or inanimacy of the subject may prove to be effective in Spain, just as it is in all the other dialects, from the data we now have.

It should be clear from the preceding, and from the design of the questionnaire, that in this first stage of our study we did not combine all object factors with all subject factors; we are in the process of doing that in the second stage of our research. It also follows that we do not yet have data on the relative strength of the various parameters when they compete, or generally interact, with each other.

We may now ask how generally have our predictions been supported. We investigated, in all, three variables for the object and four for the subject. Of the object variables, two worked according to our prediction in all dialects and one, variable (c), i.e. presence or absence of a coreferential a-phrase, did so in the five dialects for which we obtained significant differences. Of the four subject variables, one (animacy of the subject) was just discussed and shown

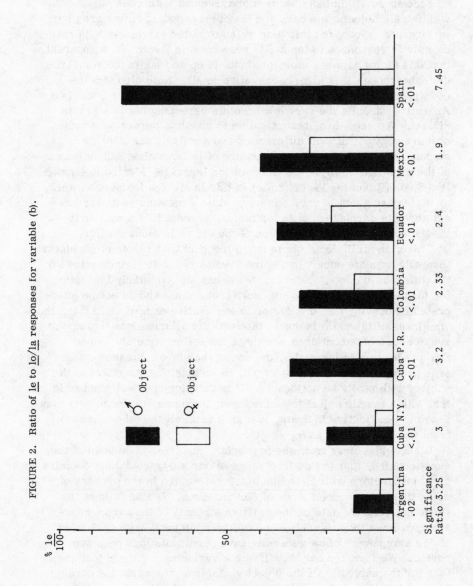

FIGURE 2. Ratio of le to lo/la responses for variable (b).

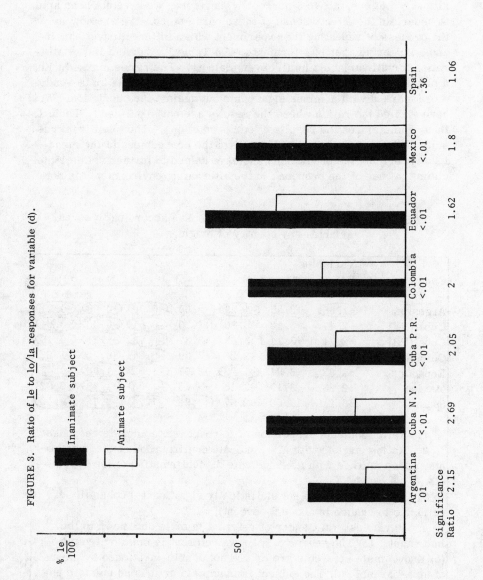

FIGURE 3. Ratio of <u>le</u> to <u>lo</u>/<u>la</u> responses for variable (d).

to work as predicted. For the remaining three subject variables we did not obtain a significant level of confidence, that is, the probability of the results being due to chance with these variables was, in all cases but one, above 5 percent. Therefore, we have not been able to ascertain the effectiveness of these parameters. We are now in the process of repeating the experiment with a different questionnaire and a larger number of informants. On Table 1 we give a list of all ratios for all variables in all seven dialects. The ratios marked with a plus sign came out as predicted--le more frequent than lo/la--and those marked with a minus sign came out against the prediction. We have circled the ratios where the results are not significant. Table 1, then, summarizes the results of our predictions. The significant results of the predictions clearly confirm the correctness of the meanings underlying the predictions and have helped to further validate the claim that use of the pronouns in the alternating environments is not

TABLE 1. Ratios of le to non-le responses according to seven variables, by country of origin.

Countries	Variables (a)	(b)	(c)	(d)	(e)	(f)	(g)
Argentina	+1.65	+2.50	-1.29	+2.65	+0.30	+0.89	+0.21
Cuba (NY)	+2.47	+3.12	+3.80	+4.20	-0.61	-0.00	+0.64
Cuba (PR)	+2.74	+5.14	+3.07	+3.37	-0.73	+1.21	+0.18
Colombia	+4.57	+3.84	+3.26	+3.39	-0.54	+0.52	-1.26
Ecuador	+4.82	+3.64	+1.22	+3.77	-1.53	+1.06	-0.45
Mexico	+2.23	+3.19	+3.16	+3.48	-1.93	+1.79	+0.32
Spain	+6.21	+11.00	+2.97	+0.92	-1.24	-0.75	-0.00

1. Ratios indicate proportion of le responses to non-le responses.
2. Ratios marked with a '+' indicate confirmation of the hypothesis; ratios marked with a '-' indicate disconfirmation of the hypothesis.
3. Ringed ratios are not statistically significant (probability of ratio due to chance is above 5 percent).
4. Variables: (a) Gender of referent is or is not known to the informant. (b) The gender of a known referent is male or female. (c) Known male referents are or are not double-mentioned by means of an a-phrase. (d) The subject is inanimate or it is an animate unknown third person. (e) The subject is 1st person or it is an animate unknown 3rd person. (f) A 3rd person subject appears before or after the verb. (g) A 3rd person subject is definite or indefinite.

a case of free variation but rather a case of selection of the most appropriate of the two meanings depending on contextual factors such as sex of the referent or animacy of the subject. Our most interesting finding, however, is what we have learned about the alternatives listed in (11) as possible accounts of the difference between dialects.

Previous approaches simply recorded the fact that in the alternating environments some countries use le more than others. This is true enough and is confirmed by our figures, which show that, over all, the percentage of le in two-participant situations differs from country to country, as indicated in Table 2. This tells us, for instance, that out of all responses in the questionnaire, the largest percentage of le over lo/la for all variables was Spain and the lowest was Argentina.

TABLE 2.   Percent of le with two participants, by country of origin.

Country	Percent le
Spain	73%
Ecuador	41%
Mexico	38%
Colombia	29%
Cuba (PR)	27%
Cuba (NY)	22%
Argentina	13%

Our approach, however, has turned up a much more interesting pattern of similarities and differences in the use of the pronouns between the different dialects. In Figure 4 we have plotted the ratios given in Figures 1 through 3. What these lines show is the absolute strength of the different strategies in each dialect. Thus in Figure 1 we see that in Argentina the ratio of gender unknown to gender known is 1.67; in Figure 2 we see that in Argentina the ratio of male to female le's is 3.25, and so forth. These points have been plotted for each dialect in Figure 5, where the ratios for each strategy have been linked. The double line running at the level of 1 indicates that the strategy has no strength at all; the percentages must be the same under both conditions to give a ratio of 1. Consequently, the closer the strategy approaches a ratio 1, the weaker it is. That is, if for any variable we were to get ratios of 1 (same percentage of le for one or the other factor), then we could truly say that, at least in terms of that contextual factor, the forms are in free variation. The farther from 1 the lines are, the less the forms are in free variation and the more the speaker is choosing the meaning that is more coherent with

FIGURE 4. Relative strength of variables (a), (b), and (d).

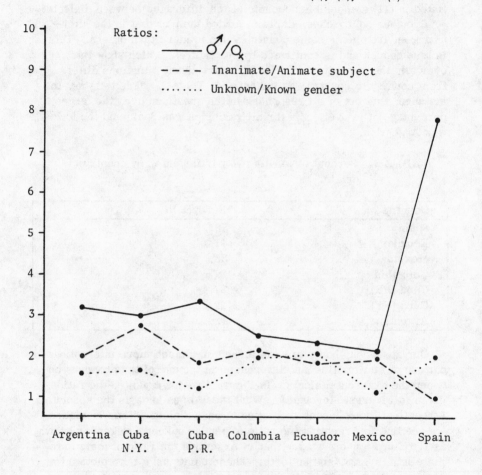

the particular contextual factor. The farther from 1 the line is, the
stronger the strategy.

It now becomes clear that in all dialects the sex of the object
(whether male or female) influences the choice of le with greater
strength than does either the animacy of the subject, or the degree
to which the gender of the object is known: the solid line runs above
the broken line, and above the dotted line. We observe, in other
words, that the relative ranking of the different strategies for choice
of le vs lo/la is the same in all dialects, despite the dramatic differences in absolute percentage of le from dialect to dialect indicated in
Table 2, and despite the differences in the absolute strength of
strategies from one dialect to another (i. e. the lines are not straight
but rather dip and rise from one dialect to the next). A striking
exception appears in Ecuador and Spain, where 'gender unknown' out-
weighs 'animacy of the subject': the dotted line rises above the broken
one. While dialects appear to exploit the opposition of le vs lo/la
according to the same strategies, the relative importance of the
strategies has been found to be different in some dialects.

Turning now to the possibilities outlined in (11), we can summarize
our findings concerning dialect differences in the following way.
First, we have shown that, based on meanings which have been validated for one dialect, we can make predictions that are borne out by
informants' responses in all areas surveyed. We thus conclude that
the meanings of the forms are the same for all dialects and, therefore, that the difference in the use of le and lo/la between dialects
must be due to something else.

Second, we have found that if several of the strategies used for the
exploitation of le and lo/la are singled out and predictions are based
on them, the responses of the informants will bear them out in the
same way for all dialects, regardless of the differences between dialects with respect to the absolute strength of each strategy. From
this we conclude that the dialects do not differ as to these strategies
either; they are shared by all dialects.

Third, our findings show that the differences that have been
noticed in the use of le and lo/la from one dialect to the other are due
to three factors, one of which was already known, namely, that the
total, overall use of le is more frequent in some dialects than in
others. In addition, we have learned that what is different between
the dialects is the absolute strength of the strategies and the way in
which these strategies are ranked.

5. Summary. The grammarian, based on the notions of direct and
indirect object, provides an analysis of the syntactic function of le and
lo which cannot account for all the data and fails every time le is used
as a direct object. Thus, leísmo is a phenomenon that exists only

when the language is seen through the particular hypothesis about le
to which leísmo is a counterexample. The dialectologist then engages
in a quantitative analysis of these counterexamples and proceeds to
tabulate the amount of leísmo in each dialect. As a result, all we
learn about the differences in the use of le is the extent to which the
hypothesis of le as indirect and lo as direct object is disconfirmed in
each particular dialect. Being dissatisfied, as anyone would be,
with this state of affairs, we were led, by viewing the phenomenon in
Form-Content terms, to ask a different set of questions, namely,
questions regarding the exploitation of the opposition between le and
lo in the communication of messages. In using le and lo, the speaker
is making a choice, not between two forms that perform two different
syntactic functions, but rather between forms that have meanings
which are exploited with the aid of inferential processes and which
remain constant in all environments. Knowing from the analysis of
le and lo what some of these standard, common inferences (called
strategies) were, placed us in a position where we could pinpoint the
areas of agreement and disagreement between dialects and led us to
discover that dialects differ in terms of the relative importance
given to (or the relative strength of) different strategies.

It should be noted that what we have learned about dialectal differences is only expressible if one views the Spanish pronouns in the
way that we have here, since, clearly, strategies are only coherent
with a meaning analysis. That is, while it is coherent for meanings
that differ in terms of degrees of participation to be exploited in order
to distinguish real world objects which can be perceived as having
different degrees of involvement in an event (for instance, male and
female referents), such an exploitation would be a mystery if the
difference between le and lo were that between indirect and direct
object or if there were no difference at all. For it is also the case
that our findings have been possible only because we have viewed
all occurrences of le as signals of the same meaning and have not
split le into two forms that carry out different functions and just
happen to sound the same, as is done under the syntactic function
hypothesis. We have shown that le is always the same and that it is
its meaning that causes it to be used invariantly in some environments
and in alternation with lo/la in others. It should be clear, then, that
our success in disentangling the problem of leísmo is a direct result of
the theoretical vantage point from which we have looked at the data.
By asking not how much le is used and what is its syntactic function,
but rather asking in which way it is used to convey messages, we
have established what relation in fact holds among different strategies; have gained new knowledge on the nature of dialectal differentiation; and have succeeded in shedding light on what previously appeared
as amorphous chaos.

APPENDIX

Questionnaire

1. No le va bien porque no _____ ayudan.
2. ¿Y Rosa? No debe estar en casa; recién _____ vieron salir.
3. ¿Dónde está Pedro? _____ llamé hace un momento.
4. Para que no haya un accidente, es mejor que nadie _____ distraiga a Jorge.
5. ¿Qué tal anda Luis? Bastante bien; el padre _____ ayuda en lo que puede.
6. ¿Qué pasó que Norberto no acertó? Fue que _____ distraje.
7. Recién _____ llamaron.
8. ¿Cómo le va a Oscar? No muy bien porque no _____ ayudan.
9. ¡Qué pena que Roberto deje los estudios! _____ llama demasiado la vida bohemia.
10. ¿Cómo van los asuntos de Tito? El padre se ocupa, y _____ ayuda en lo que puede.
11. ¿Acase fue culpa de Juan que Pepe no certara? Sí, _____ distrajo.
12. ¿Y José? Debe estar con el padre; _____ llamó hace un momento.
13. No debe estar en casa; recién _____ vieron salir.
14. ¿Cómo está Pedro? Bastante bien; _____ ayuda el hecho de que el tío haya ganado la lotería.
15. ¿Dónde anda María? Hace un momento _____ llamaron.
16. Cuando conduce Ricardo, es mejor que nadie _____ distraiga.
17. ¿Roque está? Creo que no; hace un momento _____ vio salir un empleado.
18. ¿Cómo lo va a Luisa? No muy bien, porque no _____ ayudan.
19. Para que no haya un accidente, es mejor que nadie _____ distraiga.
20. ¿Dónde quedó Augusto? Hace un momento _____ llamó un ordenanza.
21. ¿Pedro está en la oficina? La secretaria cree que no; hace un ratito _____ vio salir.
22. ¿Cómo marchan los asuntos de Cacho? Pues, _____ ayudo en lo que puedo.
23. ¿Qué pasó que Luis no acertó? _____ distrajo el ordenanza.
24. ¿Sabes dónde está Felipe? No debe estar en casa; recién _____ vieron salir.
25. ¿Jorge se arregla? No le va mal; _____ ayuda un amigo.
26. Cuando conduce Josefa es mejor que nadie _____ distraiga.
27. ¿Y Luis? El padre _____ llamó hace un momento.

28. Creo que Mauricio no está; la secretaria _____ vio salir hace un momento.

29. ¿Cómo fue que Manuel se equivocó? El ordenanza _____ distrajo.

30. No le va muy bien porque no _____ ayudan a Pepe.

31. ¿Dónde está Roberto? Recién _____ llamaron.

32. No debe haber nadie en la casa; recién _____ vieron salir a Jorge.

33. ¿Por qué no acertó Angel? _____ distrajo el ruido.

34. ¿Qué tal los negocios de Tito? Bastante bien; _____ ayuda el padre en lo que puede.

35. ¿Felipe está? Creo que no; hace un momento _____ vio salir la secretaria.

36. ¿Por dónde van? Recién _____ llamaron a Roberto.

37. ¿Qué sucedió que Jorge no acertó? _____ distrajo un ordenanza.

38. ¿Y Cacho? Hace un ratito _____ llamó el padre.

39. ¿Dónde está Agustín? No debe estar en casa; hace un momento _____ vi salir.

NOTE

1. This research was supported by a grant, which is hereby acknowledged, from the Research Foundation of the City University of New York (grant number 10144) to the first-named author.

REFERENCES

Angeles, P. 1970. Lo, le, and the Real Academia Española. Hispania 53. 442-443.

Bello, A. and R. J. Cuervo. 1847. Gramática de la lengua castellana. Buenos Aires, Sopena. (7th edition, 1964).

Cárfora, J. 1968. Lo and le in American Spanish. Hispania 51. 300-302.

Diver, W. 1969. The system of relevance of the Homeric verb. Acta Linguistica Hafniensia 12. 45-68.

García, E. (to appear). The role of theory in linguistic analysis: The Spanish pronoun system. North Holland Linguistic Series.

Gili y Gaya, S. 1969. Curso superior de sintaxis española. Barcelona, Bibliograf.

Hadlich, R. 1971. A transformational grammar of Spanish. Englewood Cliffs, N. J., Prentice-Hall.

Kany, C. 1945. American-Spanish syntax. University of Chicago Press.

Kirsner, R. 1969. The role of <u>zullen</u> in the grammar of Modern Standard Dutch. Lingua 24.101-154.

Klein, F. 1973. The role of meaning in grammatical change. Unpublished Ph. D. dissertation. Columbia University.

Reid, W. 1974. The Saussurian sign as control in linguistic analysis. Semiotexte 1. Fall Volume.

Zlotchew, C. 1969. More thoughts on <u>lo</u> and <u>le</u>. Hispania 52. 870-871.

Zubin, D. 1972. The German case system: Exploitation of the dative-accusative opposition for comment. Unpublished M. A. thesis. Columbia University.

Zubin, D. 1974. The semantic bases of case alternation in German. Paper delivered at NWAVE-III. [This volume, 88-99.]

THE SEMANTIC BASIS OF
CASE ALTERNATION IN GERMAN

DAVID A. ZUBIN

Columbia University

A German speaker, when describing an event in which physical
contact with a person occurs, may refer to that person by using either
dative or accusative case morphology, e.g. <u>Der Hund beisst ihm/ihn
in das Bein</u> 'The dog bites him (dative/accusative), in the leg'. This
alternation has presented an intractable problem for some German
grammarians and linguists, who have claimed that there is no consistent semantic distinction associated with the difference in case,
while others have claimed that an account of this alternation does not
lie within the domain of grammar at all. Before proceeding to a
semantic analysis of this alternation it will be germane to explore
some of the reasons why other analysts have failed to find a consistent
semantic basis, or have laid the alternation aside as a non-problem.

When scientific inquiry into the structure of language is approached
primarily from the viewpoint that language is an expression of thought,
there result certain biases towards the linguistic data to be analyzed.
For example, the subject-predicate distinction imported from the
logical investigation of the structure of thought plays a fundamental
role in grammatical analysis. Subjectless sentences prevalent in the
surface structure of many languages are supplied with subjects on an
underlying level of structure, thus creating the subject-predicate
relationship of a 'complete thought'. For example, subjectless sentences like (1a) and (1c) are typically assigned underlying structure
roughly corresponding to (1b) and (1d):

(1a) Mir ist kalt.
     me (dative) is cold
     'I feel cold'
(1b) Es ist mir kalt.
     it is me (dative) cold
(1c) Vor der Tür wird gesungen.
     at the door is being sung
     'There is singing at the door'
(1d) Man singt vor der Tür.
     one is singing at the door

This practice reaches absurd extremes in the analysis of discourse in which a simple statement like <u>after lunch</u> is expanded on an underlying level to supply it with both a subject and a predicate: for example, <u>the pain in my stomach started to grow worse after lunch.</u> Concerns in the philosophy of language and thought which make a distinction such as 'subject-predicate' so important include 'truth value' and the study of 'sentential synonymy' and 'paraphrase relations'.

On the other hand, preoccupation with language as the expression of thought leads to the neglect of some distinctions actually present in the surface structure, or at least to a denial of their importance for grammatical analysis. Specifically, a difference in underlying structure is allowed only when different semantic interpretations or 'readings' are apparent, in other words, when there is a semantic contrast produced by the alternation in form. For example, there is a semantic contrast corresponding to an alternation in tense form between:

(2a) Die Rokete startet (morgen)   'the rocket is taking off
     (tomorrow)'
(2b) Die Rokete startete (gestern) 'the rocket took off
     (yesterday)'

This strong contrast results in a difference in truth value: if (2a) is true it does not follow that (2b) is true. This is further shown by the clash of a past adverb with the non-past tense in (3a), and vice-versa in (3b):

(3a) *Die Rokete startet gestern 'the rocket takes off yesterday'
(3b) *Die Rokete startete morgen 'the rocket took off tomorrow'

The semantic contrast may be more subtle and show up as a difference in presupposition, as in:

(4a) Max glaubt, Marie sei schwanger
'Max believes Marie is (subjunctive) pregnant'
(4b) Max glaubt, Marie ist schwanger
'Max believes Marie is (indicative) pregnant'

Sentence (4a) with the subjunctive presupposes a belief on the part of
the speaker that Max is wrong, i. e. that Marie is not pregnant,
whereas (3b) with the indicative does not presuppose this, i. e. the
speaker is neutral to Max's belief. This difference in presupposition
is highlighted in (5):

(5) ?Max weiss, Marie sei schwanger
'Max knows Marie is (subjunctive) pregnant'

Because of the well-known incompatibility of asserting 'know that x'
when 'x' is false, sentence (5) simultaneously presupposes that Marie
is pregnant and that she isn't.

The purpose of presenting the examples in (1)-(5) has been to
illustrate how the conceptualization of language as an expression of
thought leads to reliance on truth value and presuppositional differences, and on anomalous sentences resulting from conflicts in truth
value or presupposition, for determining grammatical structure. It
is important to note the apparent weakening in semantic contrast
moving from the examples in (2) to the examples in (4). In (2a) and
(2b) the difference in tense form is associated with a semantic contrast strong enough to be intuitively obvious, and which shows up as
a difference in truth value. The mood difference between (4a) and (4b)
is associated with a more subtle semantic contrast which is not always obvious to the native speaker, and which becomes distinct only
after the presuppositional difference is pointed out. The semantic
contrast associated with the case alternation in (6a) and (6b), the
main topic of this paper, is even weaker:

(6a) Peter trat den Mann in das Bein.
'Peter kicked the man (accusative) in the leg'

where the man is in the accusative case, and:

(6b) Peter trat dem Mann in das Bein.
'Peter kicked the man (dative) in the leg'

where the man is in the dative case. The contrast gives rise to
neither a difference in truth value nor presupposition. In addition,
native speakers are not consciously aware of any difference in
interpretation at all, and linguists attempting to find a consistent

difference through intuition have failed. A German grammarian
concentrating on this problem early in the century concluded that 'I
do not dare to decide whether in this case . . . there exists a difference in the intuition of the speaker' (Behaghel 1927:352). In a recent
examination of this problem another grammarian (Starke n. d.) concluded that there is no difference in meaning when he found examples
in which dative and accusative alternate with the same verb in close
juxtaposition:

(7) Später schlugen sie ihm mit einem Hammer in die Leber
    und mit den Fäusten auf Hals und Ohren. . . . Als sie
    nichts aus ihm bekommen konnte, schlug ihn der
    verhörende Hauptmann der Guardia Civil so brutal ins
    Gesicht, dass er bewusstlos zusammenbrach und ins
    Gefängnisspital gebracht werden musste. (Weltbühne
    n. s. 18, p. 459)
    'Later they hit him (dative) with a hammer in the liver
    and with their fists on the neck and ears. When they
    could get nothing out of him the interrogating captain
    of the Civil Guard hit him (accusative) so brutally in
    the face that he collapsed unconscious and had to be
    brought to the prison hospital. '

(8) Ich trat ihn mit voller Wucht zwischen die Beine. Ich
    hatte Militärstiefel an, und ich habe selten einen Mann
    so schreien gehört vor Schmerz. . . . Der, dem ich
    zwischen die Beine getreten hatte, sprang wieder auf
    mich zu. (Grün, Irrlicht, p. 45)
    'I kicked him (accusative) with all my power between
    the legs. I had military boots on, and I have seldom
    heard a man scream so with pain. . . . The one whom
    (dative) I had kicked between the legs jumped at me
    again. '

Faced with these facts, an analyst who views language as an expression of thought will be tempted to conclude that there is no
difference in the thoughts expressed, and hence no difference relevant to the grammatical structure of the language. This alternation
of the dative and accusative case forms will be placed aside as an
interesting but useless curiosity. If, however, the problem is
approached from a different perspective, from the point of view that
language is a code, that is, a device of communication in which
morphological forms--such as the dative and accusative cases--
serve as signals with associated meanings, then the analyst is forced
to probe deeper. When dealing with morphologically discrete forms,

the orientation that language is used to communicate requires the
analyst to look for the meanings communicated by those forms.

It is not possible directly to construct an hypothesis about a difference in meaning between dative and accusative in sentences like (6a)
and (6b), (7) and (8), since as pointed out earlier, native speakers
have no reliable intuitions in this area. A previous analysis (Zubin
1972) of case meaning in other areas of the grammar of German has
revealed that an entity in the dative makes a greater contribution to
the event it participates in than an entity in the accusative. In other
words, the dative entity is more active, or more potent, or has a
greater personal interest in the event, whereas the accusative entity
is less potent or active, and more likely affected in the course of the
event. For example, a quantitative study (Zubin 1975) of a set of
predicates expressing the notion 'avoidance', as in:

(9a) Elsa meidet den Hund.
'Elsa avoids the dog (accusative)' (dog less potent)
(9b) Elsa weicht dem Hund aus.
'Elsa avoids the dog (dative)' (dog more potent)

showed that as the causal force of the entity being avoided increases,
it will more likely be in the dative case. The dog in the dative in
(9b) causes Elsa's avoidance to a greater degree than the dog in the
accusative in (9a). 'Causal force' is, of course, not the meaning of
the cases. It is inferred from the meanings of dative and accusative
--greater vs lesser contribution-- in the context of predicates expressing 'avoidance'. The more one entity causes another to avoid, the
greater its contribution to the total event. We can expect different
inferences to be made from these same general meanings in the context of the verbs expressing physical contact in (6a) and (6b). Since
physical contact can easily lead to a physical effect on the person
with whom contact is made, it will be hypothesized that a person in
the accusative will make a lesser contribution by being more greatly
affected, i.e. less potent, whereas a person in the dative will make
a greater contribution by being less affected, i.e. more potent. In
addition, it is hypothesized that the dative emphasizes the personal
interest of the individual more than the accusative. These inferences
are schematized in (10).

(10) Dative: 'greater contribution'
in the context of physical contact →less affected
more personal
involvement

Accusative: 'lesser contribution'
in the context of physical contact→more affected
less personal
involvement

To sum up, the accusative will emphasize the effect on the person, whereas the dative will emphasize his personal involvement.

To test this hypothesis 145 examples of sentences like (6a) and (6b) were culled from about 3,000 pages of running text in modern German realistic literature and journalism. Each example had a verb expressing physical contact, a dative or accusative object, and a prepositional phrase indicating the particular body part. Table 1 summarizes the data, classified according to the verb used and the case used. The verbs have been arranged according to the degree of force they express, as suggested by glosses in Cassell's dictionary and verified by two informants.

In category I the contact is light, i.e. not likely to produce a physical effect, and all sentences contain a dative. In addition, these verbs suggest a communicative interaction between the two parties, thus enhancing the personal involvement of the person being touched. Number (11) is a typical example.

(11) Der Richter klopfte ihm vertraulich auf den Arm.
"Heute sind Sie mein Gast" sagte er, laut und zutunlich.
'The Judge patted him (dat.) confidentially on the arm.
"Today you are my guest," he said, loud and obligingly.'

In category II the force of the contact expressed by the verb is greater than in category I and the dative drops to 84 percent of the sample. Number (12) is a typical example.

(12) Der Pfarrer . . . haut ihnen auf die Finger, so wie ein Lehrer Schuljungens züchtigt.
'The pastor raps them (dat.) on the fingers in the way that a teacher would punish schoolboys.'

In category III the force of the blow is still greater, often enough to produce an obvious physical effect, and the dative drops still further to 26 percent of the sample. Number (13) is a typical example.

(13) "Vorwarts, du roter Hund!" schreit er und stösst ihn in den Rücken, dass der Jupp stolpert und seine eine Krücke zu Boden fällt.
'"Get going, you red dog!" he shouts, and shoves him (acc.) in the back, so that Jupp stumbles and one of his crutches falls to the floor.'

TABLE 1. Incidence of dative and accusative objects with verbs expressing physical contact. The verbs have been classified according to the degree of force they express.

Category	Verb	Gloss from Casells	Dat.	Acc.	% Dat.	Type of contribution suggested by the verb
I	klopfen	'rap, tap'	14	0		The person receives a
	streichen	'stroke'	8	0		soft blow with com-
	tippen	'touch gently'	1	0		municative, friendly,
						or intimate intent.
	Total		23	0	100%	
II	beissen	'bite'	4	1		The person receives
	hauen	'strike'	15	1		a blow or other type
	patschen	'smack'	0	1		of contact, ranging
	schlagen	'hit, brush'	30	2		from soft to hard.
	stechen	'stab, poke'	0	1		
	treffen	'hit'	0	1		
	treten	'kick'	5	2		
	zwicken	'tweak'	0	1		
	Total		54	10	84%	
III	boxen	'box'	3	6		The person receives
	stossen	'shove'	4	14		a strong blow or
						shove, often causing
	Total		7	20	26%	him to move.
IV	fassen	'lay hold of'	0	6		The person is
	packen	'seize'	0	5		(relatively) im-
						mobilized.
	Total		0	11	0%	
	Case indeterminate			16		
	Metaphorical examples			6		
	Total N			145		

In category IV the contact is forceful in such a way as to relatively immobilize the person, so that he is always affected in a strong sense. Number (14) is a typical example.

(14) Der Jupp fasst sie um die Schultern und will ihr Gesicht sehen. Sie wehrt ihn ab.
'Jupp takes her (acc.) by the shoulders and tries to see her face. She wards him off.'

The progressive trend from dative to accusative as the force of contact with resulting effect increases and the communicative or intimate
aspect of the interaction drops out, is depicted in Figure 1.

FIGURE 1.   Decrease in use of the dative as the effect of verbal
action increases and personal involvement decreases.

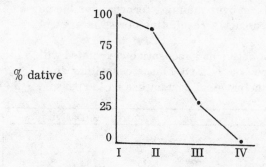

At either end of the scale of verbs in categories I and IV, where the
attraction for the dative or the accusative is strongest, we would
most likely expect native speakers to have intuitions about grammaticality, and they have. Sentences (15) and (16) are considered deviant
or ungrammatical by most speakers:

(15)   *Peter klopfte den Mann auf die Schulter, um ihn zu
          begrüssen.
          'Peter tapped the man (acc.) on the shoulder in order
          to greet him.'
(16)   *Peter packte dem Mann um die Schultern, um ihn
          festzuhalten.
          'Peter grabbed the man (dat.) by the shoulders in order
          to hold him fast.'

The reason for these judgments would now seem to be obvious. The
light contact suggested by the verb klopfen in (15) clashes semantically
with the more forceful contact suggested by the accusative. And in
(16) the forceful contact suggested by packen conflicts with the lighter
contact and intimate interaction suggested by the dative.
     An obvious indicator of the degree to which the person is affected
by being touched or hit, is the presence of a resultative clause
describing this effect, as in (17).

(17)   "Hier herrscht Ordnung!" brüllt jetzt der Handstand und
          stösst den Hoppfuss gegen die Brust, dass er rückwärts

stürzt und sein Holzbein mit einem eigenartigen, trockenen
Klang auf dem Steinboden des Fabrikhofes aufschlägt.
'"Order prevails here!" bellows Handstand now and shoves
Hoppfuss (acc.) against the chest so that he flies backwards
and his wooden leg bangs on the stone floor of the factory
yard with an unusual dry sound.'

Table 2 shows that there is an overwhelming tendency for the person
to be in the accusative when such a resultative clause is present.

TABLE 2.   Incidence of dative and accusative correlated with
the presence of a relative clause describing an
effect that the physical contact has on the person.

Relative clause	Dat.	Acc.	% Dative
present	1	8	11%
absent	83	31	73%

The presence of a relative clause corroborates the importance of
verbal meaning rather than being an independent effect, since seven
of the nine relative clauses occur with the verb stossen, which itself
heavily favors the accusative, as can be seen in Table 1.

The second part of the hypothesis claims that the dative will be
more frequent when the personal interest of the individual is somehow emphasized. One indicator of this is whether the person's face,
or some other part of his body, is involved in the contact, stemming
from the view that a person's face most clearly represents his per-
sonality and individuality, his 'personhood'. A blow to the face in
particular is more of a personal insult than a blow to another part of
the body, as in (18).

(18)   . . . glitt er und leerte den Würmertopf um, der andere
riss den Angelstock hoch und schlug mit der flachen Hand
dem Buben in das Gesicht. Das brannte--verflucht--,
er sah noch Rot vor den Augen. . . .
'He slipped and tipped the worm can over. The other
one yanked his fishing pole up and hit the boy (dat.)
with the flat of his hand in the face. That burned--
damn--, he could still see red before his eyes.'

Table 3 reveals a strong tendency for the person to be in the dative
when his face is involved:

TABLE 3. Incidence of dative and accusative correlated with
the body part involved.

	Dat.	Acc.	% Dative
face involved	26	4	87%
other body part	58	35	62%

Another factor which supports this hypothesis is the egocentricity of
speakers in the communicative process. A speaker (1st person)
tends to view himself as a more important actor in an event in which
he participates than he regards others, and thus tends to place himself in the dative rather than the accusative more often, and others
less often. Thus the expectation is that 1st person pronouns will be
skewed to the dative more than 3rd person pronouns and nouns will
be, as in (19).

(19) "Hoppfuss, das ist mein Pour le Merite, mir ehrlich
erworben, als der Lafettenschwanz meiner treuen
Haubitze mir aufs Kreuz schlug!"
'Hoppfuss, that is my Pour le Merite, honestly obtained
for me when the trail of my faithful howitzer hit me
(dat.) in the rump!!

Table 4 shows a tendency for 1st person pronouns to be in the dative.

TABLE 4. Incidence of dative and accusative in the 1st and
3rd person. The sample has been reduced to
include only those verbs which also occurred
with 1st person pronouns.

		Dat.	Acc.	% Dative
pronoun	1st	12	0	100%
	3rd	56	8	88%

Although the trend fails to achieve statistical significance, this seems
to be the fault of small sample size. Expectation that the influence of
person deixis will prove significant is heightened by the fact that the
hypothesized dative tendency of the 1st person is able to override the
accusative tendency of a resultative clause, as in (20).

(20) . . . sprang . . . ich in das Leben, das heisst in eine
Anstalt für verwahrloste Kinder, wo man mir mit dem
Knüppel so lange gegen den Magen schlug, bis ich
keinen Hunger mehr verspürte und davonlief.
'I jumped into life, that is, into an institution for neg-
lected children, where they hit me (dat.) against the
stomach with a cudgel for so long that I didn't feel
hungry any more and ran away.'

The preposition gegen suggests a strong blow, and the clause 'so long
that I didn't feel hungry any more and ran away' describes an effect
that the blows had on the speaker. But he nevertheless refers to himself in the dative.

Now that some of the factors motivating the case alternation have
been explicated, we can return to examples (7) and (8)--in which
there was claimed to be no difference in meaning of the cases--to
see if the case alternation is in fact motivated. In (7) the man is
being hit in both cases, but the second time there is an adverb
('brutally') and a resultative clause ('that he collapsed unconscious
and had to be brought to the prison hospital') describing the extreme
force of the blow and the effect it had on him. This second act of
hitting has the greatest effect on him, justifying the switch to
accusative.

In (8) there is an adverbial ('with all my power') and a clause
describing the effect the blow has on the man ('I have seldom heard
a man scream so with pain'). In addition, there is an implication in
the context that the man is temporarily knocked out of the action by
the blow. The second mention of kicking refers to the same real
world event, but this time there is no repetition of the force or effect.
The mention serves only to identify which man. So the switch from
accusative to dative is again motivated by the shift of interest in the
force and effect of the blow. Thus, examples that seemed to confirm
the analyst's suspicion that there was no difference in meaning, when
viewed from a different theoretical perspective, in fact serve to
highlight the difference in meaning between dative and accusative.

The power of this approach should be obvious. It offers a semantic
explanation as to why there should be dative-accusative alternation in
the first place, and why speakers pick one case or the other under
particular circumstances. It also supplies an explanation as to why
sentences such as (15) and (16), in which we have seen that the verb
and the case clash in the degree of force which they suggest, are
judged to be ungrammatical. In addition, this approach may provide
a more useful basis for studying the dialectal and social aspects of
the alternation of grammatical forms.

REFERENCES

Behaghel, Otto. 1927. Die Kugel traf ihn mitten ins Herz. In: Von deutscher Sprache. By Otto Behaghel. Lahr in Baden: Moriss Schauenburg. 346-352.

Grün, Max von der. 1967. Irrlicht und Feuer. Reinbeck, Rowohlt.

Starke, Günter. n. d. Konkurrierende syntaktische Konstruktionen in der deutschen Sprache der Gegenwart. Zeitschrift für Phonetik, Sprachwissenschaft und Kommunikationsforschung (ZPSK) 22 (1, 2), 25-65, 154-195.

Weltbühne. n. s. 18, 1913.

Zubin, David A. 1972. The German case system: Exploitation of the dative-accusative opposition for comment. Columbia University Linguistics Department, ditto ms.

Zubin, David A. 1975. On the distributional properties of surface morphology and their consequences for semantic analysis. Columbia University Working Papers in Linguistics 2, 189-218.

BOSTON SHORT a̲: SOCIAL VARIATION AS HISTORICAL RESIDUE

MARTHA LAFERRIERE

Southeastern Massachusetts University

1. Phonological variation is always complex, and usually hetero-geneous. A signal example of such multi-levelled complexity is found in the behavior of Boston short a̲. This sound alternates in a regular manner with not one but two different sounds; and each alternation has a different subjective value label for speakers of the dialect.

I am going to examine the range of variation in which short a̲ partici-pates. Next I consider an analysis which attributes the variation to two competing rules of greatly differing antiquity. Lastly, I discuss questions raised by this rule competition. (1) Is the mortality of a phonological rule directly proportional to its antiquity (that is, can a rule which arose several centuries ago be a productive process today)? (2) Can rules compete for the same linguistic territory? (3) How do variants come to acquire socially descriptive labels? (4) Is historical change linear or cyclic (that is, is historical change generational change which constantly repeats itself)?

2. In Boston, short a̲ ([æ]) alternates with two different sounds: low central, unrounded, tense [a], and mid-front, unrounded, tense [ε]. [1] The alternation of [æ] with low central [a] involves a slight tongue retraction, the resultant sound varying between a true central vowel [a] and a sound midway between [æ] and [a]. This general pro-cess of retraction is referred to here as the Backing of [æ] to [a].

The alternation of [æ] with the mid vowel [ε] involves a raising of the tongue with a concomitant muscular tenseness which results in a [ə] off-glide when [æ] is raised as high as [ε]. This process is referred to here as the Raising of [æ] to [ε].

Backing of [æ] to [a] occurs before the pre-palatal spirants [f],
[θ], ([ð]), [2] and [s], and the alveolar nasal [n]. It affects the following
sets of words:

(1)　　-f: half, calf, laugh, after, afternoon (daft)
　　-θ, ð: bath, path, rather (wrath)
　　-s(C): pass, ass (as in half-ass); ask, task, glass
　　　　　(grass), (Master's, i. e. M. A.)
　　　-n: aunt, can't, answer (chance)

Words in parentheses undergo Backing less frequently than the others.

Backing affects an almost closed set of words (I return to this
later). The backed [a] is identical to the sound of the orthographic
combination ar in the Boston dialect in such words as car, start,
guard, farm, and a in father, calm, palm.

Raising of [æ] to [ɛ] also occurs before spirants, including [s],
and before nasals and the voiced consonants [d], [D], [l]. It affects
a larger group of words than Backing, including some of the words
normally affected by Backing. These latter are indicated by parentheses:

(2)　　-f: rafters, careful, taffy, daft, (laugh), (half), after
　　-v: ave. (as in Mass. Ave.)
　　-θ, ð: math, Cathy, (rather), (path)
　　-s: mass, gas, class, grass, glass, (ass), cast,
　　　　basket(ball), (pass), (last) . . .
　　-š: clash, crash, cash, flash, mash . . .
　nasals: man, can, pecan, hand, land, (chance), (dance),
　　　　ham, New Hampshire, example, Yankee, Mattapan
　　　　(place name)
　d, D, l: bad, scattered, Mattapan, pal

In Boston, [æ] is usually raised only to [ˆæ], a sound which is perceptually quite distinct from the higher [ɛə] and [eə] recorded for New
York City by Labov (1972b). Raising to [ɛə], the highest position used
by my informants, occurs most frequently before nasals. The symbol
[ɛ] is therefore used here as representing both [ˆæ] and [ɛə].

Finally, the most interesting category of [æ] words is a group
which exhibits all three sounds: [æ], [a], and [ɛ]. I label this the
Mixed group:

(3) after, rather
　　last, ask, pass(ing), ass, Master's
　　can't, answer, dance, chance

Comparing the three categories of words, it can be seen that the groups labelled Raising, Backing, and Mixed share their contents to some extent. While half, laugh, and bath are almost always in the Backing category, after and afternoon, pass, ask, last, grass, glass, can't, answer alternate between Backing and Raising; and flash, cash, gas, mass, man, hand, ham could only be Raised or unaffected, but never Backed.

3. The explanation for this contemporary variation is historical: two rules of greatly differing antiquity are competing for the same phonetic territory. The environments in which both rules are most productive, that is, where they overlap, is the environment in which the competition is strongest, and thus where variation is greatest. This is the Mixed group, in which words may be pronounced as [æ] - [pæs], [a] - [pas], or [ɛ] - [pɛs].

3.1. The rule Backing [æ] to [a] is of considerable antiquity. Until about 1775, Southern British and American English had [æ] in all words under question, as well as in words which now have [æ] - cat, back, shallow, cap (Kenyon 1950:176-84). During the 17th century this short [æ] was lengthened to [ǣ] in Southern Britain and Eastern New England. By the end of the 18th century [ǣ] had been backed to [ā] in Southern Britain in several environments, among them before voiceless pre-palatal fricatives, [m], and [n].

In Southern British English a large class of words, somewhat over 150, were affected (Kenyon 1950:179):

(4)   -f: aft, after, calf, craft, daft, half, laugh, rafter, shaft, draft, graft, staff, waft, etc.

    -θ: bath, lath, path, wrath

    -s: aghast, ask, asp, bask, basket, blast . . . casket, castle, clasp, class, fast, fasten, flask . . . ghastly, glass, grasp, last, mask, mast, master, nasty, past, pass . . . plaster . . . rasp, task, vast . . .

  -m: example, sample

  -n: advance, advantage, answer, aunt, blanch, branch, can't, chance, command, demand . . . dance, France . . . glance, grant, plant . . . shan't, slant, stanch, trance

In Eastern New England, late 18th century [ǣ] was also retracted, but only to central [a], not to back [ɑ]; and fewer words were affected, especially in the -s and -n categories. A list of the affected words is given in (1). Due to its age, Backing in contemporary Boston speech must be considered a linguistically nonproductive process. That is, backed [a] has become lexicalized almost without exception before [f] and [θ], as in calf, half, laugh, bath, path; and to a somewhat lesser extent in after, rather. [a] is also the dominant form before [n] in aunt (lexicalized), can't, and to a lesser extent in chance.

Before [s] and [n], however, there is true variation between [æ] and [a], as in last, ask, pass, passing, can't, dance, change. Other words which show the alternation are glass, grass, Master's, example, which have backed [a] less often than [æ]. Variation may even occur in the same sentence. One informant, in her late forties, said:

(5) I sáid I [kæ̀nt] and I really [kânt].

Thus Backing is a process which is to a large extent crystallized. In the small class of words with [f] and [θ], and a few words with [n], [a] has become lexicalized. Backing is still vigorous only before [s] and [n].

3.2. When Backing is compared with Raising, the opposite situation is found. Raising is a vigorous and productive process; it is a much younger rule characteristic not of Southern British English but of urban American English. The Raising of [æ] to [eᵊ] as a major characteristic of New York City speech has been reported on extensively by Labov (1972a, 1972b). It has also been described for Philadelphia by Ferguson (1968) and for New Jersey by Trager (1942).

Raising, in Labov's descriptions, applies typically and most regularly before voiceless spirants [f], [θ], [s], [š]; before front nasals [m], [n]; and before voiced obstruents [b, d, ǰ, g]. All of these sounds must be followed by word boundary, inflectional boundary, or obstruent (Labov 1972b:73). Trager (1942) reports the same general patterning for New Jersey. In New York City, [æ] is raised to its highest position before a nasal or nasal + consonant.

A different and unusual situation is found, however, when we consider Raising in Boston. Note first that older Backing and younger Raising have almost the same structural descriptions--before front nasals and voiceless fricatives[2] (with the exception of [š], which is not an environment in Backing).

Theoretically, then, we should find three-way variation--[æ, a, ɛ] --in all environments. However, when Raising began to apply in Boston, it found that Backing had, as it were, gotten there first. Backed [a] had already become lexicalized in the small class of words with following [f] and [θ]--half, laugh, (after), bath, path, rather, (wrath), which in New York City typically have raised and tensed [eᵊ]. A few words with [æ] before [n] had also been usurped by Backing--aunt, can't, answer. That left [š], to which Backing was never

applicable, [s], and nasals. The environment where the greatest
variation now occurs, then, is before [s] and nasals, precisely the
environments for which both rules are still competing:

(6) Backing: [æ] → [a] / ___ [f θ | s | n]
    Raising: [æ] → [ɛ] / ___ [... | s | š | n̩ N]

All three variants can occur before [s] and [n] (Mixed Group (3)):

(7) -s: last, ask, pass, passing, ass, Master's, grass, glass
    -n: can't, answer, dance, chance

4. While Backing is virtually a nonproductive process, Raising
is just the opposite, its growing productivity reflected in its distribution across age groups:

(8)

	Original Backing Words				Original Non-Backing Words				
	1	2	3	4	5	6	7	8	9
	half	path	ask	can't	craft	math	gas	hand	bad
over 50	B	B	B	B	-	-	-	R	-
25-49	B	B	B-R	B-R	-	-	(R)	R	(R)
under 25	B-R	B-R	B-R	B-R	R	R	R	R	R

(R) indicates that Raising occurs infrequently

All informants had Raising before nasals in category 8: hand, man,
damage, pecan, Yankee. None over 50 had significant Raising before
voiced obstruents (category 9) or before spirants in either originally
Backed words (1-3) or newer words (5-7). In the middle group of
informants between 25 and 49, Raising and Backing alternated before
[s] and [n], the Mixed group (categories 3 and 4 in (8)), where the two
rules overlap. This group of informants also has occasional Raising
before [s] in newer words (category 7).

The youngest group, below 25, but especially the two 16-year-old
informants, had the greatest percentage of Raising in all relevant
environments. In fact, in this age group, Raising has invaded, and
is winning over, lexical territory from Backing. I have recorded
Raised [ɛ] before [f] and [θ] in words which meet the structural
description of Backing but were not originally affected by it, e.g.
giraffe, draft, craft (category 5); Cathy, math, ave. (as in Mass.
Ave.). Most significant is the fact that Raising has started to apply
to the sacred [a] words of categories 1 and 2--half, laugh, bath, after,
and the lone nasal can't.

The two teenagers in my sample even have tensing and a slight
Raising before the voiceless stops [t] and [k] in rat, back, exactly,
accident, actually, crack. Raising is not recorded by other

investigators in these environments, and as yet I do not have enough data to evaluate these observations.

5. When rules compete for the same phonetic territory, the results of the competition take on nonlinguistic labels. Raising is clearly characteristic of the speech of younger people. Backing, on the other hand, has a more complex social profile, which one would expect in view of its longer existence. In the first place, the greater antiquity of Backing parallels its association with older people (see chart, (8)). There is more consistent Backing in a greater number of words in categories 1-4 among older speakers than among those in the other two age categories. This is especially significant in categories 3 and 4, where Backing is still an active process. Thus the oldest informant, Pat, in her early seventies, used Backed [a] almost without exception in half, laugh, after, afternoon, bath, path, wrath, rather, ask, passing, last, task, basket, answer, can't, aunt. Her son Mike, 27, had Backed [a] in ask, laugh, last, half, but neutral [æ] or Raised [ε] in after, craft, rafters, rather, wrath, passing, pass, task, can't, answer. These examples are taken from reading passages, where his Raised [ε] was quite Raised and tensed, especially in can't, answer, rather, and rafters. In casual speech, however, Mike used a Backed [a] in can't, answer, rather, ass, half-assed, instead of the Raised [ε] of his reading style.

The second feature of Backed [a] is its association, as one would expect, with Boston identity. People in the middle or older group who have lived in Boston most of their lives, or who have returned permanently to Boston and associate themselves with the city, use Backed [a] frequently and regularly in speaking and reading. This is true whether they live in the city proper, as do Pat in Charlestown, Mrs. B, 52, in Dorchester, Vic, 31, in South Boston, Mike, 27, in Charlestown, or in a surrounding town, as do Stel, 64, in Cambridge, Bim and Charlotte, late sixties, in Brookline, and the two teen-agers, from Cambridge and Medfield.

While [a] is a sign of Boston identity, it is also a stigmatized feature for those people whose ties to the city are more precarious because of higher education or prolonged residence outside the New England area. Yet people who label [a] as stigmatized tend to use it themselves. Mike, 27, a graduate student in linguistics, had slightly Raised [ε] in his reading style but backed [a] in his casual speech in the same words--answer, rather, can't, pass, passing, ask. His subjective opinion is that he no longer has many Boston phonological characteristics in his speech. Yet his reading style clearly reveals a superimposition of the Raising rule over the bedrock of the Boston Backing rule, which dominates his casual style.

A third feature of Backing is its use as a hypercorrect indication
of erudition. The word <u>master</u> is normally not subject to Backing;
however, a colleague in her fifties told me at a cocktail party that
her son was 'going for his [ma· stəz]'. Another woman in her late
fifties tried to impress a group of younger people by telling them she
needed only a few more credits for her [ma· stəz]. Other words ob-
served to contain an erudite [a] are <u>class</u>, <u>glasses</u>, <u>dance</u>, <u>example</u>,
and both vowels in the expression 'he/she's a [hǎf + às]' or '[hǎf + àst]'.

6. In summary, I have presented an analysis of variation in
Boston short <u>a</u>. The word classes with the most extreme variation
are the results of two rules competing for the same phonetic territory. The early Modern English Backing rule is still active, although restricted, in the Boston dialect, indicating that there is presumably no limit on the length of time a phonological process may
continue to function in a language. A grammar can reflect processes
from a much earlier stage as long as there is true allophony at some
level of speech.

An old rule, however, may have taken on a complex series of
nonlinguistic labels--local identity, stigmatized form, and even
hypercorrect form. The question which must be investigated now
is whether hypercorrection in this case is an independent factor or
whether it is related to the identity label. The fact that hypercorrection, which indicates a prestige target, and stigmatization,
are both labels for Backed [a], may be only an apparent contradic-
tion. These two seemingly opposite labels reflect not linguistic but
social levels.

Finally, I would like to suggest that sound change is cyclic rather
than linear. Backing is associated with nativeness, and is viewed by
the college-educated informants in my survey as stigmatized, even
by those who themselves use Backed [a] in casual speech. In a
formal situation, older people tend to Back more and Raise less.
But younger people in a formal situation Raise more and Back less.
Also, older informants attribute a wider range of functions to [a]
(erudite, native, prestige/stigmatized) than they do to [ε]. Thus, it
appears that as people get older, they tend to Back more and Raise
less.

NOTES

1. The study of short <u>a</u> was conducted on 14 informants who were
natives of Boston and neighboring cities. The ages of the informants
were: 72, 68, 65, 64, 56 (oldest group); 49, 49, 48, 41, 31, 27
(middle group); 25, 16, 16 (youngest group). All interviews were
recorded on a Realistic cassette-type recorder with hidden

microphone; the machine had very good fidelity. The interviews consisted of three reading passages containing key words (formal style) and free conversation (casual style).

    2. Rather is the only relevant word with a voiced spirant [ð].

REFERENCES

Ferguson, C. F. 1968. 'Short a̲' in Philadelphia English. Mimeographed.

Kenyon, John Samuel. 1964. American pronunciation. Ann Arbor, George Wahr.

Labov, William. 1972a. The isolation of contextual styles. In: W. Labov, Sociolinguistic patterns. Philadelphia, University of Pennsylvania Press. 70-109.

Labov, William. 1972b. The internal evolution of linguistic rules. In: Linguistic change and generative theory. Edited by Robert P. Stockwell and Ronald K. S. Macaulay. Bloomington, Indiana University Press. 101-171.

Laferriere, Martha. 1973. The Boston-area dialectology project. Talk given at Harvard School of Education, Language Seminar, April.

Trager, George. 1942. One phonemic entity becomes two: The case of 'short a̲'. American Speech 15. 255-58.

VARIATION AS A TOOL
IN LINGUISTIC AND CULTURAL RECONSTRUCTION

MURIEL R. SAVILLE

Georgetown University

From at least the time of de Saussure through the work of Chomsky, interest in linguistic theory has been focused on an idealized system of oppositions and structures which are abstracted from the supposed vagaries of individual performance. Even the most empirically oriented dialectologists and anthropological linguists have strained their variable data through a methodological or analytical grid and have produced artificially uniformized descriptions which purport to characterize dialects or even whole languages. This kind of principled abstraction, which was apotheosized by Chomsky as the 'ideal speaker-hearer', and which made linguistics the envy of the other social sciences, has almost completely dominated the value system of the science until recently. As a consequence, it is difficult to find descriptions by professional linguists which admit to variation in their data, except insofar as it is accounted for by autonomous systemic conditioning, or relegated to the notorious closet of free variation. Only since the work of Labov and Hymes have linguists begun to examine linguistic performance itself, and to discover unexpected systemic regularities, as well as ways to accommodate variation within linguistic theory and analysis.

Most of the studies to date have examined variation in the languages of socially complex societies, such as English, French, and Spanish, and have found interesting relations between this variation and factors of style, class, and origin. Such observations clearly relate to the broader longitudinal question of how linguistic changes arise and spread, and should ultimately give us greater insight into the operations of these processes.

During the past several years I have been interested in examining linguistic variation within a less urbanized society, namely that of the Navajo and other Apachean tribes, and in considering how variable data can be used in the process of linguistic classification and ethnohistorical reconstruction. For the purposes of my research, I have made use of 19th century word lists compiled primarily by travelers, missionaries, and military personnel quite unsophisticated in linguistics, but conscientiously trying to record the language they heard--including its variability. At the end of this paper under the heading Apachean is a listing of the languages studied and sources utilized during this phase of research.[1] I have recently added data from Northern and Pacific Athabaskan languages for comparative purposes. These are listed in the regional grouping as suggested by Hodge, with the different sources utilized listed under each, and with the different names which were used to refer to what were probably the same tribes.[2]

Hodge's grouping by region within the Northern division is being used for the moment as linguistic grouping as well, but the data thus far suggest at least five clusters of languages will emerge in the final analysis with a number of intermediate or more isolated dialects apart from the clusters. Furthermore, within the Eastern region of the Northern division, Dogrib and Yellowknife appear to be more similar to some dialects of Chipeweyan than the relationship between these Chipeweyan dialects and others also reported as Chipeweyan, and other questions will undoubtedly arise as the analysis continues.[3]

An example of the phonological variation which is encountered in closely related languages (or dialects) may be illustrated with the Apachean terms for 'three', 'turkey', and 'father' in Table 1. An alternation between [t] and [k] even occurs within a single language, as word-list entries for Navajo, Mescalero, and Jicarilla attest.[4]

The linguistic variation revealed by these archival data raises problems for the traditional approach to the classification of linguistic groups. Just as we take the Second Sound Shift to distinguish High German from Low German, so Hoijer in 1938[5] separated the Apachean languages into Western Apachean (including Navajo, San Carlos [19th century Pinal Apache and Arivaipa], Mescalero, Chiracahua, and White Mountain [19th century Coyotero, Pinaleño, and Mimbreño]) and Eastern Apachean (including Jicarilla, Lipan, and Kiowa Apache), primarily on the basis of the [t]:[k] correspondence. Hoijer reported only [t] in Western Apachean and [k] in Eastern Apachean. That the data are not so neat, however, can be readily seen from the occurrence of both [t] and [k] in each region on Table 1.

Such variable data form a problem for the Stammbaum, or family tree, model of language classification, which rests on the assumption that linguistic groups separate unequivocally, and that sound laws

TABLE 1. Alternation of [t]:[k] in Apachean.

Western	Eastern
'three'	
ka (N-Thompson ca 1871)	k'aî-i (J-Wilson 1889)
t'ai (M-Bartlett 1851)	kági (L-Mooney 1855)
ɽage (A-Loew 1874)	kāggi (KA-Gatschet 1884)
kah-yae (Me-Cremony 1863)	
'turkey'	
tássi (Ch-Ruby 1886)	katche (L-Berlandier 1829)
koz-zhee (N-Shaw ca 1884)	xa'dshe-e (L-Gatschet 1884)
kār-zhée (C-Chapin 1867)	
'father'	
shǐ-thá (C-Smart 1866)	shǐ-tātha (J-MacElroy 1875)
sh-ee-kai-e (PL-Whipple 1850)	shi-kái-e (J-Wilson 1889)
petɽa (A-Loew 1874)	
N - Navajo	PL - Pinaleno
M - Mimbreño (Coppermine)	J - Jicarilla
A - Arivaipa	L - Lipan
Me - Mescalero	KA - Kiowa Apache
Ch - Chiracahua	

operate without exception. As dialectologists have long been fond of pointing out, these assumptions often do not apply to differentiations within what is essentially a single dialect area such as that of the Apachean languages. Even more confounding is the situation where not only do different words follow different patterns of correspond-ences, but intradialectal variation for particular forms exists. Here a different model for treating linguistic relationships is needed: one that can incorporate the facts of linguistic variation.

A good candidate field to examine for the existence of possible models is archeology, which is very much concerned with the facts of variation in its work. Variations in artifact frequencies and distributions are at the heart of archeological classifications and reconstructions, used to establish frameworks of temporal and spatial relationships between cultures. The possible relevance of archeo-logical models to work utilizing language data is therefore very promising, and deserves close consideration.

One such model is the seriation technique developed by George Brainerd and W. S. Robinson. Originally applied to collections of artifacts from different archeological sites to determine the degree

of similarity between them, the Brainerd-Robinson technique can be
applied to collections of linguistic data for the same purpose.
Bernardo Vallejo first used it with synchronic data on Cuban Spanish, [6]
and I have modified it slightly to apply to these collections of archival
data from the Athabaskan languages. The technique is especially useful precisely where the Stammbaum model fails, for it does not require dichotomous presence/absence differences, but operates with
relative degrees of similarity between samples from a continuum to
place them in a series (hence 'seriation'). Since the relative fre-
quence of variable features differs between different samples, the
index of similarity between samples can be simply calculated and the
samples arranged in a series.

Let me briefly review this seriation procedure using three phonological correspondences and the data entered in Table 2. A number
of words were identified in which one of these correspondences might
occur and the total number of possible occurrences of each form was
tabulated; e. g. in words containing a [t]:[k] correspondence, the [t]
occurred in 80 percent of the possible positions in Navajo data, never
in Jicarilla, always in Chipeweyan, and 90 percent of the time in
Kutchin. In words containing a three-way [n]:[d]:[nd] correspondence,
Navajo speakers used [n] 99 percent of the time, Slave speakers used
[n] 67 percent, [nd] 33 percent, and [d] not at all, and so forth.

The difference in the percentage of occurrence for each sound between each pair of languages or group of languages is calculated and
subtracted from 100--or identity. This assigns a similarity index,
which is plotted on a table or matrix, such as illustrated in Table 3,
with the indices placed at the intersection of each two languages or
groups, which are listed by column or row. The columns and rows
are then shifted about until they most closely approximate a situation
with the highest index figures along the diagonal and a continuous decrease in the magnitude of the numbers away from the diagonal in
both directions. The resulting sequence of sources should then reflect the relative relationships among them along the dimensions of
time and/or space.

Table 3 presents a seriation of the Apachean dialects according to
the three phonological correspondences tabulated in Table 2. Note
that Kiowa Apache (KA) is most distantly related to Navajo (N) with
a similarity index of 17, and closest to Jicarilla (J) and Lipan (L)
with indices of 75 and 72, respectively.

The results of the seriation procedure closely agree with Hoijer's
(1956) lexicostatistical ordering of the Apachean dialects, [7] providing
further independent confirmation of that technique as a tool in linguistic classification. This is perhaps all the more ironic, in that
Hoijer based his well-known critique of lexicostatistics on the
material he used in his own classification.

TABLE 2. Occurrence of phonological variables.

	[t]:[k]	[y]:[z]	[n]:[d]:[nd]
Southwestern Division:			
Navajo (N)	80:20	79:21	99: 1: 0
Western Apache (WA)			
Pinal Apache	100: 0	50:50	60: 0:40
Mimbreño	100: 0	75:25	50:10:40
Arivaipa	100: 0	33:67	71:14:14
Coyotero	79:21	22:78	60:17:23
Mescalero	86:14	33:67	38:25:38
Pinaleño	100: 0	0:100	33:33:33
Chiracahua	100: 0	0:100	
Eastern Apache (EA)			
Jicarilla	0:100	33:67	42:26:32
Lipan	0:100	33:67	30:27:43
Kiowa Apache	0:100	0:100	13:50:37
Northern Division:			
Eastern (N-E)			
Chipeweyan	100: 0	64:36	80: 0:20
Slave	100: 0	60:40	67: 0:33
Hare	78:22	67:33	78:11:11
Northwest (N-NW)			
Tanaina	100: 0	80:20	67:17:17
Kutchin	90:10	10:90	59:24:18
Southwest (N-SW)			
Nahane	91: 9	67:33	60:40: 0
Sekani	83:17	25:75	50:50: 0

Table 4 utilizes similarity indices based on the regional groups indicated in Table 2, and including the Northern data tabulated there. The fact that many of the same features which show variation within Southwestern Athabaskan also vary within Northern Athabaskan suggests that the variation is quite old in the family. Since one of the major questions regarding the history of the Southwestern Athabaskans is where they originated in the north, seriation may be able to help point to a solution by indicating to which of the northern groups they may be most closely related.

There is a great spread of differences in the variable occurrence of [t]:[k], [y]:[z], or [n]:[d]:[nd] in both Southwestern and Northern

TABLE 3. Similarity index among Apachean tribes (phonology).

	N	PA	M	A	C	Me	PL	Ch	J	L	KA
N		66	69	70	68	54	50	33	33	34	17
PA	66		69	73	65	71	58	67	41	48	19
M	69	69		67	74	74	69	75	49	34	28
A	70	73	67		74	62	75	56	49	50	29
C	68	65	74	74		88	80	73	65	51	39
Me	54	71	74	62	88		82	93	59	49	34
PL	50	58	69	75	80	82		83	43	42	35
Ch	33	67	75	56	73	93	83		42	22	33
J	33	41	49	50	65	59	43	42		85	75
L	34	48	34	50	51	49	42	22	85		72
KA	17	19	28	29	39	34	35	33	75	72	

TABLE 4. Similarity index of Northern to Southwestern languages (phonology).

	N	N-E	N-SW	N-NW	WA	EA
N		85	78	75	72	39
N-E	85		83	90	83	45
N-SW	78	83		91	85	55
N-NW	75	90	91		92	53
WA	72	83	85	92		60
EA	39	45	55	53	60	

Athabaskan, with Navajo and Kiowa Apache occupying the extremes in the Southwest, and Chipeweyan and Sekani in the North. Further, the figures reveal an interesting and surprisingly consistent pattern of similarity and difference between pairs of Northern and Southwestern languages, with Navajo, for example, showing the greatest similarity to languages to which Lipan shares the least similarity, and vice-versa. This pattern could be highly significant, but further analysis and comparison along other dimensions, including lexicon and grammar, must be done before any definitive conclusions can be drawn. In particular this is true because the number of cognates involved in dealing with the Northern languages is smaller, hence the figures are less reliable.

The regional grouping of languages as entered in Table 4 represents one effort to improve the reliability of the calculations at this stage. Note that Navajo appears to be closest to the Eastern Division of Northern Athabaskan (N-E), but Eastern Apachean (EA) least so.

Western Apachean (WA) calculates closest to the Northwest Division of the Northern language group (N-NW).

A trial check was made at this point to see if the set of phonological correspondences posited by Sapir[8] would exhibit more regularity than the three just discussed, or if they would indicate different groupings in the North, or different patterns of relationships between Northern and Apachean languages. Two correspondences checked for this purpose were Chipeweyan [θ] to Navajo [s] or [z] and Chipeweyan affricate [tθ] to Navajo [ts]. Although these were listed separately by Sapir, I suspect more complicated alternations are involved along a single dimension. The Chipeweyan word for 'star', for instance, is recorded as θun and Navajo as son, but Sekani speakers evidently alternated between son and tson (at a ratio of 1:2 in my data).

Furthermore, in the term for 'tongue', recorded as θadi in Chipeweyan and tsad in Navajo, Coyotero Apaches use tsad, zad, and žad.

The [θ] variant seems never to occur in Apachean languages, but is variable in Northern usage. In terms for 'yellow', for instance, Slave uses both -tθo and -tso, and in final position, Sekani uses both k'os and k'oθ for 'neck'.

In the data I have analyzed thus far, Chipeweyan, Yellowknife, and Dogrib consistently use [θ] in these contexts, and Slave does over 70 percent of the time, which correlates with the regional grouping of these languages in an Eastern category. I have not yet encountered a [θ] in Hare, which suggests it should be grouped elsewhere, as do the data tabulated in Table 2. Another classificatory question arises with Kutchin, which uses [θ] more than 60 percent of the time--the only language grouped in the Northwest region in which [θ] occurs at all.

Clearly, the addition of this and perhaps any other variable correspondences will indicate some changes in posited relationships. The most important would be the greater distance between Navajo and the Eastern division of the Northern languages, which in Table 4 appear to be the nearest Navajo/Northern linkage.

Table 4 might also suggest that Navajo is closer to all of the Northern languages than it is to Eastern Apachean, but this merely illustrates the inadequacy of shared phonological correspondences alone to indicate degrees of relationship beyond the range where lexical items are almost entirely cognate.

Using all of the word lists noted at the end of this paper and the fifty lexical items which occurred most frequently, I calculated the similarity indices which are recorded in Table 5. These represent the percentage of shared lexical items between each pair of regional groupings. Using this criterion the Apachean languages cluster in the upper left corner of the matrix, as would be expected from their geographical proximity. It is interesting to note that Navajo also appears to be closest to the Eastern region of the Northern division according to these lexical calculations, with all Apachean languages somewhat closer to the Southwest than they are to the Northwest division of the Northern languages.

TABLE 5. Similarity index of Northern, Southwestern, and Pacific languages (lexicon).

	EA	WA	N	N-E	N-SW	P	N-NW
EA		77	77	67	68	66	60
WA	77		80	69	67	64	67
N	77	80		73	68	68	60
N-E	67	69	73		75	65	62
N-SW	68	67	68	75		70	61
P	66	64	68	65	70		60
N-NW	60	67	60	62	61	60	

My very limited consideration of Pacific data suggests the closest tie is with the Southwest division of the North, next with the Eastern division of the North and the Southwestern Apachean languages almost equally, and most distant from the Northwest division of the North.

I would like to suggest a few tentative conclusions based on this analysis to date:

1. That neither the Pacific nor Apachean groups migrated from single regions in the North, but rather from along a wide front in the Southwest and Eastern regions.

2. That different waves of migration could well have originated in a limited area and remained as a unit in resettlement, as most of the ancestral Navajo migrated from a single location in the Eastern division of the North.

3. That the sound changes implied in the phonological correspondences [t]:[k], [y]:[z], and [n]:[d]:[nd] have a very great time depth in Athabaskan. The change from [t] to [k] is probably due to the strong velar aspiration common after [t] and might easily have resulted from a process of drift within languages or dialects without the need for regional diffusion.

4. That the [ts]:[s] alternation is also very old, but that the [θ] variable was an innovation in the Eastern division of the North following the time of the Apachean exodus.

5. Finally, from a theoretical point of view, it is most interesting to note that the phonological and lexical systems of these languages have changed at differential relative rates.

This differential rate of change lends even more weight to the conclusion that no analysis of a single aspect of language is sufficient for positing relationships--in time or in space. I hope I have succeeded in showing that variable data can supply important bases for linguistic classification that have been largely ignored through an era of descriptive 'regularization', and particularly that such 'neat' analyses as characterized both structuralist and transformational efforts cannot adequately reflect the nature or content of Athabaskan languages.

APPENDIX

Archival Resources

APACHEAN:
Navajo
   N - Navajo, Navaho
      Simpson 1849, Eaton 1852-53, Whipple 1855, Bristol 1865, Nichols 1866-68, Willard 1868, Powell 1870, Thompson 1870, Thompson 1871, Arny 1874, Loew 1874, Shaw 1884, Hough 1901

Western
  PA - Pinal Apache
      Gatschet 1883
   A - Arivaipa, San Carlos
      Palmer 1867, Loew 1874
   C - Coyotero, Sierra Blanco, Apache, White Mountain
      Smart 1866, Chapin 1867, Sherwood nd, White 1876, White 1874-75, Mearns ca 1880, Reagan ca 1903
   M - Mimbreño, Coppermine
      Bartlett 1851, Gibbs 1855
  PL - Pinaleño
      Whipple 1855
  Me - Mescalero
      Mooney 1855, Cremony 1863, Bennett 1889-94
  Ch - Chiracahua
      Ruby 1886

Eastern
   J - Jicarilla
      MacElroy 1875, Wilson 1889, Russell 1898
   L - Lipan
      Berlandier 1829, Mooney 1855, Gatschet 1884

KA - Kiowa Apache, Ná-isha Band
     Gatschet 1884

NORTHERN:
Eastern
  YK - Yellowknives, Tatsanottine, South Shore Chipeweyan
       Russell 1894
  DR - Dogrib, Thlingchadinne
       Russell 1894
  Sl - Slaves, Liard Slaves, Etchaottine, Etchareot-Tine,
       Achotoetenni
       Kennicott nd, Kennicott ca 1869, Ross, Kennicott and Petitot
       nd
  Cw - Chipeweyan, Chipewyan, Chipwyan, Tinne, McKenzie River
       Dialect, Caribou Eaters
       Ross 1858, Anderson 1858, Kennicott 1862, Petitot 1869,
       Ross, Kennicott and Petitot nd, Bompas 1890, Russell 1894
  Ha - Hare, Kawchodinne, Kat'a-gottiné, Katcho-gottiné, Nnèa-
       gottiné
       Kennicott 1863, Petitot, 1865, Petitot 1869, Ross, Kenni-
       cott and Petitot nd

Northwestern
  Ku - Kutchin, Louchoux, Kootchin, Kutchakutchin, Hong (Han?)
       Kutchin
       Ross 1862a, Ross 1862b, Petitot 1869, Kennicott ca 1869,
       Roehrig 1874, Russell 1894
  Tan - Tanana, Upper Tanana
        Geoghegan 1904-06
  Tai - Tanaina, Kenai, Cook's Inlet Bay, Bay of Kenai, Kandünă,
        Kankünats Kŏgtana
        Lisiansky ca 1803-06, Wowodsky nd, DeMeulen 1870,
        Roehrig 1874, Staffeief and Petroff 1885-86
  Ing - Ingalik, Anvik Dialect
        Chapman 1904
  Tl - Tlatskanai, Klatskanai
       Anderson 1858, Turner nd
  Kw - Kwalhioqua, Willipah
       Anderson 1858

Southwestern
  Nah - Nahane, Nehaunay-Kaska, Nehawnay
        Kennicott 1862, Ross 1862, Roehrig 1874
  Sk - Sekani, Sicanny, Sickannie
       Ross 1848, Ross nd, Pope 1865, Roehrig 1874

Ca - Carrier, Takulli, Tahcully
   Anderson 1858, Turner nd, Roehrig 1874, Morice 1890
Cl - Chilcotin, Tsilkotin
   Morice 1890

Pacific:
 Um - Umkwa, Umpqua
    Anderson 1858, Turner nd
 Tu - Tututunne, Tootooten
    Anderson 1858
 Hu - Hupa, Hoopah, Hopah
    Anderson 1858, Turner nd
 Mat - Mattole
    Li 1930
 Hay - Haynarger
    Anderson 1858
  AC - Applegate Creek
    Anderson 1858
 Nab - Nabiltse
    Anderson 1858

NOTES

1. Except for Loew's 1874 manuscript (listed under both Navajo and Arivaipa) which was published in Gatschet's Zwölf Sprachen in 1876, and Berlandier's 1829 manuscript on Lipan which was found in the British Museum, all of these sources are in the Anthropological archives of the Smithsonian Institution.

2. Except for Li's Mattole description in the Pacific division, all are again manuscripts found in the Smithsonian Anthropological archives.

3. In the Southwestern region of the Northern division, Chilcotin is included by Hodge, but not by J. P. Harrington, who identifies Chilcotin as a Pacific language in his field notes. The data I am working with which were recorded by Morice suggest a somewhat intermediate position for Chilcotin, but closer lexical and phonological alliance to the North. (Harrington's data have not yet been included in this analysis.)

4. After plotting the locations of each Navajo source, these data suggest that the [t]:[k] alternation within that language was geographically distributed, that a distinction between Eastern and Western Navajo can be posited, with isoglosses running north and south along the Lukachukai Mountains on the New Mexico-Arizona border. (Previously reported in 'Diversity in Southwestern

Athabaskan: A Historical Perspective', Navajo Language Review,
1(2). 67-84, 1974.)

    5. Hoijer, Harry. 'The Southwestern Athapaskan Languages',
American Anthropologist, 40. 75-87, 1938.

    6. Vallejo-Claros, Bernardo. La distribución y estratificación
de /r/ /r̄/ y /s/ en el Español Cubano. Unpublished dissertation.
University of Texas at Austin, 1970.

    7. Hoijer, Harry. The Chronology of the Athapaskan Languages.
IJAL, 22. 219-232, 1956.

    8. Sapir, Edward. The Concept of Phonetic Law as Tested in
Primitive Languages by Leonard Bloomfield. In: Methods in Social
Science: A Case Book. Edited by Stuart A. Rice. Chicago, Uni-
versity of Chicago Press, 1931. (As discussed by Harry Hoijer in
'The Athapaskan Languages', Studies in the Athapaskan Languages,
University of California Press, 1963.)

SYNTACTICALLY VS. PRAGMATICALLY CONTROLLED ANAPHORA

IVAN SAG
Massachusetts Institute of Technology

JORGE HANKAMER
Harvard University

0. It has long been known that certain anaphoric expressions, though generally interpreted by reference to some linguistic antecedent, do not require such an antecedent, but can be controlled by some aspect of the nonlinguistic (we will say 'pragmatic') environment. This is the case, for example, with ordinary definite third person pronouns:

(1) My brother's a doctor, and he says your hair will fall
    out if you eat that.
    Sue introduced me to her mother.
    Anyone who eats that will lose his hair.
    If the unicorn were a possible animal, it would certainly
    be a herbivore.

(2) He's saying that your hair will fall out.
    Her hands are trembling.
    I hope it's a herbivore.

The examples in (1) illustrate syntactically controlled anaphora with definite pronouns. The examples in (2) illustrate instances of what we call 'pragmatically controlled' (or 'deictic') anaphora. Each of the examples in (2) is well formed in a context which, without linguistic antecedent for the pronoun, nevertheless contains enough pragmatic information to allow (more or less) unambiguous determination of its intended referent. [1]

What has not (to our knowledge) been observed before[2] is that there are anaphoric processes[3] which (with reservations to be elaborated herein) <u>must</u> be syntactically controlled. [4] Consider the contrast in the following utterance-context events:

(3)   [Hankamer attempts to stuff a 9-inch ball through a
        6-inch hoop]
       # Sag: It's not clear that you'll be able to. [5]
(4)   [Same context]
       Sag: It's not clear that you'll be able to do it.

There is a subtle but distinct difference in acceptability between these two utterances in this context: the anaphoric process which leaves a pro-form <u>do it</u> as anaphoric VP can more readily be pragmatically controlled than the process known as VP Deletion, which leaves behind no pro-VP, but only a bare AUX or stranded complementizer.

The utterance in (3) is fine, of course, if there has been previous linguistic context in which mention has been made of getting the ball through the hoop:

(5)   Hankamer: I'm going to stuff this ball through this hoop.
       Sag: It's not clear that you'll be able to.

For further illustration of the contrast we offer another example:

(6a) [Sag produces a cleaver and prepares to hack off his
        left hand]
       # Hankamer: Don't be alarmed, ladies and gentlemen,
          we've rehearsed this act several times, and he
          never actually does.
(6b) [Same context]
       Hankamer: . . . he never actually does it.

Notice, however, that once the <u>do it</u> anaphor has appeared in a discourse, it can itself serve as controller for syntactically anaphoric VP Deletion:

(7)   Hankamer: At least he never has yet.

which is well formed in the context of (6b), where <u>do it</u> has already been introduced pragmatically.

So it seems that syntactic anaphora can be controlled by a pragmatically anaphoric item. The difference comes out quite clearly
when the two are reversed in order in the same sentence:[6]

> [Sag attempts to rip Boston phone directory in
>   half]
> (8a) Hankamer: I don't think you can do it, but I know some-
> one who can.
> (8b) #I don't think you can, but I know someone who can do it.

The purpose of this paper is to investigate this difference between
syntactically and pragmatically controlled anaphora, and to show that
there is a class of rules which, like VP Deletion, resist pragmatic
control (although we will see that various factors interfere to produce
exceptions of various interesting kinds). We will argue that the class
of rules which require syntactic control is just the class of anaphora
rules for which evidence is available that they are syntactic deletion
rules, and which produce 'null anaphors', i.e. do not leave behind a
pro-form.

1. Syntactic deletion anaphora and pronominalization anaphora

1.1 Grinder and Postal (1971) have argued, on the basis of sentences like (9)-(10), that VP Deletion must be a syntactic deletion
rule, relating intermediate structures like (9)-(10a) to surface structures like (9)-(10b):

> (9a) I've never ridden a camel, but Jorge has ridden a
>   camel$_i$, and he says it$_i$ stank horribly.
> (9b) I've never ridden a camel, but Jorge has, and he
>   says it$_i$ stank horribly.

> (10a) I don't keep gerbils in my office, but Jorge keeps
>   gerbils in his office, and they$_i$ eat holes in his books.
> (10b) I don't keep gerbils in my office, but Jorge does,
>   and they$_i$ eat holes in his books.

The essence of their argument is that the right clauses of these
sentences contain a pronoun which must have an antecedent, but the
surface structures of the (b) sentences contain no NP which could be
the antecedent for the pronoun. Note that the instance of the NP a
camel in the left clause of (9b) cannot serve as antecedent for a
definite pronoun:

> (11) *I've never ridden a camel, and it stank horribly.[7]

On the basis of this 'missing antecedent' phenomenon, Grinder and Postal argue that an interpretive theory of VP-anaphora (and, they claim, any identity-of-sense anaphora) which attempts to generate the structures containing null anaphors directly, without deriving them from an intermediate stage where the anaphoric VP is syntactically represented, must be rejected.

Ross (1969) also gives several arguments that VP Deletion is a syntactic deletion process. In sentences like (12), if the anaphoric right clause is derived by VP Deletion, the appearance of the distributionally restricted item <u>there</u> and the plural agreement are straightforwardly accounted for; otherwise some unpleasantly ad hoc mechanisms will have to be called into play. [8]

(12) Some people think there are no such rules, but there $\begin{Bmatrix} \text{are.} \\ \text{*is} \end{Bmatrix}$

In sentences like (13)-(14), the collocation WH+<u>to</u> and the observed restriction that the WH cannot be <u>why</u> in this collocation are accounted for directly under an analysis which derives such sentences by a combination of WH fronting and VP Deletion, since the pre-deletion versions exhibit exactly the same collocation and restriction. [9]

(13) He knows how to dress, but I don't know how to.
(14) *He knows how to get high, but he doesn't know why to.

Finally, an otherwise reducible auxiliary fails to undergo reduction before the null VP:

(15) Paul Anderson's fat, and $\begin{Bmatrix} \text{I am} \\ \text{*I'm} \end{Bmatrix}$ too.

This inability of normally reducible items to reduce has been shown (King 1970) to correlate with the presence of an immediately following deletion site. [10]

As indicated in the last three notes, there are conceivable 'interpretive' approaches which evade some of these arguments. It is not the purpose of this paper to contemplate the viability of interpretive approaches to anaphora, i.e. whether grammars can be constructed so that null anaphors are interpreted at some superficial level. What is of interest for the present is that there is a class of rules, which we will characterize as 'deletion anaphora', which give evidence of the existence of syntactic structure at some level of representation which is absent (or at least invisible) in surface structure. Any interpretive theory which is to be consistent with this kind of evidence must provide, as a substitute for the deletion relation, a system of syntactically present and active but (at least phonologically) null constituents.

1.2 Bresnan (1971) has shown that the missing antecedent arguments cannot be constructed to show that do it anaphora is a deletion process:

(16) *Jack didn't cut Betty with a knife--Bill did it, and it
      was rusty.
      [where it = the knife Bill cut Betty with]

The judgments are delicate, but it is generally agreed there is a difference between this sentence and the corresponding one with VP Deletion, which allows control of it from the missing antecedent.

Bresnan shows, in fact, that in general sentential it anaphora-- of which she assumes, probably correctly, that do it is a special case--fails to exhibit the missing antecedent phenomenon:[11]

(17) *Jack didn't get picked off by a throw to first, but it
      happened to Bill, and it singed his ear.
      [where it = the throw to first that singed Bill's ear]

She suggests that the correct generalization should be that anaphoric processes that leave pro-forms behind do not exhibit the missing antecedent phenomenon, whereas anaphoric processes which leave no pro-form do. [12]

Notice that Ross's arguments that VP Deletion is a syntactic deletion process do not go through for do it anaphora: there are no there-insertion sentences anaphorized with do it, there is no argument on the basis of the how to/*why to contrast, since do it is manifestly a VP in its own right, and can take the relevant adverbial modifiers (do it this way, do it for this reason), and there is no argument based on the reduction prohibition. In fact, so far as we know, this is representative of the situation with respect to pronouns in general; aside from the ingenious argument of Grinder and Postal, which suggests that one(s) pronominalization involves syntactic deletion, there seem to be no arguments that pronominalization involves deletion of syntactically present constituents. [13]

1.3 We have noted that there is a correlation, for the VP anaphora rules, between the existence of evidence that the rule is a syntactic deletion and its inability to operate under pragmatic control. We advance the following general claim:

Claim: It is just those anaphoric processes which consist
in syntactic deletion, leaving no pro-form in place
of the deleted structure, that require syntactic
control.

We thus distinguish deletion anaphora, which involves deletion
resulting in an 'incomplete' surface structure, i. e. a surface structure in which a normally present constituent is absent entirely, and
pronominal anaphora, where there is an anaphorically interpreted
item actually present as a constituent in surface structure. Our
claim is that deletion anaphora requires an antecedent in actual linguistic structure, so that 'null anaphors' produced by deletion cannot
normally be interpreted under pragmatic control; but that in general,
pronominal anaphors may be so controlled.

Thus, for example, as pointed out in Section 0, ordinary definite
pronouns do not in general require syntactic control. Sentential it
pronominalization can also occur, although less readily, with nonsyntactic control, as in the following situation:

(18) Hankamer [observing Sag successfully ripping phone
          book in half]:
      I don't believe it.
(19) Sag [same circumstance]:
      It's not easy.

When we consider nominal Identity-of-Sense anaphora, the claim
appears to be borne out, although the judgments become somewhat
delicate. We find nonsyntactic control of indefinite pronouns like
one(s) perfectly OK:

(20) [Sag produces two apples]
      Hankamer: Can I have one?
(21) [Observing Max ride by on his camel]
      Daddy, buy me one.
      Did you ever ride on the one Sue used to have?

But for the version of Identity-of-Sense anaphora (commonly referred
to as Genitive-Head Deletion) which deletes the head entirely, leaving
only a genitive modifier, nonsyntactic control is somewhat more
difficult:[14]

(22) #Have you ever ridden on Sue's?

The judgment is admittedly delicate, but in the course of several
presentations and discussions of this paper we have found that a

majority of speakers concur in the opinion that (22) is odd in the context specified in (21) in a way that the examples given in (21) are not.

It is a fact, however, that pragmatic control is felt to be much more palatable with nominal null anaphora than with VP null anaphora. This is a troublesome and interesting fact; it seems to indicate that the size of the null anaphor determines to some extent its nonsyntactic controllability, and that this factor interacts with the independent difference between deletion anaphora and pronominalization anaphora to produce a scale of judgments fading off toward imperceptibility. It makes sense, of course, that it will be easier to interpret a missing N from pragmatic context than a missing VP; the latter case involves more guesswork.

If this is correct, then in the case of an anaphoric process which deletes almost all of a clause we would expect the requirement of syntactic control to be particularly strong. There is such a rule, the rule of Sluicing, which derives sentences like (23b) from sources like (23a):

(23a) We were looking for somebody, but I can't remember
       who we were looking for.
(23b) We were looking for somebody, but I can't remember
       who.

Ross (1969) has argued overwhelmingly that this rule must be a rule of syntactic deletion.

Sluicing, like the other anaphora rules discussed here, can be syntactically controlled from previous linguistic context, even with a change of speakers:

(24) Hankamer: Someone's just been shot.
      Sag: Yeah, I wonder who.

But it cannot be pragmatically controlled, as the following example demonstrates:

(25) [Hankamer produces a gun, points it offstage and fires,
          whereupon a scream is heard]
      #Sag: Wow, I wonder who.

We conclude, then, that our claim is substantiated at least for the cases of deletion anaphora which produce incomplete surface structures above the level of NP structure, with the larger null anaphors showing the restriction more clearly. Clause-sized null anaphors, produced by Sluicing, are almost impossible to interpret pragmatically; VP-sized ones are easier, but still pretty clearly require syntactic control; and when the null anaphor is the size of a mere N, the requirement of syntactic control, while perceptible, is considerably diminished in effect.

2. Ellipsis rules. In this section we examine the class of rules which effect ellipsis in clauses. These are the rules which delete constituents from variable locations in a clause under identity with corresponding constituents in some other clause. Their properties are discussed in Hankamer (1971), and arguments that any rule of this type must be a syntactic deletion are given in Hankamer (1973).[15]

2.1 Stripping. Stripping is a rule which deletes everything in a clause under identity with corresponding parts of a preceding clause, except for one constituent (and sometimes a clause-initial adverb or negative):

(26) Alan likes to play volleyball, but not Sandy.
(27) Gwendolyn smokes marijuana, but seldom in her own apartment.

This rule can operate across a speaker boundary. Notice that the two clauses in each of the examples can be spoken by different speakers, and the resulting discourses are well formed, as is the following:

(28) Hankamer: Listen, Ivan, he's playing the William Tell Overture on the recorder.
Sag: Yeah, but not very well.

Here the response not very well results from the application of Stripping to the full clause But he isn't playing the William Tell Overture on the recorder very well.
This stands in marked contrast to the following discourse, where the extralinguistic context might be expected to provide sufficient information to control Stripping pragmatically:

(29) [Sag plays William Tell Overture on recorder]
#Hankamer: Yeah, but not very well.

The ill-formedness of this discourse shows that Stripping requires syntactic control.[16]

2.2 Gapping. Gapping is an ellipsis rule which applies in coordinate structures to delete all but two major constituents from the right conjunct under identity with corresponding parts of the left conjunct.

(30) Ehrlichman duped Haldeman, and Nixon, Ehrlichman.

Gapping too can operate across a speaker boundary, as is shown by the following discourse:

(31) Hankamer: Ivan is now going to peel an apple
      Sag: And Jorge, an orange.

Once again, we observe that although it doesn't matter whose utterance controls Gapping, it nevertheless must be an utterance, not merely a situation. Consider the following discourse:

(32) [Hankamer produces an orange, proceeds to peel it,
           and just as Sag produces an apple, says:]
      #And Ivan, an apple.

As you can see, this discourse ranks high on the bizarreness scale. We conclude that Gapping requires syntactic control.
    The rule of Gapping can also delete subjects, [17] as in

(33) Mitchell lied to the committee, and is now serving his sentence.

And, as by now should come as no surprise, subject-Gapping requires syntactic control, as the following discourse shows:

(34) [Hankamer is still peeling his orange]
      #Sag: And is dropping orange peels all over my foot.

    It has been suggested to us that what is wrong with examples like (32) and (34) is perhaps not the lack of syntactic control for Gapping, but the impossibility of getting an isolated conjunct beginning with and; in other words, that the sentences are independently ungrammatical because and can only occur between surface conjuncts. This, however, does not appear to be true, for there are contexts in which utterance-initial and is possible, with no preceding discourse:

(35) Hankamer: [observing Sag playing pretty good ragtime
           piano] And he doesn't even have a left hand!

Other examples are pretty easily called to mind. It seems that such cases involve essentially pragmatic omission of an understood left conjunct, which is just what would have to be possible to allow the utterance-initial <u>and</u> in examples like (32) and (34). And in fact, if you put the verbs back in (and the subject in (34)), the bizarreness disappears:

(36) [Same context as (32)]
     And Ivan is going to peel an apple.
(37) [Same context as (34)]
     And he's dropping orange peels all over my foot!

We must conclude that the strangeness of (32) and (34) is not due to the fact that the conjunction is not flanked by conjuncts, but rather to the attempt to gap under pragmatic control.

We have shown in this section that two ellipsis processes, Gapping and Stripping, can be controlled syntactically across a speaker boundary from a discourse antecedent, but cannot be controlled pragmatically. For other ellipsis rules, such as Comparative Ellipsis, it is impossible to construct examples where they apply across sentence boundaries at all, so it is impossible to test them for pragmatic control. So far as we have been able to determine, there are no counterexamples to our claim: ellipsis rules which can be shown to involve deletion cannot operate under pragmatic control.[18]

3. Conclusion. Elsewhere (Sag and Hankamer (to appear)) we argue that the claim made in Section 1.3 must be modified somewhat to take into account various instances of anaphoric processes that leave pro-forms behind but act like they don't, and vice versa. We argue, in fact, that there are two coherent classes of anaphora phenomena that must be distinguished (which we term Deep Anaphora and Surface Anaphora). The notions of syntactically and pragmatically controlled anaphora, as developed in this paper, play a crucial role in determining to which class a given anaphoric process belongs.

NOTES

1. The examples in (1) can also, with some strain, be read with pragmatic control of the pronoun--then, of course, it is <u>not</u> coreferent with the NP which is its antecedent on the syntactically controlled reading.

The examples in (2), and again also the examples in (1), can also be syntactically controlled in discourse, with the linguistic antecedent in a previous sentence. It is clear that this intersentential control is syntactic and not just a case of pragmatic control, for the pronoun can, as in the examples in (1), have no real-world referent:

(i) Do you know what happens to anyone who eats this stuff?
--Yeah, <u>his</u> hair falls out.
(ii) Is the unicorn a possible animal?
--I don't know, but if <u>it</u> is, it's certainly a herbivore.

2. Shopen (1972) discusses the possibility of pragmatic control of anaphoric processes in some detail, but does not note the distinction observed here.

3. We use the term 'anaphoric process' to refer to any grammatical device which allows the interpretation of an element to be chosen from an infinite number of potential values, the choice in a particular instance being determined by context. This usage is intended to be neutral as to whether the proper formulation of the grammatical device is a syntactic transformation, an interpretive rule, or whatever.

4. There are, of course, strictly sentence-internal processes, such as reflexivization, which are and always have been recognized as strictly syntactically controlled.

5. We introduce the cross-hatch (#) as an indication that the sentence so marked is incompatible with the indicated context (presuming, of course, the absence of any relevant previous linguistic context).

6. We read these with normal (noncontrastive) intonation in the first clause, so that the main stress falls on <u>do it</u> in (8a) and on <u>can</u> in (8b). If the sentences are read with contrastive stress on <u>you</u> in both examples, (8b) becomes for some people more nearly conceivable as a discourse-initial utterance. This is a mysterious effect, but seems to have nothing to do with pragmatic control of VP Deletion. What seems to be the case is that VP Deletion, which ordinarily (like all anaphoric processes) is reluctant to operate backwards in conjoined structures, can marginally do so if some element outside the VP in the left conjunct is contrastively stressed. Thus (8b) becomes exactly as good as (i):

(i) I don't think YÓU can, but I know sómeone who can rip phone books in half.

7. The <u>it</u>, of course, may have another antecedent in discourse; then (11) is grammatical:

(i) Al, why did you refuse to ride the camel$_i$?
Al: I've never ridden a camel, and it$_i$ stank horribly.

Sentences like (9)-(10b), however, are grammatical even in the absence of a discourse or pragmatic antecedent for the pronoun.

8. The arguments given here were designed against an interpretive theory which does not employ 'empty' nodes which can undergo syntactic rules, as proposed, for example, in Wasow (1972). Under this proposal, anaphoric or elliptical structures start out as syntactically fully developed underlying structures, except that some of the nodes are empty. These structures can then be transformed by syntactic transformations to produce elliptical derived structures, the empty parts of which get interpreted by interpretive rules which refer to other parts of the derived structure.

This proposal amounts to an admission that the anaphor is related to a syntactically real underlying representation. What distinguishes this from a deletion analysis is no longer the claim that anaphorized structures are not present at any stage in syntactic representation, but that the lexical items are never inserted.

This is not the place to go into an exhaustive analysis of the consequences of this proposal. The matter is taken up in more detail in Sag and Hankamer (to appear) and by McCawley (1974). For the moment, let it suffice to say that it is not at all clear that such an interpretive theory is distinct in any empirical way from a deletion theory, the central claim of which is that the anaphorized material is syntactically represented at some stage, and that it can be null just in case there is an identical antecedent structure.

9. This argument, however, does not go through against the syntactically active empty node version of the interpretive theory.

10. One could, of course, devise an interpretive theory employing empty nodes in 'surface structure' which would be interpreted under control from a filled node elsewhere in the structure, and say that reduction is blocked when there is an immediately following empty node. It is not clear that such a theory would differ in any interesting way from one involving syntactic deletion.

11. Postal (1972) disputes the generality of Bresnan's observation, claiming that there are cases of sentential it containing missing antecedents. The delicacy of the judgments involved makes it very difficult to evaluate the arguments in this controversy, but the fact remains that there is a difference between VP Deletion, which readily allows missing antecedent effects for all speakers, and sentential it (including do it) anaphora, which in general do not. It is this difference that we are interested in.

12. This suggestion should probably be modified to say that 'definite' pronouns do not exhibit the missing antecedent phenomenon, since Grinder and Postal show that indefinite pronouns like one can contain missing antecedents.

We also discuss, in Section 3, an anaphoric process which does not involve a pro-form (i. e. the 'anaphor' is null) and which does not exhibit the missing antecedent phenomenon. We show, however, that this process is not deletion anaphora.

13. Identity-of-Sense pronominalization with <u>one(s)</u> is the only anaphoric process we know of that both gives some evidence (albeit scanty) of involving syntactic deletion and appears to substitute a pro-form for the missing constituent.

14. There is another anaphoric process in NP's, closely related to the Genitive-Head Deletion discussed here but with slightly different properties (see Andrews 1974), which might be called Quantity-Head Deletion:

(ia) I asked for one orange, and she gave me three.
(ib) I asked for three oranges, but she only gave me one.
(ic) She went to look for oranges, and she found several.
(id) How many did she find?
(ie) I didn't think there were any.

The <u>one</u> in (ib), like the <u>three</u> in (ia), is a quantity expression, and must be distinguished from the pronoun <u>one</u>, which appears in (ii):

(ii) I asked for an orange, and she gave me one.

The pronominal <u>one</u> occurs only unstressed, whereas the quantity <u>one</u>, like other quantity expressions, may occur with stress; also the quantity <u>one</u> occurs before adjectives, whereas the pronoun <u>one</u> occurs after adjectives, and both can occur in the same NP:

(iii) Give us one blue one.

This rule of Q-Head Deletion is a deletion anaphora rule; no pronoun replaces the missing head of the NP, and missing antecedent arguments are easy to construct:

(iv) I don't own any camels that have fleas, but Bela owns three, and they keep getting in his beard.

We predict then that pragmatic control will be more difficult for Q-Head Deletion than for <u>one(s)</u> pronominalization, and though again the judgments are delicate, we find that this is the case:

(v) [Observing camel, no previous discourse]
     My uncle owns one.

(vi) [Same context]
     #My uncle owns three.

The difference, however, is disturbingly small, and the prohibition against nonsyntactic control can be overridden by various factors which we have not investigated, such as high predictability in a stereotyped environment, as when one says to a pretzel seller:

(vii) I'll take three.

15. In addition to the arguments given there, it is possible to construct Grinder-Postal type arguments based on the missing antecedent phenomenon for each of these rules. To illustrate, for the rule of Stripping:

(i) Bill took his coat off, but not Sally. She never takes if off.

In this sentence the pronoun it can refer to Sally's coat, even though the surface structure contains no NP which could control the anaphora, and the sentence is clearly good in a context where the pronoun could not be pragmatically controlled.

In order to construct a missing antecedent argument for Gapping, we must consider an idiolect such as that of only one of the authors of this paper, in which sentences are accepted which violate the No-Ambiguity Constraint proposed in Hankamer (1973). The crucial property for our purposes is the ability to gap an object NP along with the verb as in

(ii) Sally took her clothes to the laundromat, and Herman, to the dry cleaner.
[From . . . and Herman took his clothes to the dry cleaner]

Speakers who can stomach (ii) on the intended reading are also happy with (iii), showing that the gap can contain a missing antecedent:

(iii) Sally takes her clothes to the laundromat, and Herman, to the dry cleaner, even though he knows they're all wash-and-wear.

16. The possibility of pragmatic control in the following example provides a counterexample to the simple claim made in the text:

(i) Not in my wastebasket, you don't.

We have not the space here to go into the details of this very interesting phenomenon, but it appears that the requirement of syntactic control holds only for strictly declarative sentences, sentences with the

illocutionary force of statements. In the case of examples like (i),
the illocutionary force is clearly not declarative, but peremptory;
and in imperatives and exhortatives VP deletion also can take place
under pragmatic control:

    (ii) [Hankamer brandishes cleaver, advances on Sag]
        Sag: Don't! My God, please don't!

Similarly, if you see that an acquaintance has dyed his hair green,
you can say:

    (iii) You didn't!

    What is clear is that in each of these cases the illocutionary force
is not declarative (although what exactly it is in some cases, as in
(iii), is far from clear). So far as we have been able to determine,
the restriction holds perfectly (with the caveat stated at the end of
Section 1) for declarative sentences. We have no idea why there
should be such an effect on the behavior of anaphoric processes
conditional on the illocutionary force of the utterance.
    17. Arguments that such sentences result from Gapping and are
not instances of VP conjunction reduction are given in Hankamer
(1973).
    18. There is a peculiar class of pragmatic contexts where cer-
tain of these violations lose their offensive character. In particular,
when two or more people are party to a nonlinguistic event or situation, the longer the event or situation continues, i. e. the longer all
parties concerned are observing a particular event without saying
anything, the more 'linguistic' the context becomes. That is, once
an event or situation has been observed long enough in silence, it
becomes part of a tacit discourse between the observers, and it can
trigger syntactically controlled anaphora, as in the following
example.

    (i) Sag (to Hankamer): [after watching a pygmy pole vaulter,
        not three feet tall, spit on his hands, rub them up and
        down on the shaft of his pole, eye the bar which is fixed
        at 19'3", take a thirty-yard running approach, and
        successfully clear the bar by an inch and a half]
        It looks like he can!

Other related examples include the rather comic effect achieved
in the Sherlock Holmes story where Watson, asleep in an easy chair,
is being observed by Holmes. Watson writhes and squirms in his
chair, obviously dreaming intensely. Just at the point where Watson

is about to fall off onto the floor, Holmes utters a sentence like:

(ii) No she won't.

Clearly, the intended effect is that Holmes has been reading
Watson's mind. The events of Watson's dream have become a
common linguistic context, one which is capable of triggering syntactically controlled anaphora, as in (ii), which is an instance of VP
Deletion. Although such contexts as these do permit smaller violations of control restrictions, as in the last two examples involving
VP Deletion, we know of no such examples involving more severe
violations.

REFERENCES

Andrews, A. 1975. One(s) deletion in the comparative clause. In:
Proceedings of the Fifth Annual Meeting of the Northeast Linguistic
Society. Edited by E. Kaisse and J. Hankamer. Cambridge,
Mass., Harvard University Press. 246-256.

Bresnan, J. 1971. A note on the notion 'identity of sense anaphora'.
Linguistic Inquiry 2.589-596.

Grinder, J. and P. Postal. 1971. Missing antecedents. Linguistic
Inquiry 2.269-312.

Hankamer, J. 1971. Constraints on deletion in syntax. Unpublished
doctoral dissertation, Yale University.

Hankamer, J. 1973. Unacceptable ambiguity. Linguistic Inquiry
4.17-68.

Jackendoff, R. 1972. Semantic interpretation in generative grammar.
Cambridge, Mass., The M. I. T. Press.

King, H. 1970. On blocking the rules for contraction in English.
Linguistic Inquiry 1.124-136.

McCawley, J. 1974. How to get an interpretive theory of anaphora
to work. Unpublished paper.

Postal, P. 1972. Some further limitations of interpretive theories
of anaphora. Linguistic Inquiry 3.316-399.

Ross, J. R. 1969. Guess who? In: Papers from the Fifth Regional
Meeting. Chicago, Chicago Linguistic Society. 252-286.

Ross, J. R. 1972. Act. In: Semantics of natural language. Edited
by Harman and Davidson. Dordrecht, P. Reidel Publishing Co.
70-126.

Sag, I. and J. Hankamer. To appear. Deep and surface anaphora.

Shopen, T. 1972. A generative theory of ellipsis. Unpublished
doctoral dissertation, UCLA. Reproduced by the Indiana University
Linguistics Club.

Wasaw, T. 1972. Anaphoric relations in English. Unpublished
doctoral dissertation, M. I. T.

SOME ASPECTS
OF CONDITIONAL SENTENCE PRAGMATICS

PHILIP J. TEDESCHI

University of Michigan

0. Conditional sentences[1] have many uses, many functions. The relationship between the meaning of a conditional sentence and the meaning of its consequent, appearing as a surface sentence, is an extensive, varied relationship. Often the illocutionary force of a conditional sentence differs from the illocutionary force its consequent sentence would have if it stood alone.

Various classes of antecedent sentences affect the illocutionary force of sentences in particular ways. Some classes of antecedent sentences will be examined with respect to their effect on several syntactic classes of consequent sentences. Heringer has already examined a particular class of antecedent sentences and his work will be drawn upon (Heringer 1971).

Three specific types of consequent sentences are considered here: declarative sentences whose usual illocutionary force is that of a statement, yes/no questions whose usual illocutionary force is that of a request, and 'admonitive' sentences, e.g. you should do S, whose usual illocutionary force is that of a suggestion. These consequent sentences are examined with various types of antecedent sentences and the resultant illocutionary force is discussed. The consequences which this data implies for the performative analysis are then considered.

1. Declarative sentences. Conditional sentences with antecedents and consequents that are declarative sentences are the classic conditional sentences of logic. I am not concerned with this class in this paper. Certain types of antecedent sentences, however, can be used

in conditional sentences affecting the illocutionary force of the conditional sentences, changing the force exhibited by the consequent sentence. Consider sentence (1):

(1) You're wrong.

This declarative sentence is used by a speaker to inform his addressee of the speaker's opinion of the addressee's opinions/statements/ beliefs. . . . The same declarative sentence appearing as the consequent of a conditional sentence has a different function, although approximately the same illocutionary force.

(2) If $\left\{\begin{array}{l}\text{I understand you correctly}\\\text{I'm not mistaken}\\\text{my thinking is correct}\\\text{you haven't misled me}\\\text{I haven't been misled}\end{array}\right\}$, you're wrong.

The antecedent sentences in (2) temper the abrupt, somewhat rude statement made by (1). The use of the conditional does not change the determination of the truth value of (2). The speaker intends (2) to be true iff (1) is true. Essentially, the antecedent sentence serves to protect the speaker, to lower somewhat his responsibility for the direct illocutionary force of sentence (1). In many ways, the conditional sentences in (2) function similarly to the sentences in (3):

(3) I $\left\{\begin{array}{l}\text{think}\\\text{believe}\\\text{It is my opinion that}\end{array}\right\}$ you're wrong.

The conditional form thus is used partially as a politeness device. Determination of the truth value of the antecedent is not really necessary for determination of the truth value of the sentence, i.e. in this case the truth value of the consequent sentence.

In general, when the antecedent contains an expression referring to the correctness (truth value) of the propositional attitude of the speaker, the conditional sentence is used as a politeness device, used further to reduce the speaker's responsibility for the illocutionary act. If the speaker of (2) were proven wrong, i.e. his addressee's statements were correct, the speaker could answer that:

(4a) he misunderstood the addressee
(4b) he was mistaken
(4c) his thinking about the addressee's topic was incorrect

$$\left.\begin{array}{l} \text{(4d)} \\ \text{(4e)} \end{array}\right\} \text{he was misled}$$

All of the sentences in (4) would have further discourse continuations rationalizing away the error of the speaker.

Using a purely Gricean approach, we would analyze these sentences as material conditionals and determine their function through the device of conversational implicature. Basically, since the maxim of relevance is violated--clauses such as if I'm not mistaken are not directly relevant--the listener would through a decision process (cf. speech act inferences in Searle 1969) realize that the conditional sentence form is being utilized for purposes other than directly stating a material conditional. This decision process would lead further to the realization that the antecedent is used as a politeness device to temper the direct statement.

There are other conditional declarative sentences which are not to be analyzed truth-functionally. Consider:

(5a) I'll eat my hat.
(5b) If Nixon is innocent, I'll eat my hat.
(6a) We would know he's guilty.
(6b) If Rosemary had not pushed the button, we'd know he's guilty.
(7a) He's honest.
(7b) If Ford is dense, he's honest.

Rhetorical conditionals, (5), counterfactuals, (6), and concessive conditionals, (7), all have different illocutionary force from normal conditional sentences. Rhetorical conditionals use an absurd consequent to imply the falsehood of their antecedent, i. e. present a reductio ad absurdum argument as a statement that the antecedent is as false as the consequent. Counterfactuals presuppose the negation of their antecedent and, as Karttunen noted, invite the inference that their consequent is false (Karttunen 1971:567). Hence, counterfactuals are not used directly truth-functionally. Their uses are varied but primarily they express the speaker's belief in a possible consequence of an event which did not occur. In concessive conditionals, the speaker admits the truth of the antecedent to state a consequent which changes (almost orthogonally) the subject of discourse or which often is at odds with the consequent. Honesty and stupidity are more or less orthogonally related--the speaker of sentence (7) concedes a fault in order to express a virtue.

The change in illocutionary force becomes more obvious with nondeclarative sentences. Declarative sentences do not vary in function as much as nondeclarative sentences. The same form can be a warning, request, or order, depending on context and/or manner of delivery as in sentence (8), uttered in the given contexts.

(8) Watch out for their linebacker.
    (i)   coach to team during practice session
   (ii)   coach to referee having noted infractions on part of opposing team
  (iii)   coach yelling to blocker during the course of a play

Similarly, delivering a sentence in conditional form results in a different illocutionary force from that in the sentence consisting of the consequent alone.

    2. Imperatives. An imperative uttered as the consequent of a conditional sentence usually presents an order and qualifications on when it is to apply. There are many ways, of course, in which an imperative can be qualified. Some qualifications temper the performative force of the imperative and reduce it from the order force it would have standing alone to a request. Often the qualification of an imperative is used to convey 'uninvited' inferences that the imperative itself does not convey.

    The first type of illocutionary acts conveyed by conditional sentences with consequents that are imperatives to be discussed is what we might call 'directions'. The antecedent refers to a remote possible event and, in general, the sentences are used to convey directions as to what should be done in the event the antecedent obtains.

(9) Grab something that floats.
(10) Bail out and pull the ripcord.
(11) Break the circuit before $\left\{ \begin{array}{l} \text{you remove} \\ \text{removing} \end{array} \right\}$ the fuse.

Sentences (9)-(11) could be felicitously uttered as orders in some situations. Such sentences, however, are perhaps more often used as directions telling what to do in an emergency of some sort. In this latter use they are often uttered in a conditional sentence; the antecedent specifies the emergency situation.

(12) If you fall into the water, grab something that floats.
(13) If your engine quits, bail out and pull the ripcord.
(14) If the lights go out, break the circuit
       before $\left\{ \begin{array}{l} \text{you remove} \\ \text{removing} \end{array} \right\}$ the fuse.

The sentence in (14) is particularly the type of warning one might find written on a fuse box--directions which appear syntactically as orders.

Basically, all conditional sentences of this type can be paraphrased by the use of <u>whenever</u> in place of <u>if</u> (cf. Sadock 1974).

The basic form of a conditional order consists of reference to a temporally close possible event in the antecedent, followed by an imperative in the consequent.

(15a) Tell the repairman about the washing machine.
(15b) If the repairman comes, tell him about the washing machine.
(16a) Tell the teacher why you were absent.
(16b) If you go to class tomorrow, tell the teacher why you were absent.
(17a) Paint the garage.
(17b) If it doesn't rain tomorrow, paint the garage.
(18a) Take out the garbage.
(18b) If it isn't raining right now, take out the garbage.

The illocutionary force of sentences (15)-(18) is that of an order. A close paraphrase of these sentences is obtained by use of <u>when</u> replacing <u>if</u> rather than <u>whenever</u>. In a sense, sentences (12)-(14) are 'generic' orders--'whenever situation A obtains, do B'-- uttered by a general authority often having the illocutionary force of a strong suggestion rather than an order due to their temporal re- moval from the antecedent event and due to the weakness of the 'authority'. Sentences (15)-(18) are real conditional orders. Sen- tences (12)-(14) are used by the speaker (be it a marine sergeant or the electric company) to absolve himself of responsibility in the event of an emergency. In (15)-(18) the speaker is taking full responsibility for the order. The speaker has given directions through the condi- tional sentence for what to do if and when a certain situation obtains. The antecedent here merely qualifies conditions under which the illocutionary force applies.

In sentences (15)-(18) the speaker wants the consequent to be accomplished. Sentences (12)-(14) are somewhat vague as to the desires of the speaker. Consider:

(19) If an officer walks by, salute.

This is a generic order equivalent to sentences (12)-(14), but clearly it could be uttered by a speaker who really does not care whether the consequent is accomplished, by a speaker who is merely passing on a generic order which he may feel is ridiculous.

The expectation value of the occurrence of the antecedent event in sentences (15)-(18) is much higher than that of sentences (12)-(14), but (15)-(18) refer to only the first occurrence of the relevant event whereas (12)-(14), being more general, refer to any occurrence of the relevant event.

Consider the following direct order conditional sentences, however:

(20a) Go out and play.
(20b) If you've finished your homework, go out and play.
(21a) Begin handling the new order.
(21b) If you're done with that job, begin handling the new order.
(22a) Don't worry about this new order.
(22b) If you're continuing work on the project, don't worry about this new order.

Although sentences (20)-(22) appear to be of the same syntactic and semantic type as sentences (15)-(18), they may differ in function. These sentences can be used as basic conditional orders. Often, however, conditional sentences with aspectual verbs in their antecedents in the present perfect tense are used to invite the 'uninvited' inference that the antecedent be fulfilled. They function as a suggestion to complete/continue the relevant event. Generally, the consequent sentence refers to an event desired by the addressee; the sentences can be considered as 'inducements'. The causal or sufficiency connection established by the speaker through use of the conditional form, between completion/continuation of one event and occurrence of an event desired by the addressee, 'induces' the addressee to complete/continue the antecedent event. Note that sentence (21) only functions this way if it is assumed that beginning a new task is desired by the addressee.

Conditionals are also used as hedges on imperatives, reducing the illocutionary force of the imperative.

(23a) Pick up some soap on your way home.
(23b) If you think of it, pick up some soap on your way home.
(24a) Take out the garbage.
(24b) If you're not too busy, take out the garbage.
(25a) Visit Joe at the hospital before you leave.
(25b) If you remember, visit Joe at the hospital before you leave.
(26a) Stop and get some lettuce for dinner.
(26b) If you have time, stop and get some lettuce for dinner.
(27a) Bring your friend home for dinner.
(27b) If the occasion arises, bring your friend home for dinner.

(28a) Pluck some chickens.
(28b) If you don't have anything better to do, pluck some
       chickens.

This use of conditional sentences seems to correspond to an instance of R. Lakoff's Rule 2 politeness (Lakoff 1973:298). The
speaker is opening up options for the addressee and in doing so,
mutes the performative force of the imperative to a suggestion. In
a completely felicitous order the speaker is not giving the addressee
any options other than obeying or not. With a conditional hedge the
addressee has the additional option of determining whether the condition described in the antecedent, dealing with his psychological state,
holds. If this condition does not hold, he can interpret the order as
not having been given. The conditions which 'cause' the order to be
felicitous do not hold.

Similar results are obtained when the predicate of the antecedent
refers to other kinds of internal states of the addressee. He is being
given more options. These options reduce the illocutionary force of
the imperative to a suggestion.

(29a) Close the window.
(29b) If you're cold, close the window.
(30a) Don't finish the project.
(30b) If you're too tired, don't finish the project.
(31a) Drink some water.
(31b) If you're thirsty, drink some water.
(32a) Have a beer.
(32b) If you're thirsty, have a beer.

There is an additional result which the utterances of sentences
(29)-(32) have in common. The speaker's reference to an internal
state of the addressee, a state which must be self-determined, re-
moves responsibility for alleviating the state from the speaker to
the addressee. Sentence (32b) in particular might be used by a
speaker to inform a guest to take care of himself, whereas (32a) is
an invitation. Like most other politeness devices, conditional sentences can easily be used ironically. Any of sentences (23)-(32) can
be uttered ironically in certain situations.

Heringer has discussed a special class of conditional orders in
which the qualifying antecedent is one of the conversational postulates
usually associated with ordering (and with other performative forces). [2]

(33a) Take out the garbage, if I may ask you to.
(33b) Make your bed, if you haven't already.

(33c) Take out the trash, if you wouldn't mind.
(33d) Take out the trash, if you want to.

With the antecedent following the consequent, these sentences do seem
to have the illocutionary effect of an order, but less force than the
consequent standing alone has. The antecedent referring to a conversational postulate associated with ordering seems added as an afterthought more or less equivalent to tags such as won't you added to an
imperative as an afterthought to lessen its illocutionary force.

With the antecedent initial, the illocutionary force seems more
muted and the imperative even more request-like.

(34a) If I may ask you to, take out the garbage.
(34b) If you haven't already done so, make your bed.
(34c) If you wouldn't mind doing so, take out the trash.
(34d) If you want to do so, take out the trash.

Note the similarity between the following pairs of orders:

(35a) Take out the garbage, $\begin{cases}\text{won't you?} \\ \text{if you would.}\end{cases}$
(35b) Make your bed, $\begin{cases}\text{won't you?} \\ \text{if you would.}\end{cases}$

3. Yes/no questions. Sentences that are yes/no questions are
used as consequents in conditional sentences for a variety of reasons.
The most basic form, perhaps, is that in which the antecedent specifies the conditions under which the illocutionary force of a request
obtains:

(36a) Will you paint the garage?
(36b) If it doesn't rain tomorrow, will you paint the garage?
(37a) Will you ask John to see me?
(37b) If John shows up, will you ask him to see me?
(38a) Will you explain the 'A over A' convention to me?
(38b) If you've read Aspects five times, will you explain
       the 'A over A' convention to me?

Note that in sentence (38b) the antecedent of the conditional states one
of the conversational postulates of a request: 'the speaker assumes
that performance of the action requested is possible.' Note that in
one of its uses (38) is akin to a concessive conditional and might be
paraphrased by:

(39) Since you've read <u>Aspects</u> five times, will you explain
   the 'A over A' convention to me?

In sentence (38) the speaker is stating a reason why the addressee
should (at least, should be able to) comply with his request, i. e.
again a conversational postulate of requests is involved in the qualification. Sentence (38) might be used ironically to imply that the
addressee had not really read <u>Aspects</u> five times, in which case it
is similar to a rhetorical conditional, and the absurdity of the request
in the consequent leads to the negation of the antecedent. Consider:

(40) If you're so rich, why don't you drive a Cadillac?[3]

Sentence (40) is a paradigm example of a concessive conditional used
to request information, but it is usually used ironically as a challenge
to a statement of a speaker.
   An additional type of antecedent frequently associated with conditional requests is one in which the speaker establishes a causal or
sufficiency connection between a possible future act of the speaker
beneficial to the addressee and the act requested, the consequent.

(41) If I give you five dollars, will you mow the lawn?
(42) If I give you a 'C', will you promise never to take
   another linguistics course?

The conditional form may be used as a hedge to reduce further the
illocutionary force of the yes/no question from a request to that of a
suggestion and to increase the politeness measure of the request.

(43) If you think of it, $\begin{cases} \text{please} \\ \text{will you} \end{cases}$ take out the garbage?

(44) If you have time, $\begin{cases} \text{please} \\ \text{will you} \end{cases}$ stop at the store and pick up
   some bread?

(45) If you're thirsty, will you get us some beer?

Just as with orders, referring to a state internally determined by
the addressee weakens the performative force of the request--makes
it more polite. The sentences in (43) and (44) are akin to those
studied by Heringer in which a conditional request is qualified by an
antecedent referring to the intentions and/or desires of the addressee.[4]

(46) If you don't mind my asking
   you to, $\begin{cases} \text{will you take} \\ \text{do you mind taking} \end{cases}$ out the garbage?

(47) If I haven't already asked, $\begin{cases} \text{will} \\ \text{can} \end{cases}$ you tell me when you're
   leaving?

(48) Will⎫ you clean the cat box, if you don't mind?
     Can⎭

(49) Will you allow me to see her, if you can?

(50) Will you   ⎫ open the window, if you don't mind my asking?
     Do you want to⎭

(51) Will you see what's wrong with Jane, if you haven't already?

As Heringer has noted, there are restrictions on the type of qualifying clause that can be used with requests and other speech acts. Certain 'intrinsic' conversational postulates of the various speech acts cannot be used to qualify those speech acts. In particular, an indirect speech act based on a given conversational postulate cannot appear in a conditional sentence with a sentence based on that postulate in the antecedent (cf. Heringer 1971:Chapter 4).

4. Admonitives.[5] The situation with respect to admonitives appearing as consequents of conditional sentences parallels the imperative and yes/no question cases. The conditional can be used to establish the conditions under which the performative force, usually that of a suggestion, is to apply:

(52a) You should plant the tree.

(52b) If it rains tomorrow, you should plant the tree.

(53a) Why don't you tell John about Mary?

(53b) If John comes, why don't you tell him about Mary?

The use of conditional can hedge the already weak performative force of the suggestion:

(54a) You should see a dentist.

(54b) If you have time, you should see a dentist.

(55a) You should get yourself a beer.

(55b) If you're thirsty, you should get yourself a beer.

(56a) You should get yourself a beer.

(56b) You should get yourself a beer, if you want one.

(57a) You should visit John at the hospital.

(57b) If you can remember, you should visit John at the hospital.

By using an antecedent that refers to an internal state of the addressee, the speaker lessens his responsibility for the suggestion. Having his addressee determine an internal condition involving the desires/ intentions of the addressee before the illocutionary force associated with the consequent applies, places some of the responsibility evolving from consequences of the action suggested on the addressee. If in sentence (54b) the result of seeing the dentist is disastrous for the addressee, the speaker can rationalize that the action follows as much from the decision of the addressee re the antecedent as from his suggestion in the consequent. Of course, the hedges also serve a politeness function. Like almost all politeness devices, these hedges can easily be used ironically.

(58) If you don't like it here, why don't you go back where you came from?
(59) If you want to, you should turn in your paper on time.

The conditional can function as a suggestion that the antecedent be made to obtain. This particularly applies when the main verb of the antecedent is an aspectual verb and the consequent is an event desired by the addressee.

(60) If you $\begin{Bmatrix} \text{'ve finished} \\ \text{'re done with} \end{Bmatrix}$ your homework, you should go out and play for awhile.
(61) If you're continuing to work on your paper, you should forget about the assignment.
(62) If you're still working on the Johnson job, you should forget about the new order.

In cases like (60) and (61), the consequent is an event which the speaker assumes is desired by the addressee. Although there are many types of illocutionary force that could be considered, the three foregoing cases serve to illustrate some problems inherent in several of the basic assumptions of generative semantics.

5. Performative analysis. The various uses of conditional sentences as pragmatic devices qualifying illocutionary force present several problems for performative analysis. According to an assumption of generative semantics, all utterances in their logical forms have as the highest predicate a performative verb and only one performative verb occurs in a single logical structure (cf. Ross 1970; Lakoff 1972). Further, adverbs, especially sentence adverbs, are analyzed as higher predicates having as their argument the sentence they modify (Lakoff 1970:Appendix F and 1972:549-53).

Recently, the interaction of these two assumptions has been strongly questioned. Fraser notes that even if the performative analysis is adopted, certain adverbs and other constructions can and do occur as higher predicates commanding the performative (Fraser 1971:2-3). Morgan raises further questions about the interaction of these assumptions stating that adverbs can and do modify abstract performative verbs (Morgan 1973:415). Davison in particular has noted the problem with conditional sentences and the performative analysis (Davison 1973a and 1973b). [6]

In many of the sentences that have been considered here, it is obvious that the illocutionary force of the consequent sentence is not applied until the antecedent sentence obtains. In particular, the generic orders, called 'directions' herein, in which the illocutionary force of the order applies whenever the antecedent obtains, seem to require an analysis with the predicate representing if commanding the performative of the consequent clause. In addition, the quantifier representing the 'genericity' of these sentences would command both the IF predicate and the performative predicate of the antecedent clause. Perhaps a still higher performative of STATEing could command these predicates, but at least one of the assumptions of performative analysis would have to be changed to analyze these sentences. [7] Another alternative is to discard the analysis of sentence adverbs as higher predicates, but this alternative is the least attractive. Consider the following examples:

(63) If it doesn't rain, paint the garage tomorrow.
(64) If John comes, have a beer.
(65) If the pail is full, will you take out the garbage?
(66) If it doesn't rain, I'll take you to the zoo tomorrow.

Sentence (63) may not convey an order to the addressee unless the antecedent is satisfied; sentence (64) may not be an invitation unless the antecedent is satisfied; sentence (65) may not be a request until the condition is satisfied; sentence (66) is ambiguous. [8] If we consider situations in which the antecedent does not obtain, then it seems that imperatives, yes/no questions, and other syntactic forms like 'I bet you . . .' do not have the illocutionary force of orders, requests, bets. Promises and suggestions and other forms do seem to have the same illocutionary force, however.

Note that with surface performative verbs certain utterances predicted by an analysis with the performative verb highest are impossible, whereas the equivalent utterances under an assumption that the performative of the consequent is commanded by IF are acceptable sentences.

(67a) If it doesn't rain, I order you to paint the garage.
(67b) I order you, if it doesn't rain, to paint the garage.
(67c) I order you to paint the garage, if it doesn't rain.
(67d) *I order you if it doesn't rain to paint the garage.
(67e) *I order you to if it doesn't rain, paint the garage.
(67f) *I order you to paint, if it doesn't rain, the garage. [9]

(68a) If Michigan beats OSU, I'll bet they're still not ranked
       number one.
(68b) I'll bet, if Michigan beats OSU, they're still not ranked
       number one.
(68c) I'll bet Michigan's still not ranked number one if they
       beat OSU.
(68d) *I'll bet if Michigan beats OSU they're still not ranked
       number one.
(68e) *I'll bet Michigan's still not, if they beat OSU ranked
       number one.
(68f) *I'll bet Michigan's still not ranked, if they beat OSU,
       number one.

As Davison noted in her thesis, reason adverbial if-clauses can
usually be associated with the performative. Their function seems to
be to imply that a felicity condition holds rather than to state that it
is the case. Heringer, however, has given evidence that in certain
instances--his nonessential felicity conditions--the conditions themselves can appear as the antecedent clauses. Adoption of an analysis
which would permit nonperformative predicates in a logical structure
above the performative yields an additional benefit. The change in
illocutionary force of various performatives can be explained by
meaning postulates referring to the predicates which dominate or
are clause mates of the performative predicate. For example, consider:

(69) If you want to, take the garbage out.

Sentence (69) would have an analysis approximated by (70):[10]

(70)

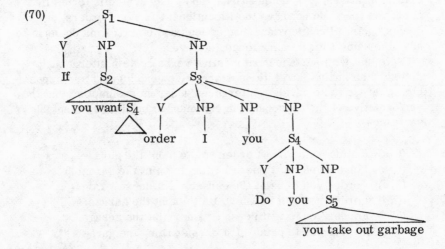

A general meaning postulate could be written to explain the change in illocutionary force of the performative ORDER in (70) to the conveyed request as follows:

(71) IF $(S_1, (_{S_2} \text{ ORDER } (I, \text{ YOU}, (_{S_3} \text{ DO } (YOU, S_4)))))$

If in the structure in (71) the highest predicate of S_1 refers to the intentions/desires of the addressee of S_2 with respect to S_3, then the conveyed illocutionary force is a request. [11]

NOTES

I am indebted to A. L. Becker, A. Borkin, J. Lawler, C. Pyle, and M. Sinclair for their comments and insights. Many sections of this paper have benefited from their intuitions. Of course, all remaining errors are the sole responsibility of the author.

1. In this paper conditional sentences are restricted to mean 'If . . ., . . .' sentences and their linear permutations.

2. The following examples are all from Heringer (1971:Chapter 4). My sentences (33a-33d) are his (4.5) (f), (4.9) (w), (x), (aa), respectively. In general, sentences (23)-(32) are related to Heringer's observations. Although the antecedents in (23)-(32) do not directly refer to the conversational postulates associated with the performative of the antecedent, they certainly do entail the conversational postulate associated with the desires/intentions of the addressee.

3. Example due to J. Lawler, personal communication.

4. The following examples are drawn from Heringer (1971:Chapter 4). My sentences (52), (53), (54), (55), (56), (57) are his (4.22) (c), (4.25) (c), (f), (j), (4.27) (c), (e), respectively.

5. The term 'admonitive' has been coined in order to have a term to apply to sentences with the syntactic form 'you should do S.' To the best of my knowledge, 'classical' linguistic analysis does not provide us with a term for this syntactic form.

6. There is strong logical evidence that operators binding variables should occur higher than performatives. If McCawley's analysis of referring NP's is extended to the deictic pronouns of the performative clause, then the λ-operator of Church's calculus should probably be accepted to bind the variables in the sentence. This abstraction operator would logically have to occur higher than the performative predicate.

7. Either the highest predicate assumption or the assumption of only a single occurrence of a performative in a given structure would have to be dropped. In general, along with Sadock (1974) I tend to doubt the validity of a performative STATE used with statements and

lean rather toward a logical structure with λ-operator to establish the deictic facts.

8. This ambiguity can be explained by considering the difference between 'promise to' and 'promise that'. With the latter interpretation (66) is a promise; with the former it does not acquire the illocutionary force of a promise until the antecedent obtains.

9. The intonation of the (d) sentences in (67)-(69) is crucial. They are not to be intoned with 'parenthetical' intonation, i.e. as a sentence adverb on the higher clause that has been transformationally lowered to a sentence-initial position, but rather as adverbial clauses modifying the embedded sentence. Commas have been used to suggest the intonation contours distinguishing the (b) from the (d) sentences. The syntactic point becomes much clearer with antecedent clauses like If you want to.

10. This structure is a complete fudge. I do not believe that if if is to be analyzed as a higher predicate it would be atomic. The structure would undoubtedly be more complex with a complex structure, probably involving CAUSE, going through various raising and deletion transformations, then lexicalizing as if.

11. It is also possible that further examination will reveal that adverbials modifying performatives should be treated as syntactic amalgams arising from an independent deep structure and attached via transderivational rules to the main clause. There are some functional reasons for arguing that all if clauses are derived via amalgams, but the evidence is not yet sufficiently developed to advance this claim (cf. Lakoff 1974:330-39).

In this postulate, by refers I also mean to include those cases where the highest predicate of the antecedent entails information about the desires/intentions of the addressee.

This postulate is only written for the 'order' performative, but it could easily be extended to the 'request' and 'suggestion' cases. Many other postulates or some similar devices are needed to handle the other problems raised by the data but the statement of these postulates is simplified if the if commands the performative.

REFERENCES

Davison, A. 1973a. Performative verbs, felicity conditions and adverbs. Unpublished dissertation, University of Chicago.

Davison, A. 1973b. Words for things people do with words. In: Papers from the Ninth Regional Meeting. Chicago, Chicago Linguistic Society. 114-22.

Fraser, B. 1971. An examination of the performative analysis. Bloomington, Indiana University Linguistics Club.

Grice, H. P. 1967. Logic and conversation. Unpublished lecture notes.

Heringer, J. T. 1971. Some grammatical correlates of felicity conditions and presuppositions. Unpublished dissertation, Ohio State University.

Karttunen, L. 1971. Counterfactual conditionals. Linguistic Inquiry 2.566-69.

Lakoff, G. 1970. Irregularity in syntax. New York, Holt, Rinehart and Winston.

Lakoff, G. 1972. Linguistics and natural logic. In: Semantics of natural language. Edited by D. Davison and G. Harman. Dordrecht, D. Reidel. 545-665.

Lakoff, G. 1974. Syntactic amalgams. In: Papers from the Tenth Regional Meeting. Chicago, Chicago Linguistic Society. 321-44.

Lakoff, R. 1973. The logic of politeness: Or, minding your P's and Q's. In: Papers from the Ninth Regional Meeting. Chicago, Chicago Linguistic Society. 292-305.

Morgan, J. L. 1973. How can you be in two places at once when you're not anywhere at all? In: Papers from the Ninth Regional Meeting. Chicago, Chicago Linguistic Society. 410-27.

Ross, J. R. 1970. On declarative sentences. In: Readings in English transformational grammar. Edited by R. A. Jacobs and P. S. Rosenbaum. Waltham, Mass., Ginn and Co. 222-72.

Sadock, J. 1974. Toward a linguistic theory of speech acts. New York, Academic Press.

Searle, J. R. 1969. Speech acts. Cambridge, At the University Press.

INDIRECT SPEECH ACTS:
A NATURAL CLASS OR NOT?

ALICE DAVISON

State University of New York at Stony Brook

Some speech acts convey meaning and illocutionary force less
directly than other speech acts. Whether or not indirectly expressed
speech acts form a discrete class or whether they represent a point
or several points on a continuum of explicitness is not an issue to be
raised here.[1] Given that speech acts with the same illocutionary
force and conveyed propositional content do differ in the way that
these are conveyed, I would like to raise the question here of whether
indirect speech acts have anything in common beyond the property
that they indirectly convey a speech act. The answer to that question
has consequences for the major proposals which have been made
fairly recently to account linguistically for indirect speech acts.

The first problem to deal with is to delimit the scope of the question. What sentences or kinds of sentences should be investigated to
determine the properties of indirect speech acts, out of all the sentences which somehow or other convey something other than their
literal meaning? The first sentence types to be studied in the context
of a linguistic theory of speech acts were the whimperatives, as in
(1a, b),

(1a) Can you hand me the pliers?
(1b) Would you pass the Bombay Duck?

which were noticed by Sadock[2] because they have the surface form and
(sometimes) the intonation of questions, but the illocutionary force of
imperatives (Sadock 1970). Green (1970, 1973) demonstrated that
the range of illocutionary force actually goes from mild suggestion to

brusque command if one looks at a wider range of surface forms of
this sort. Her papers, and Sadock's papers on whimperatives and
queclaratives, investigate the possibilities of discourse cooccurrence,
possible appropriate replies for example, and syntactic cooccurrences,
such as <u>after all</u> in the queclarative in (2):

(2) After all, does linguistics mean a damn thing to politicians?

This sort of detailed analysis deals with a class of speech acts defined
by a specific combination of surface structure and conveyed illocutionary force, and generally shows that the conveyed illocutionary
force is more important than surface illocutionary type in determining
cooccurrence. McCawley (1973) has shown, for the class of exclamations expressed as questions, as in (3), that these utterances differ in
many ways from real questions. On the basis of the properties of
such explicitly defined classes of utterances, Sadock and Green were
brave enough to propose semantic structures for the indirect speech
acts they considered, structures which in some way combined elements defining the surface form and the conveyed illocutionary force.
These structures turned out not to be free of problems, and in any
case were not easily extendable to other types of indirect speech acts.
    Gordon and Lakoff, in their very illuminating paper (1971), focus
on the literal illocutionary force and propositional contents of the indirect speech act, and propose a set of conversational postulates
based on the felicity conditions of the act conveyed, or on general
principles of conversation. By these postulates a given sentence may
conversationally imply another speech act. For example, the requests
in (1) may be conveyed, in this analysis, by questioning the addressee's
ability (1a) or willingness (1b) to do something, which is what the
speaker wants done. Conversational postulates predict that connections between speech acts will exist where in fact they do, but they also
predict connections where they do not exist. Gordon and Lakoff are
careful to note that certain illocutionary acts cannot be conveyed indirectly, for example, those in (3), though the same surface forms
can be used indirectly, as in (4).

(3a) *May I command you to bomb New Haven? (* as a command)
(3b) *Let me fire you for dereliction of duty. (* as an act of
        firing)
(3c) *I must (have to) pronounce you man and wife. (* in a
        marriage ceremony)

(4a) May I say that I deplore the recent bombing of New Haven?
(4b) I must ask what you know about this outrage, and where
        you were at 2 a.m.

(4c) Allow me to offer my deepest sympathy.

(4d) May I ask you not to play your cornet at 3 a. m.

The normal meaning of the sentences in (4) is the conveyed meaning; (4a), for example, would be nonsensical in its literal meaning, which asks permission to say what has just been said.

Gordon and Lakoff are rather noncommittal on the subject of sentences like (5a), (6a), and (7a), which sometimes conversationally imply something other than the literal meaning.[3] Example (5a) could mean any one of the sentences (5b-f), or others I haven't thought of.

(5a) It's rather chilly in here.

(5b) Shut the window (door, etc.).

(5c) Turn off the air-conditioning.

(5d) Turn on the heating.

(5e) Light a fire.

(5f) I'd rather not stay in here.

The intonation often gives away some of the speaker's real purpose in saying something; example (5f) might be a more likely interpretation if the tone is apologetic, and less likely if the tone is brisk and emphatic. I would like to argue that (5a) and others like it--(6a) and (7a) discussed further on--belong on the outside edges of a class of linguistically relevant indirect speech acts, if there is one, or at some further point on a scale of indirectness than, for example, the sentences in (1), (2), and (4). A case could be made, however, for saying that the literal meaning and the conveyed act are linked by the same kind of implicature as in the whimperatives in (1). For example, (5a) might imply that the speaker has some reason for wanting the addressee to do something about the temperature, and thus fulfills one of the felicity conditions on a sincere request. A chain of propositions would relate the literal and the conveyed acts: a statement about situation X conversationally implies that the speaker wants something done to change X, and that in turn implies that the hearer, knowing from the situation (somehow) what will best change X, should do that thing. Double implicature will be discussed later.

Consider some similar examples. One of my colleagues told me that his Southern grandmother asks people to pass the chicken by saying (6a).[4]

(6a) Will you have some more chicken?

(6b) Have some chicken.

(6c) Pass me the chicken, please.

(6d) It's time for the next course.

(6e) It's time for you to go home.

I think that most people would think that (6a) means (6b), though they might be polite and offer the chicken first to an older person. It would not be clear, except to someone who knew the family code, exactly what (6a) is intended to mean when said by this person; ordinarily, it would mean (6b), or possibly (6d) or (6e), instead of (6b).

Another example based on a real situation is (7a), which is the way that Queen Elizabeth complains, in writing, of some flaw in the Guards' appearance or performance.[5]

(7a) Is it customary for the Guards to wear purple socks?
(7b) I don't know but it seems strange.
(7c) I do know it's not customary, and I don't like it, don't do it again.
(7d) Apologize for the lapse.

Unless one knew the source of the sentence (7a), and other circumstances, the sentence would appear to be a real question, a request for information rather than an expression of criticism. Sentence (7b) would represent the speaker's assumptions and intentions, rather than (7c) and (7d). Sentence (7a) is, in fact, used as a rebuke.

In the three cases just discussed, two or more meanings are possible, and which meaning is conveyed is clear only if the circumstances of the utterance are known. The more that a hearer[6] knows about the circumstances, the more easily the hearer is able to pick out the likeliest conveyed meaning. In all three cases also, the speaker could reasonably disavow a conveyed meaning, provided that the intonation used is consistent with the literal meaning. While someone might claim that in saying (7a) no criticism was intended, I don't think that someone could claim that he or she was only asking permission in (4a, c, and d), or only asking about ability and willingness in (1), without being accused of linguistic cheating.[7]

Having pushed this sort of indirect speech act more or less to one side, we are left with a somewhat more manageable residue, which can be more readily identified by surface structure type. The largest range of surface structure forms is discussed in Heringer (1972), which extends the Gordon and Lakoff postulates to general principles surrounding speech acts. The examples which follow are intended to be a representative sample of surface structure types. Their non-literal meaning is virtually always apparent, and their surface structure forms belong to some finite list. Concerning these indirect speech acts, there are two important questions. (1) Are they different in any consistent and nonobvious way from the direct speech acts which correspond in illocutionary force and propositional contents? (2) Are indirect speech acts similar to each other in any way? The semantic composition analyses proposed for whimperatives by Sadock

and Green would suggest that there would be differences from direct
speech acts, while the conversational postulates analysis would seem
to say that a conveyed act and a directly performed act would not be
different, and also perhaps that all acts conveyed by a conversational
postulate would be similar. [8]

There are two ways that I know of in which direct and indirect
speech acts differ. Not every direct act has a perfect counterpart
indirectly expressed. One can make ordinary statements about facts,
such as (8a) and (8b):

(8a) Today is Saturday.
(8b) The Battle of Hastings was in 1066.
(8c) Does your dog have fleas?

The question in (8c) might be quite banal and commonplace. But
indirect expression of these speech acts is never neutral in tone.
Stating and asking the counterparts of (8) indirectly sounds rather
strange if the speech acts are meant to be the same as (8).

(9a) (?) May I tell you that today is Saturday?
(9b) (?) I must ask you if your dog has fleas.
(9c) (?) Let me ask if your dog has fleas.
(9d) (?) Can I say that the Battle of Hastings was in 1066?
(9e) (?) Would you believe that the Battle of Hastings was
      in 1066!
(10a) Can I get you to tell me if your dog has fleas?
(10b) Won't you believe that I love you?

The speaker seems to be saying, by using the surface forms in (9),
that there is something disturbing, or upsetting, something to
apologize for, in performing the illocutionary act, though the act is
performed anyway. If so, it would follow that indirect expression is
not possible for speech acts for which it is inappropriate to apologize,
or to consider intrusions;[9] the sentences in (3) are strange, then,
because their illocutionary force and their surface form are incompatible. The sentences in (4) express, in somewhat milder form, the
speaker's feeling that the addressee may not like or welcome the
speech act. If used initially in discourse, the speech act apologizes
for intruding on the addressee. Other indirect forms, such as those
in (10), emphasize what is said, implying previous attempts at stating something; the speaker using the sentences of (10) would sound
rather desperate or exasperated.

Ordinary direct speech acts can occur in connected sequences.
Indirect speech acts sound rather strange if several of them occur

all at once. In (11) I have tried to concoct semantically plausible
sequences, which nevertheless sound definitely strange.

(11a)　??* May I say that I doubt that these maps are entirely
accurate. Can I inform you that the distances between
Srom and Saraneb are not consistent on several of the
maps, and I must say that I cannot see how the projec-
tions from the first angle match those from the second.
Let me say that I am not sure that you observed all this
at first hand. [10]

(11b)　?? I must request you to do me a favor. Could I ask
you to get me a quart of milk and half a dozen eggs,
and may I ask you to pick my coat up at the cleaner
and mail this letter? Why don't I give you a $5 bill
now and could I ask you to give me the change later?

The strangeness arises from there being so many indirect speech
acts in sequence; any single such act in sequence with ordinary speech
acts would be perfectly possible. It is hard to see how a restriction
on excessive use of indirect speech acts could be expressed in terms
of conversational postulates. The special expressive value of indirect form might be accounted for as the environment in which the
postulates apply (designated by * in Gordon and Lakoff 1971). But
sequences of indirect speech acts could only be blocked by preventing
the relationship of implicature from holding. In effect, a speech act
could not convey another by conversational implicature if an indirect
speech act has preceded. But such a description of the strangeness
in (11) would mean that all but the first indirect speech act in each
sequence have their literal meaning as the conveyed meaning of the
utterance. It seems to me, however, that (11a) consists of indirectly conveyed statements and (11b) of indirectly conveyed requests, expressed in an excessive way, rather than sequences of
speech acts directly expressed by the surface forms. The restrictions seem to be on the use of indirect form rather than on the
mechanism of implicature. The indirect form is in a sense redundant
after the first indirectly expressed act has expressed something about
the speaker's attitude.

Restrictions on syntactic cooccurrence follow the conveyed
illocutionary force. The studies of whimperatives, queclaratives,
and question exclamations mentioned earlier show that in general the
indirect speech act investigated shares the cooccurrence possibilities of the corresponding direct speech act. The after all in (2) is
possible, though the sentence has the form of a question, because the
speech act conveyed is a statement, a reminder of some fact. Ordinarily, questions cannot be prefixed by after all, though statements

can. I have noted elsewhere (Davison 1975) that indirect speech acts take the same reason clauses as the corresponding direct speech act, and not reason clauses appropriate to the literal meaning. [11] This fact can be stated in terms of conversational implicature. A given combination of illocutionary act and syntactic constituents is well formed if the illocutionary act implies another speech act of the right illocutionary force. [12] What would be harder to describe would be such combinations which are well formed if the illocutionary act does not imply another speech act, or which are well formed for some conveyed acts and not others, with no apparent differences among them. I would like to discuss here some examples of such apparently arbitrary differences.

The first concerns questions conveying other speech acts. Example (12a) is a rhetorical question which implies the negative statement in (12b).

(12a) Who needs crooked politicians?
(12b) Nobody needs crooked politicians.

It is not possible to convey a negative statement with some speech act which itself conveys the rhetorical question. The sentences in (13), in which I have tried to do such a thing, are all very peculiar, though (13d) is the least bad, if said with the right intonation, and destressing of would you.

(13a) *I must ask you who needs crooked politicians.
(13b) *May I ask who needs enemies, with friends like that?
(13c) *Can I get you to tell me who needs a dope like that?
(13d) ?Would you tell me who gives a damn about them?

Yet (14a) and (14b) questions, conveying a request, can in turn be expressed indirectly, as in sentences (14c-e), which I have found myself saying on occasion.

(14a) Would you move your car?
(14b) Would you mind moving your car?
(14c) Could I ask if you'd mind moving your car?
(14d) Can I ask if you'd be able to park further over?
(14e) I must ask if you'd be so kind as to move your car,
      which is blocking the garage.

Double implicature seems to be possible if the end result is a request rather than a negative statement, and even triple implicature as in (14e). In any case, restrictions on multiple implicatures can be described only by complicating the statement of the postulates.

Negatives and tags may not occur in yes/no questions if they are indirectly conveyed. Sentences (15a) and (15b) are ordinary negative and tag questions, and while they are different from plain yes/no questions in assumptions that the speaker makes, and perhaps in other ways, the differences do not explain why (16) and (17) are impossible.

(15a) Those are real diamonds, aren't they?
(15b) Isn't that a Rembrandt over there?

(16a) ?*May I ask if that isn't a Rembrandt over there?
(16b) ??Isn't that a Rembrandt over there, may I ask?

(17a) *May I ask if those are real diamonds, aren't they?
(17b) *Those are real diamonds, aren't they, may I ask?

Sentence (16b) might be barely possible, but oddly, the indirect expressions of questions in (18) are much better.

(18a) I wonder if that isn't a Rembrandt over there.
(18b) I don't suppose that's a Rembrandt over there?
       (rising intonation)
(18c) I'd like to know if that isn't a Rembrandt over there.

The rule of Slifting (described in Ross 1973) moves complement clauses and adjoins them to the left of the original embedding structure as a coordinate clause, leaving the rest of the structure as a tag. The rule applies freely to some indirectly expressed requests, mainly whimperatives, as in (19):

(19a) Pass the Bombay Duck, would you?
(19b) Shut the door, could you?
(19c) I'll be there at 3, tell them.

But other indirect requests, notably ones containing an overt verb of requesting, do not undergo Slifting:

(20a) *Pass the Bombay Duck, may I request?
(20b) *Shut the door, let me ask you.
(20c) *Leave immediately, I must ask you.
(20d) *Leave at once, you may.

It would be hard to state, much less explain, the difference between two questions conveying requests, such as (19a) which is well formed if Slifting applies, and (20a) which is not well formed if Slifting

applies. Such a statement in terms of conversational postulates
would have to mention very specific surface structures and postulates.

Sentence adverbials like <u>naturally</u> and <u>obviously</u> occur with statements, but not with questions and requests (21). Some indirect expressions allow sentence adverbials and others do not, as in (22).

(21a) Obviously that's not very satisfactory.
(21b) Naturally, they'll put up a fight.
(21c) *Obviously, is that very satisfactory?
(21d) *Naturally, put up a fight. (* as a command, rather
than a suggestion)

(22a) Let me say (that) obviously we can't do that.
(22b) May I say that naturally I'll do everything I can.
(22c) ??Can I get you to believe that obviously they won't
like it?
(22d) ??Would you believe that naturally I'll do everything
I can?

As in the previous cases, some indirect expressions can be combined
with the same adverbials with which the conveyed act can be combined, while others, apparently similar, cannot.

I have tried to demonstrate that indirect speech acts have some
unique properties not shared by the direct counterparts; minimally,
the indirect expression in itself expresses something. Indirect speech
acts also differ among themselves as to what the surface form does
express, and also in possibilities of cooccurrence and rule application. None of these differences are predicted by conversational
postulates; indeed, it is hard to think what they would be predictable
from. Indirect speech acts would seem to resemble primarily the
conveyed speech act and to differ from it in odd ways, and in this
respect they behave like idioms, as Sadock has suggested (1972).
But the relationship between conveyed meaning and literal form and
meaning is not so arbitrary or opaque as it very often is for idioms.
The conversational postulates analysis in its original form, and extensions proposed by Heringer and others, explain why a certain surface form can convey a given speech act, even if the actual occasions
for these relationships are somewhat more limited than one might
suppose. If it is the case that a speech act is conveyed by another of
a certain form and meaning, conversational postulates show why.
But they do lack the power to predict and explain many features of
indirect speech acts, some of which I have sketched here.

Clearly, much more must be discovered about the actual nature
of indirect speech acts, in discourse and in other syntactic combinations. Description of indirect speech acts has to be based on the

semantic and syntactic nature of these structures, which at present is not very well known. I am sorry to say that I have no comprehensive alternative to propose, and can only conclude by saying that indirect speech acts are something else.

NOTES

This is a slightly revised version of a paper given October 26, 1974, at the Third NWAVE Conference, Georgetown University. I am grateful to Don Larkin for his initial encouragement, which led to my submitting an abstract, and to Mark Aronoff for comments and the use of his linguistic intuitions.

1. Earlier discussions of indirect speech acts have treated them as a class or as specific classes in which a given surface structure type expresses a specific type of illocutionary act. The Gordon and Lakoff conversational postulates delimit a class, by specifying which structures can convey which other speech acts. It may well be the case that the 'class' of indirect speech acts has no sharp boundaries. It may be that, as Fraser suggested in the discussion, there is a continuum of explicitness in speech acts, with those containing overt verbs specifying the illocutionary force, at the most explicit end, ordinary direct speech acts next, etc. I find the idea attractive for the explanation it affords for the function of overt performative verbs, but its existence is compatible with the assumptions that indirect speech acts have special properties worth investigating, and that linguistic phenomena cannot be adequately described unless a great deal is known about their properties.

2. Jespersen, who noticed many things that have come to be recognized as important syntactically, describes requests having the form of questions in Jespersen 1931:250-51, and 1969:40.

3. Sentences like this are easy to feel ambivalent about. The relationship between literal meaning and conveyed meaning can be quite arbitrary, and yet here there is a fairly clear systematic connection, discussed further on.

4. I am grateful to D. S. Petrey, Department of French and Italian, State University of New York at Stony Brook, for this example.

5. This example was constructed on the basis of information given me by J. de Courcy, formerly of the Irish Guards.

6. Or, of course, the recipient of a written communication.

7. People who take whimperatives literally are just as infuriating as those people who pass just the butter and not the dish, when asked to pass the butter. The real-world properties of butter determine what the speaker means the hearer to do, just as the nature of

requests, which require that the addressee be willing, explains why the whimperative form can be used for a request.

8. Gordon and Lakoff note that some speech acts are more brusque or imperious than others. This is true of speech acts conveyed by speech acts concerning speaker-based felicity conditions (Gordon and Lakoff 1971:81).

9. This account was based on my intuitions about when I would use the indirect form, and a short period of self-observation. It seems to cover the behavior of other people also, as reported by Don Forman in the discussion.

10. This example was suggested to me by a psychiatrist's account of his treatment of a person who claimed to have explored outer space. Serious examination of the 'documents' showed glaring inconsistencies.

11. For example:

(i) Where's Sam Goody's, because you've been there before.
(ii) *I don't know where Sam Goody's is, because you've been there before.
(iii) *I want to know where Sam Goody's is, because you've been there before.
(iv) Turn on the heat, because it's chilly in here and I don't know where the thermostat is.
(v) *It's chilly in here, because I don't know where the thermostat is.

Examples (ii) and (iii) are bad if they are intended to be synonymous with (i); (v) is bad as a counterpart of (iv). The main point I wish to make is that indirect speech acts like (ii), (iii), and (v) do not have the full range of reason clauses (related to felicity conditions on the performative verb) that are possible with ordinary direct speech acts.

12. Conversational implicature does not, however, explain why indirect speech acts seldom, if ever, behave syntactically like the counterparts of the literal form and meaning, rather than the acts conveyed.

REFERENCES

Davison, Alice. 1975. Indirect speech acts and what to do with them. In: Syntax and semantics, Vol. III. Edited by Peter Cole and Jerry Morgan. New York, Academic Press. 143-186.
Gordon, David and George Lakoff. 1971. Conversational postulates. Papers from the Seventh Regional Meeting. Chicago, Chicago Linguistic Society. 63-84.

Green, Georgia M. 1970. Whimperatives: Schizophrenic speech
acts. Unpublished paper.

Green, Georgia M. 1973. How to get people to do things with words.
In: Some new directions in linguistics. Edited by Roger W. Shuy.
Washington, D. C., Georgetown University Press. 51-81.

Heringer, James T. 1972. Some grammatical correlates of felicity
conditions and presuppositions. Working Papers in Linguistics, 11.
Columbus, Ohio, Department of Linguistics, Ohio State University.

Jespersen, Otto. 1931. A modern English grammar, Vol. IV.
London, George Allen and Unwin. Reprinted 1970.

Jespersen, Otto. 1969. Analytic syntax. New York, Holt, Rinehart
and Winston.

McCawley, Noriko. 1973. Boy! Is syntax easy! Papers from the
Ninth Regional Meeting. Chicago, Chicago Linguistic Society.
369-377.

Ross, John R. 1972. The category squish: Endstation Hauptwort.
Papers from the Eighth Regional Meeting. Edited by Paul
Peranteau et al. Chicago, Chicago Linguistic Society. 316-28.

Ross, John R. 1973. Slifting. Proceedings of the 1969 Paris
Symposium on Formal Linguistics. Edited by M. Gross, M.
Halle, and M. Schützenberger. The Hague, Mouton. 133-69.

Sadock, Jerrold M. 1970. Whimperatives. In: Studies presented
to Robert B. Lees. Edited by J. Sadock and A. Vanek. Edmonton,
Alberta, and Champaign, Ill., Linguistic Research, Inc.

Sadock, Jerrold M. 1971. Queclaratives. Papers from the Seventh
Regional Meeting. Chicago, Chicago Linguistic Society. 223-31.

Sadock, Jerrold M. 1972. Speech act idioms. Papers from the
Eighth Regional Meeting. Chicago, Chicago Linguistic Society.
329-39.

THE ROLE OF INTONATION
IN SIGNIFYING SPEAKER INTENT

BRUCE FRASER

Boston University

Introduction. Even to the most casual observer it is obvious that
a speaker usually, if not always, intends to convey a great deal more
than he says. Recent work within the fields of linguistics, philosophy,
sociolinguistics, anthropology, and adjacent areas has focused on this
point, and we have now a growing body of speculation specifying how
to account for the fact that we mean more than we actually say. See,
for example, Fraser (1975), Gordon and Lakoff (1971), Searle (1969),
Grice (1967), for some representative research. None of these
scholars, however, has seriously addressed the following question:
to what extent does the intonation of the utterance determine how the
utterance is to be interpreted? Or, to invoke the title of this paper,
what is the role of intonation in signifying speaker intent? The
following represents a small, preliminary attempt to get at this
question.

   I am well aware that certain sentences are characteristically
used in more than one way. For example, a speaker may utter It's
getting late and intend to have it count as a simple report (say, during a discussion about whether we should go to the movies tonight),
as a complaint (say, when waiting for the waiter to arrive to take the
order prior to the theater), or as a request that we leave (say, if the
speaker were my wife, whom I had brought to a party of linguists).
But we are not aware of whether or not the speaker in one or more
of these utterances of the same sentence signifies his intended message through the use of a particular intonation pattern.

   To get some evidence which bears on the question of intonation and
utterance-meaning, we designed an experiment to determine if native

164

English speakers could accurately judge the intended use of a series
of utterances when these were removed from their conversational
setting. We selected the following six test sentences, which have a
relatively direct interpretation and an indirect interpretation as well.

		Direct	Indirect
		Direct	Indirect
(a)	Spend more time studying	Order	Suggestion
(b)	You must eat in that restaurant	Order	Recommendation
(c)	Could you do that before the operation	Question	Request
(d)	Can you lift your right arm	Question	Request
(e)	Shouldn't you be on your way to N. Y.	Question	Suggestion
(f)	Do you have to keep the lights on	Question	Suggestion

We hypothesized that while there was a class of possible intonation
patterns consistent with the direct interpretation, whenever the
speaker intended the indirect interpretation to be taken, he would
signify this by utilizing a distinctive intonation pattern, not drawn
from this class.

Method. Three male native speakers of English served as speakers
of these test sentences. Each speaker was asked to consider each of
the six sentences and to consider a context in which one of the interpretations of the sentences might be most appropriate. Then the
speaker was asked to imagine himself in this situation, create whatever conversation was necessary to evoke the mood, and then utter
the example sentence with the intended interpretation. The three
speakers uttered each sentence twice, once for each intended interpretation, thereby providing a total of 36 utterances (three speakers
x six sentences x two interpretations = 36). These 36 utterances
(preceded by a statement of this number) were arranged at approximately five-second intervals on a tape in two groups of 18 utterances
each. The same sentence was never placed in succession on the tape,
though two of the speakers uttered successive utterances one time in
each group. Each group contained some utterances of a sentence with
the direct interpretation, some with the indirect interpretation.
The subjects were 22 white, female college students who had
little or no linguistic training. The experiment was carried out in
two parts.
Subjects were first given a questionnaire containing the six test
sentences intermingled with seven additional examples. Each of the
13 sentences was arranged as illustrated by the following example:

Would you like a piece of cake
Example: Question 1 2 3 4 5 6 7 Offer

Subjects were instructed via written directions to indicate for each
sentence how they thought the sentence might be used in an ordinary
conversational situation. Selecting (1) in the foregoing example would
signify that the sentence could be used only to make a question, not an
offer, and vice-versa for selecting (7). Selecting (4) would signify
that the sentence might be used equally well for both interpretations,
depending on the context. Subjects were instructed to ignore any
opinions about how a sentence is most often used. At no time was
the term 'intonation' mentioned.

These questionnaires were collected and the subjects were given a
second rating sheet. Subjects were informed that they would hear a
series of 18 sentences spoken by several native English speakers and
that each sentence was recorded when the speaker was using the sentence for one of the two purposes indicated on the rating sheet. The
rating sheets did not contain the sentences, but only the utterance
numbers and rating information, for example:

1. Question 1 2 3 4 5 6 7 Suggestion
2. Suggestion 1 2 3 4 5 6 7 Order
3. etc.

Subjects were to indicate, using the same criteria as in the earlier
questionnaire, their opinion of how the sentence was intended. After
finishing the first group of 18, the subjects were given a second rating
sheet and completed the second group of 18 utterances.

Results. Subject judgments on the questionnaire sentences are
presented in Table 1.

The numbers to the right of each example in Table 1 indicate the
number of subjects who judged the sentence had only the first reading
(those who selected (1) or (2) on the rating scale), followed by the
number who judged the sentence could have both readings (those who
selected (3), (4), or (5) on the rating scale), followed by those who
judged the sentence could have only the second reading (those who
selected (6) or (7) on the rating scale). For example, 14 subjects
judged that (a) could have both interpretations, 5 judged that (b) could
have only the Order reading, and 4 judged that sentence (e) could have
only the Suggestion reading. Of the 22 subjects in this experiment,
only one maintained her initial judgments about the use of these sentences; all others changed their opinions when they heard the actual
recorded utterances. Changes in judgment were of two sorts: (1)
moving from an initial judgment of only a single interpretation to the

TABLE 1.

(a) Spend more time studying	Ordr/Sugg	7/14/1
(b) You must eat in that restaurant	Ordr/Rec	5/ 7/10
(c) Could you do that before the operation	Ques/Sugg	5/12/5
(d) Can you lift your right arm	Ques/Req	8/12/2
(e) Shouldn't you be on your way to N. Y.	Ques/Sugg	4/14/4
(f) Do you have to keep the lights on	Ques/Sugg	5/10/7
(g) Why aren't you cleaning your room	Ques/Sugg	8/10/4
(h) Why not try that one	Ques/Sugg	0/10/12
(i) Can I see that	Ques/Req	4/10/8
(j) Will you get here by 8	Ques/Req	7/12/3
(k) Can't you try another	Ques/Req	3/15/4
(l) You could help me now	Stat/Req	2/10/10
(m) That would be wrong	Stat/Ques	16/ 4/2

could-be-either position; (2) a polarity switch to the other interpretation. In less than 1 percent of the 792 judgments (36 utterances x
22 subjects) was the polarity switch in the wrong direction (i. e. having first judged, for example, that (b) could be used only as an Order
and then, when hearing it intended as an Order, judging it to be a
Recommendation). On the other hand, more than half of the subjects
changed their minds on two or more of the six sentences, usually on
at least two of the six utterances of the sentence that they heard.

The subject judgments on the 36 utterances were analyzed to determine how consistent they were in recognizing the speaker intent.
The original data was rearranged so that for each sentence, all the
utterances with one of the intended interpretations were to receive a
rating of (1), while the second interpretation was to receive a rating
of (7). The subject judgments for each intended interpretation for
each sentence (3 speakers x 1 sentence x 22 subjects) were then
averaged. The difference in the two averages for each sentence was
taken to be the degree of separation in recognizing speaker intent.
The results are presented in Table 2.

TABLE 2.

Sentence	Difference in average rating
(a) Spend more time studying	3. 4
(b) You must eat in that restaurant	2. 5
(c) Could you do that before the operation	1. 1
(d) Can you lift your right arm	0. 43
(e) Shouldn't you be on your way to N. Y.	0. 43
(f) Do you have to keep the lights on	0. 26

In an effort to corroborate the judgments of the subjects that the utterances were indeed actually different, we analyzed the fundamental frequency (f_0) contours of half of the utterances.[1] This group of 18 analyses contained each of the six sentences three times (once by each speaker), with two of the three utterances with one intent, one with the other. The results corresponded to the subject judgments on two grounds.

First, the intonation contours of the three speakers for a sentence when uttered with one of the interpretations intended were roughly the same. Moreover, for a given sentence, the contours for the two intents differed markedly (both visually and in terms of relative frequency change) in at least one part, thereby appearing to signal the different speaker intent.

Second, the degree of intonation difference was much greater for the first two sentences ((a) and (b)) than for the remaining four ((c), (d), (e), and (f)). The frequency difference at the peak of the contour over studying and must was considerably more than the differences between the rising contour of the questions in opposition to the other interpretations of the interrogative forms in (c)-(f). But as I have indicated, subjects were most clear in their judgments of speaker intent for sentences (a) and (b), and much less clear in (c)-(f); thus, the degree of intonation difference also corresponds to the subject judgments.

Discussion. I want to stress what the preceding presentation should have made evident: this work must be taken only as a suggestion of where future, serious experimentation might take us. I think, however, there are several points that might be made.

First, the judgments on the questionnaires and the subsequent judgments on the utterances reveal once again that native speakers are not necessarily reliable informants. That many of the students when making the questionnaire judgments did not consider more than one intonation contour was evident from their comments subsequent to the presentation of the utterances. But the opposite side of the coin is that many linguists present their 'crucial' examples with a particular intonation pattern, thereby possibly prejudging the interpretation.

Second, this sort of experiment raises the question of whether the direct interpretation intonation contours form one equivalence class, with the indirect contours forming another. This may be too strong. For example (cf. Sag and Liberman 1975), it may be only that there is an intonation contour which can guarantee that the direct interpretation is understood. Or, it may be that although there are contours which clearly indicate either the direct or indirect interpretation, they are used only if confusion might result; the rest of the time the contour is left to vary within broad limits. Moreover, although I have referred to these intonation contours as if they were clear, discrete, and well defined, this view is a great oversimplification.

Third, although both perceptually and acoustically the intonation seemed to vary systematically in terms of speaker intent, no control for timing, duration, or amplitude was made. Any one of these might have been responsible for the observed experimental results.

Fourth, we have no way of knowing the extent to which subject expectation influenced judgments. We tried to select the semantic content of each sentence to be equally compatible with each of the two interpretations, but no check was run on this. If, for instance, the example in (d) had been Can you resemble your pet rabbit, the meaning would have surely been taken to be that of a direct question, and a foolish one at that. In addition, it may be that a sentence such as (e) with a negative modal is nearly always used to convey a suggestion rather than a question; thus, even with a strong question intonation, subjects might have had to overcome a strong suggestion bias.

Finally, the use of staged utterances has a number of obvious disadvantages, the worst being the high likelihood that extraneous, nonconversational factors may be introduced and influence the experimental results.

NOTE

1. Thanks are due to John Allen and Doug O'Shaughnessy of MIT for making available their pitch extraction system as well as for assisting me in the actual analysis. Since the data was used as corroborative rather than primary data, and since there was only a single sampling from each speaker for a given utterance-meaning, the actual contours are not presented.

REFERENCES

Allen, J. and D. O'Shaughnessy. 1974. Fundamental frequency contours of auxiliary phrases in English. Ditto, MIT, Cambridge.

Fraser, B. 1975. Hedged performatives. In: Syntax and semantics III: Speech acts. Edited by J. Morgan and P. Coles. New York, Academic Press. 177-210.

Gordon, D. and G. Lakoff. 1971. Conversational postulates. In: Papers from the Seventh Regional Meeting. Chicago, Chicago Linguistic Society. 63-84.

Grice, P. 1967. Logic and conversation. Ditto, University of California, Berkeley.

Sag, I. and M. Liberman. 1975. The intonational disambiguation of
   indirect speech acts. In: Papers from the Eleventh Regional
   Meeting. Chicago, Chicago Linguistic Society. 487-497.
Searle, J. 1969. Indirect speech acts. In: Syntax and semantics
   III: Speech acts. Edited by J. Morgan and P. Coles. New York,
   Academic Press. 59-82.

TOWARD A DEFINITION OF IRONY

ALICE R. MYERS

University of Michigan

Irony is a little bit like the weather: we all know it's there, but so far nobody has done much about it. In this paper I raise some questions that will have to be answered before irony can be adequately explained, although it is not possible yet to provide much more than the beginnings of answers to those questions. The procedure will be to work from intuitions which, hopefully, are largely shared by native speakers, in an attempt to lay out the parameters within which an explanatorily adequate definition may be constructed. A later step in research on irony must be to test these assumptions empirically.

The two traditional definitions of irony have been: (A) saying something other than what is meant; (B) saying the opposite of what is meant. These stock definitions are inadequate in three ways. First, they do not account for the data, in that they include cases of nonirony and exclude some cases of irony. Second, they do not predict some interesting syntactic peculiarities of irony. And third, they give no insight into why language should permit such an apparently perverse means of communication.

1. Accounting for the data. Definition (A), 'saying something other than what is meant', would predict that instances of conveyed meaning such as those treated in Gordon and Lakoff (1971) would be ironic since the speaker is understood to be saying something other than what he means:

(1) It's cold in here.
(2) Would you mind closing the window?

171

(3) Can you get the window?

Sentences (1) through (3) can all be taken by the hearer to mean
'Please close the window'. Definition (A), then, would have to be
more tightly constrained to rule out such instances of conveyed
meaning from a characterization of irony.

On the other hand, 'saying something other than what one means'
would exclude cases of irony where on a certain level the speaker
does, in fact, mean what he says, while the context includes a
referent known to the hearer which renders the statement ironic.
For example, (4), which can be said by a driver to a passenger in
his car after another car has just cut in front without signalling:

(4) I love people who signal.

is literally true yet contextually ironic, because the person who is
in some sense 'referred' to did not signal, and is not included in the
set of [people who signal]. [1]

The second definition to be considered, 'saying the opposite of
what one means', appears to handle at least those cases where
irony is built on a single lexical item. (Underlining here and
throughout indicates ironic portions.) Thus,

(5) <u>Smooth</u> move,

when the addressee has just done something especially klutzy;

(6) <u>Lovely</u> weather we're having, isn't it?

after three days of rain;

(7) I always <u>wanted</u> to spend the summer in Ann Arbor,

said by Larry Horn at the 1973 LSA Summer Institute, who presumably hadn't.

But definition (B) would predict that saying

(8) There's a book on the table

when there is no book on the table would be ironic, too. Grice's
example of the windowless car is a similar case: we pass an
abandoned car with shattered windows and I say, 'Oh, look at that
car with all its windows intact'. I may have committed a social
error--you will not talk to me if I say things like that very often--
but I have not communicated irony.

These examples suggest that irony fills a judgmental or emotive function, i. e. I give you my judgment of Harry's stupidity when I say (9):

(9) Harry's a real genius.

With sentences (5)-(7) I communicate my opinion that dropping the cream pie was klutzy, that three days of rain is lousy weather, and that Ann Arbor is not my idea of a summer resort. When I speak of the book on the table or the windows in the car, I am communicating fact, not judgment. The 'fact' may be wrong, but it is not ironic because it is not judgmental. A definition of irony, then, will have to include this judgmental aspect.

Furthermore, definition (B) wrongly excludes cases where no clear opposite exists, such as (10):

(10) He's merely the greatest find since Kareem Abdul-Jabbar, that's all.

In (10) the speaker does not mean not merely, nor does he expect the hearer to substitute an opposite lexical item for merely. Or consider a sentence like (11):

(11) Everyone knows you never make any mistakes.

In what sense does this utterance say the opposite of what is meant? We will have rough going if we continue to look for a single lexical item. Is the opposition to be everyone/no one? knows/guesses? you/I? never/always? and so on. In fact, what everyone knows is [NEG S], i. e. 'it is not the case that you never make any mistakes', or in other words, that the scope of the negation is the entire sentence.

Consider also the ironic use of complex predicates:

(12) Sure, John killed Mary,

where the irony is ambiguous between (13) and (14):

(13) Mary died, but John didn't cause it.
(14) John tried, but Mary didn't die.

There are other possibilities, e. g. she was already dead. These all derive from the components of the complex predicate kill: CAUSE, BECOME, NOT ALIVE. (Example (12) has the same

intonation for all readings; if <u>John</u> is stressed, the reading shifts
to 'not John, but someone else killed Mary'.)

Irony includes negation then, but not all utterances can be simply
negated. Consider, for example, ironic speech acts such as questions or thanks. In a volleyball game once, when methods of rotation
were being discussed, one player said, 'Don't make it too complicated', and another responded with:

(15) It's like a circle. Think you can handle a circle?

Searle's (1970) felicity conditions on speech acts specify that in a
properly executed question the speaker does not know the answer
and wants to know it, but in (15) the speaker was not really questioning whether the hearer had the intelligence to follow a circular
rotation pattern, nor did she expect an answer. Next, imagine a
circumstance where you are standing in front of a heavy university
building door, juggling books and a half-empty coffee mug, and
someone goes in but doesn't hold the door open for you. You say

(16) Thanks.

The felicity conditions on thanking require that an act be done which
benefits the speaker, and that the speaker feel gratitude, neither of
which applies in (16). Here again, some cases of ironic usage are
excluded by definition (B). Felicity conditions may be viewed as the
analog of truth functions in speech acts where simple true-false
distinctions do not apply. Thus a question is not true or false, but
it may be felicitous or infelicitous. Clearly then, the notion of
felicity will have to be utilized in some way in defining irony.

Traditional definitions are inadequate because they do not explain either all or only ironic utterances. Definition (A), 'saying
something other than what is meant', wrongly includes conveyed
meaning and excludes utterances which are literally true but contextually ironic; definition (B), 'saying the opposite of what is meant',
wrongly includes nonjudgmental opposites and excludes cases where
no clear opposite exists. Definition (A) looks hopeless. Definition
(B), actually a subset of (A), appears salvageable, if it is fixed up
to include the judgmental aspect of irony, and the role of negation
interacting with felicity conditions.

2. Syntactic peculiarities. There are some interesting syntactic
facts about irony which, at present, I can point out but not yet explain, although I will suggest how they might be explained. If these
facts can be accounted for in the existing grammatical theory, they
may not have to be predicted by the definition.

First of all, a sincere (restrictive) relative clause may be embedded in an ironic matrix, but not vice versa (generally). Thus,

    (17a) I <u>love</u> people who don't signal.
=(17b) I hate people who don't signal.

Example (17b) represents the real meaning, or sincere paraphrase, of (17a), and shows that the higher verb, <u>love,</u> is to be taken ironically, with the embedded clause remaining a comment on the true state of affairs, i.e. someone didn't signal. For many people, sentence (18a) is an impossible ironic utterance ((18b) is again a sincere paraphrase):

    (18a) *I hate people <u>who signal</u>.
=(18b) I hate people who don't signal.

(I think people who think (18a) is effective as an ironic utterance are reading the scope of the irony over the entire S:

    (19) It is not the case that I hate people who signal,

or treating the sentence as if the irony were on the top verb, so that the sincere reading would be:

    (20) I love people who signal.

The reading I wish to force, however, is one where only the meaning of the embedded clause undergoes a change.)

Here are two more examples of sentences where the matrix is to be taken ironically, but the relative clause is sincere:

    (21a) I <u>love</u> people who smoke cigars on the bus.

In (21a) the embedded S represents a true state of affairs; the matrix is ironic. A sincere reading would be

    (21b) I hate people who smoke cigars on the bus.

Similarly,

    (22a) I <u>love</u> people who don't refill the ice cube trays.

Again, the embedded S is true of a particular state of affairs; the matrix is ironic. The sincere reading would be:

(22b) I hate people who don't refill the ice cube trays.

Now, if these utterances are reconstructed in an attempt to embed an
ironic S in a sincere matrix, they are bad, i. e. they fail as ironic
communication:

(23a) *I hate people who don't smoke cigars on the bus. [2]
=(23b) I hate people who smoke cigars on the bus.
(24a) *I hate people who refill the ice trays.
=(24b) I hate people who don't refill the ice trays.

Notice that another kind of restrictive relative, specifically one
which is not presupposed, accepts irony freely and does not entail
irony in the matrix:[3]

(25) I met a man who's really liberated: he thinks it's OK
for women to work as long as they're home in time to
fix dinner.

The hypothesis I want to present is that embedded material which is
presupposed cannot be ironic if the higher S is sincere because that
would erase the presupposition which is in some way integral to the
matrix it is embedded in. The claim for relative clauses, in its
strongest form, would be that there can be irony in the top S with
the lower, presupposed, S sincere; there can be irony in both places;
but there cannot be irony only in the lower when the lower is presupposed.
      The second syntactic fact to notice is that irony in sentential
complements is constrained in certain ways and shows some parallels
with the constraint on irony in relative clauses. Example (26) shows
that it is acceptable to have an ironic matrix with a sincere, or true,
sentential subject:

(26) Listening to Jerry talk is really exhilarating.

And (27) has irony at both matrix and embedded levels:

(27) Your skillful juggling of the plates at the party last
night certainly was impressive. (You only broke
three.)

But a sentence with irony in the sentential subject and no irony in
the top S is unsuccessful as an act of communication:

(28) *That Harry's a real genius surprises me. (His
      brother is quite bright.)

Emotive factives appear to favor cases where irony in the lower
sentence entails an ironic reading in the higher. Thus (27) cannot
mean (29):

(29) Your unskillful juggling was impressive.

but can only mean (30):

(30) Your unskillful juggling was not impressive.

A third syntactic problem, as Cutler (1974) has noticed, is that
some conjoined sentences, namely, those with a commonality of
subject, cannot be half ironic and half sincere:

(31) *Harry's a real genius and Fred's a nice guy.

Presumably, the failure of (31) lies in the fact that the speaker intends the first conjunct to be taken as false in terms of 'what he
really means', and the second conjunct as straightforwardly true.
But since the conjunction of T and F is F, the principle suggested
by Morgan (1973), that it generally makes for more efficient communication if the parties deal in truths rather than falsehoods,
would not be served.
    Probably there are other syntactic frames which reject irony.
Those mentioned here look suspiciously islandy. Much is currently
being done to find an explanation for why the Ross constraints exist.
The current research on what is assertable and how it is manifested
(Schmerling 1973; Shir 1973) has, I think, direct bearing on what
can be ironic. The problem is certainly not just syntactic: it is not
possible to specify what can and cannot be ironic on purely syntactic
grounds, in the same way that it is not possible to specify what is
assertable, purely on syntactic grounds.

    3. Pragmatics. An informed definition of irony cannot be
concocted until we understand how and why irony works. One way
to characterize irony would be to say that it breaks or fails to
satisfy the conditions on the speech act it is in the shape of. So an
ironic statement breaks the sincerity condition that the speaker
believes what he says; an ironic question breaks the sincerity condition that a speaker wants to know the answer. Ironic thanks breaks
the sincere gratitude condition. It might also be possible to write
felicity conditions for irony itself, [4] e.g.:

preparatory Speaker believes the hearer shares his assumptions or has the necessary information to understand the irony.

sincerity Speaker believes the opposite or negative of part or all of what he says.

But these conditions seem to be describing something very peculiar about the act of communication. If, as is probably the case, the function of irony is to communicate a judgment or opinion, why doesn't the speaker say it outright? And how is the hearer able to process the ironic utterance properly?

Grice's (1967) conversational maxims have proved useful tools for some kinds of linguistic study, for example, Gordon and Lakoff's (1971) analysis of conveyed meaning. The pertinent maxims are:

Quantity Be as informative as, but more informative than, necessary.

Quality Tell what you believe to be true.

Relation Be relevant.

Grice himself, and Zwicky and Sadock (1973) suggest that irony is a result of the suspension of the quality maxim. But the quantity maxim is also flouted, in at least two ways, and must therefore be acknowledged in some way in a definition of irony. First of all, in understatement, the speaker is purposely and obviously saying less than circumstances warrant. (Recall Grice's claim that when a maxim is flouted on purpose, the result is a conversational implicature; in Gordon and Lakoff's terms, some conveyed meaning is entailed.) For example:

(32) You were a little under the weather last night.

Translation: You threw up on the rug, fell in the punch bowl, and backed your car through the garden.

Secondly, one of the clues that a statement is to be taken ironically is redundancy, particularly at the beginning and end of the utterance (redundant items are underlined):

(33) Oh yeah, sure, you're going to be the next Vice President.

This violation of the maxim of quantity is in the other direction from that of (32): it affirms too much, thereby throwing into question the speaker's sincerity.

Grice's Cooperative Principle is an umbrella maxim: Make your contribution appropriate to the stage, purpose, and direction of the conversation. This maxim is found in various forms, and with reference to various facets of social behavior, in the works of Sacks and Schegloff (together and separately), Goffman, and Garfinkel. The main theme that comes up over and over in their work is the trust people have that social interaction will proceed along its normal, tacitly rule-governed course, and that someone will not purposefully throw a monkey wrench into the works. That is, if social interaction proceeds smoothly and securely, everybody wins, and it's in everyone's best interest to maintain a good working order.

Thus Sacks and Schegloff point out the regular expectable sequences of beginnings and ends of conversations and of turn-taking during a conversation. And Garfinkel (1972), after experiments 'that involved departures from an anticipated course of ordinary affairs, regardless of whether the departure was gross or slight', found that the subjects always recognized 'that the experimenter was engaged in double-talk, irony, glosses, euphemism, or lies'.

The 'how' of irony can perhaps best be explained by Grice's maxim of relevance. By 'how' I do not mean the technical aspects of how irony is fashioned, but how it is that speaker and hearer are able to deal with irony as part of the conversation and go on from there. Irony functions as what Schegloff (1968) calls 'sanctioned disruption'. It is the hearer's trust in the speaker's intention to keep his contributions relevant, in order to keep the conversation going until there is good reason to stop, that ensures the hearer's willingness to hunt around for what is 'really' meant. The role of opposition is important to note here because, as Hale (1973) has pointed out, opposites differ from each other in only one feature; if a speaker cannot possibly mean what he is saying, and the hearer knows that, either from shared knowledge or clues provided by the speaker, then the nearest place to look is the opposite, just one feature away. One breaks the rules of quantity, of quality, but never the rule of relevance. It is this rule that the hearer assumes, trusts, presupposes that the speaker will adhere to above all others.

But why, after all, should the means to communicate by opposition be provided or even tolerated by the language? In order to attempt to answer this, it is necessary first to see when irony is used.

In conversational use, irony serves two purposes that I can ascertain from observation, one inclusive, the other exclusive. That is, sometimes irony is used to reinforce solidarity, camaraderie between or among members. The exclusive function serves to elevate the speaker's own position at the expense of his hearer, via a put-down or a one-up ploy. It is in this latter category that sarcasm belongs, as a use of irony for the particular purpose of causing hurt.

But these ends, of reinforcing camaraderie, or of elevating one's own position at the expense of another, could be achieved in different ways, much more straightforward ways, it would seem. To serve an inclusive function, we might say:

(34) I like you.
(35) I'm glad we're here, enjoying things together.

or, exclusively:

(36) You talk too much.
(37) You sure are dumb, Harry.

Robin Lakoff (1973) has pointed out that in normal conversation, Grice's maxims are frequently broken. Lakoff summarizes all of Grice's rules into one: Be clear. She sets against the clarity maxim, the maxim of politeness. The two together make up the Rules of Pragmatic Competence. She claims that the two frequently conflict and that when they do, it is usually the case that politeness supersedes. The rule of politeness has three components:

Don't impose.
Give options.
Make the hearer feel good--be friendly.

Examples (34) and (35) obey the first rule: they are reserved for relationships with a fair degree of intimacy, but in ordinary conversation they constitute emotional imposition.

On the other hand, examples such as (36) and (37) break the third rule. Notice that in exclusive irony it is the appearance that counts: you can make somebody feel absolutely rotten, but on the surface have maintained the appearance of politeness. It is perhaps for this reason that negatively stated irony fails more often than positively stated irony. A negative statement intended ironically as a compliment is far more open to misinterpretation, even among friends, than is a positive one intended as criticism because it breaks two rules: a rule of clarity (say what you mean) as well as a rule of politeness. In contrast, 'blame-by-praise' breaks only a rule of clarity, and that rule is, as Lakoff suggests quite convincingly, usually secondary to the rule of politeness.

Searle's work on felicity conditions provides an insight into how a speaker produces irony; Grice's maxims suggest how a cooperative hearer is able to understand an ironic utterance as such; Lakoff's politeness principles at least partly explain why irony works at all. The definition of irony that evolves out of the questions and components considered here will still be a working definition. Undoubtedly, counterexamples will turn up, the analysis of which will provide at least a more sophisticated working definition, and hopefully an explanatorily adequate definition.

NOTES

1. Ann Borkin has pointed out to me that sentence (4) is not really 'literally' true either, since <u>love</u> does not accurately represent whatever appreciation we feel for people who do signal. <u>Love</u> qualifies as hyperbole here, but hyperbole is not (I claim) part of irony. In hyperbole, one may not mean quite all of what one says, i. e. in saying <u>greatest</u> one means <u>very good,</u> but the difference between the two judgments does not cross the center point of the scale of whatever is being measured. In understatement, on the other hand, that center point is crossed, so that in saying <u>a little</u> ironically, one conveys <u>a lot.</u> Hyperbole, then, treats judgments on the same half of the scale; understatement treats judgments on opposite sides of the center point of the scale, although they do not reach to the extent of polar opposites.

2. The embedded negative in (23a) is a bit unfair, because negatively stated irony does not behave the same way positively stated irony does. This is because the sets to choose from are different. For example, the opposite of

   (i) people who live in trees

is

   (ii) people who don't live in trees.

But if the first, and overt, statement is

   (iii) people who don't live in trees

there is no clear opposite to select, because people who don't live in trees might live on the ground, on river boats, in basket-balloons, etc. In other words, the set of choices is too large. All this notwithstanding, I have left the example as is because (24a) with an embedded positive also doesn't work, so the failure of (23a) is not just because of the negative.

3. Hooper and Thompson (1973) point out that some relative clauses on indefinites can be assertable.

4. One would not want, however, to have to posit a higher performative of irony, something like I hereby ironize.

REFERENCES

Cutler, Anne. 1974. On saying what you mean without meaning what you say. Papers from the Tenth Regional Meeting. Edited by Michael W. La Galy et al. Chicago, Chicago Linguistic Society. 117-27.

Garfinkel, Harold. 1972. Studies of the routine grounds of everyday activities. In: Studies in social interaction. Edited by David Sudnow. New York, The Free Press (Macmillan and Co). 1-30.

Goffman, Erving. 1971. Relations in public. New York, Harper and Row.

Gordon, David and George Lakoff. 1971. Conversational postulates. Papers from the Seventh Regional Meeting. Edited by Douglas Adams et al. Chicago, Chicago Linguistic Society. 63-84.

Grice, H. P. 1967. Logic and conversation. Unpublished lectures from William James Lectures, Harvard University.

Hale, Kenneth. 1973. Psychological reality and the role of abstract semantics among Australian aborigines. Talk given at the University of Michigan, April 4.

Hooper, Joan B. and Sandra A. Thompson. 1973. On the applicability of root transformations. Linguistic Inquiry 4.465-97.

Lakoff, Robin. 1973. The logic of politeness: Or, Minding your p's and q's. Papers from the Ninth Regional Meeting. Edited by Claudia Corum et al. Chicago, Chicago Linguistic Society. 292-305.

Morgan, Jerry L. 1973. How can you be in two places at once when you're not anywhere at all? Papers from the Ninth Regional Meeting. Chicago, Chicago Linguistic Society. 410-24.

Sacks, Harvey and Emanuel A. Schegloff. No date. On turn-taking. Mimeo.

Schegloff, Emanuel A. 1968. Sequencing in conversational openings. American Anthropologist 70.1075-95.

Schegloff, Emanuel A. and Harvey Sacks. 1973. Opening up closings. Semiotica 8.279-387.

Schmerling, Sue F. 1973. Aspects of English sentence stress. Unpublished Ph. D. dissertation, University of Illinois.

Searle, John R. 1970. Speech acts. Cambridge, The University Press.

Shir, Nomi E. 1973. On the nature of island constraints. Unpublished Ph. D. dissertation, Massachusetts Institute of Technology.

Zwicky, Arnold and Jerrold Sadock. 1973. Ambiguity tests and how to fail them. Ohio State University Working Papers in Linguistics. 16. 1-34.

ON THE ANALYSIS OF SENTENCE ADVERBS:
EVIDENCE FROM
EXPLICIT PERFORMATIVE SENTENCES

GILLIAN MICHELL

University of Western Ontario

Bruce Fraser, in his 1971 article 'An examination of the performative analysis', raises a number of problems for the analysis proposed in Ross (1970). My paper attempts to show that one of these problems, if more fully analysed, does not, in fact, constitute counterevidence to Ross's proposal, while it has implications for the analysis of another linguistic problem, sentence adverbs.

One of the claims of the performative analysis is that the verb conveying the illocutionary force of a sentence--that is, of course, the performative verb--must be the highest verb of that sentence in logical structure. Fraser suggests that explicit performative sentences with -ly adverbs--that is, sentence adverbs--are counterevidence to this claim, because sentence adverbs are analysed by many linguists as having an underlying source which results in their dominating the rest of the sentence in which they occur. For example, sentence (1a) would be related to the sentences in (1b), and to these would be ascribed an underlying structure like (1c), in which the performative concede is not the highest predicate.

(1a) Obviously I concede the election.
(1b)   i. That I concede the election is obvious.
       ii. It is obvious that I concede the election.

184

(1c)

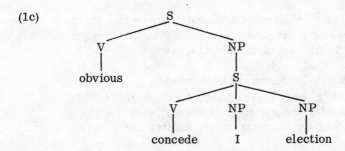

I am going to present evidence to show that this is not the right analysis of such sentences and that, although syntactically it might appear that sentence adverbs can be in construction with a range of different illocutionary acts, semantically they must in fact be associated with a related assertion; that is, sentence adverbs actually occur in construction with assertions only, and this fact needs to be incorporated into the description of sentence adverbs.

First of all, I would like to point out that it is not clear that the sentences of (1b) could be an intermediate stage in the derivation of (1a) from (1c). Evidence for this is that all speakers do not agree that (1b) and (1a) are equivalent illocutionarily. That is, while (1a) clearly counts as a concession for all speakers, (1b) is for many only an assertion describing a concession and not the actual performance of a concession. Therefore, the sentences in (1b), for which (1c) is a reasonable source, are poor choices as paraphrases to reflect the meaning and force of (1a).

I plan to show that the kind of sentence exemplified by (1a) differs significantly from sentences for which (1c) seems more appropriate; namely, ones in which a sentence adverb is in construction with a sentence which is not explicitly performative and which counts as an assertion.

By 'a sentence which is not explicitly performative' I mean any surface sentence which does not express its illocutionary force directly with a lexically realized performative verb. Sentence (2a), for example, is an assertion which does not have <u>I assert</u> dominating it in the surface form, as (2b) does, and sentence (2c) is an indirect request used to express the direct request of (2d).

(2a) He promised to pay me back.
(2b) ?I assert that he promised to pay me back.
(2c) Can you lend me another dime?
(2d) *I request that you lend me another dime.

In Schreiber's 1971 analysis of sentence adverbs, he gives evidence for distinguishing at least two classes of sentence adverbs: evaluative adverbs, as in (3), and modal adverbs, as in (4). [1, 2]

(3) astonishingly, fortunately, incredibly, interestingly, ironically, luckily, naturally, oddly, paradoxically, predictably, regrettably, strangely, surprisingly, unbelievably, understandably, unfortunately, unluckily

(4) allegedly, apparently, certainly, clearly, conceivably, evidently, obviously, possibly, presumably, probably, undoubtedly, unquestionably

He describes the characteristic differences in the semantic interpretation of sentence adverbs from one class or the other as in (5):

(5) . . . while an evaluative adverb presupposes the positive truth value of the (surface) predication with which it is in construction and offers an evaluation (value-judgment) of it, a modal adverb assigns a degree of likelihood (a probable truth-value) to the associated predication (Schreiber 1971:88).

One aspect of this characterization is of particular relevance to this discussion; that is, that the interpretation of these adverbs is crucially related to the truth value of the associated predications.

Now it should be noted that Schreiber's semantic description is based on the behaviour and interpretation of sentences where the sentence adverb is in construction with a sentence which counts as an assertion. So also is the semantic theory of Thomason and Stalnaker. They propose a set of semantic criteria which are sufficient conditions for any adverbial to be sentence modifying. Their Criterion 4, they claim, approaches being both a necessary and sufficient condition. [3]

(6) Criterion 4: Only if Q-ly occurs as a sentence modifier can one paraphrase the sentence by deleting the adverb and prefacing the resulting sentence by It is Q-ly true that (Thomason and Stalnaker 1973:205).

For example, (7b) would paraphrase (7a), and (8b) would paraphrase (8a).

(7a) Unfortunately Argle has disappeared.
(7b) It is unfortunately true that Argle has disappeared.

(8a) Apparently he didn't like the new house.
(8b) It is apparently true that he didn't like the new house.

Both these analyses, then, have in common the feature that the truth of the sentence associated with the adverb is an integral part of the semantic description. This follows, since the truth conditions of sentences are of central importance in the theory of reference. The relevance of truth conditions to explicit performative sentences is different, however. While performative sentences do have truth conditions (Lewis 1970:58-59), these are greatly overshadowed in importance by their felicity conditions.

When we look at a performative sentence in construction with a sentence adverb, it becomes apparent that this difference in the relevance of truth conditions is important. In sentence (1a), what the speaker believes is obvious is not the truth of <u>I concede the election</u>. Rather, it is obvious that conceding is perhaps the reasonable or appropriate thing to do. For contrast, consider sentence (9), an assertion which is very close in form to (1a).

(9) Obviously I am conceding the election.

This might be said in a context where, for example, the speaker is in the process of writing a statement indicating his concession. This is simply an assertion about the truth of the sentence associated with the adverb.

It may not be obvious yet that this is a kind of meaning distinction that must be accounted for in a grammar. But consider the kind of reason clauses that can be added to a sentence like (1a), as in (10).

(1a) Obviously I concede the election.
(10a) . . . since I'm 374 votes behind now.
(10b) . . . since I've realized I don't want to be in politics anymore.
(10c) ??. . . since I'm writing my concession speech.
(10d) *. . . since I'm saying I give up.

The reasons in (10a-b) are appropriate reasons for performing the illocutionary act involved, while the reasons in the questionable sentences (10c-d) are reasons for believing that <u>I concede the election</u> is a true description of a state of affairs. Note that the reasons in (10c-d) can be attached to (9) to form the perfectly acceptable sentences of (11), which are not explicitly performative and do not count as acts of conceding.

(9) Obviously I am conceding the election,
(11a) . . . since I'm writing my concession speech,
(11b) . . . since I'm saying that I give up.

This is in line with Davison's observation (1973) that if a reason clause modifies a performative, it is always connected with felicity conditions on successful performance, and generally implies that a felicity condition holds.

It is clear, then, that there is a meaning distinction between surface sentences with sentence adverbs which are simply assertions and those which are not. This suggests that the descriptions of Schreiber and of Thomason and Stalnaker must be modified, and that sentences like (1a) must be analysed differently.

I am going to argue that sentence adverbs that occur in surface sentences in construction with explicit performatives should be analysed as relating underlyingly to a particular condition on illocutionary acts. This analysis will suggest the kind of underlying source that such sentences might have.

Fraser described the meaning of a sentence like (1a) as follows:

(12) . . . in [such a sentence], the speaker concedes that he
has been defeated and then makes a clarifying comment
about the appropriateness to make this concession (1971:3).

That is, Fraser is claiming that the adverb relates to conditions of appropriateness. My own first approximation of the meaning of these sentences mentioned appropriateness too, as well as reasonableness. However, these approximations can be refined: we can say, rather, that the adverb always relates to why the speaker is performing that particular act.

The following example should make it clear that there can be a difference between the reason why a speaker is performing an illocutionary act and the reason why that act is appropriate: if in a backgammon game your opponent doubles you, it is only appropriate--or reasonable--to accept the double if there is a good chance you can still win the game. But in sentence (13), the speaker gives as his reason for accepting, an admission which shows that he knows he is behaving inappropriately.

(13) Obviously I accept the double, since I don't know when
to quit.

Now the reason that a speaker has for performing an act is the same reason that causes him deliberately or intentionally to perform that act. It seems, then, that by using the sentence adverb <u>obviously</u>

in (1a), the speaker is calling his hearer's attention to the obviousness of what causes him to have the intention of performing this act.

This relates to a condition on all illocutionary acts, discussed by
Heringer (1971), Fraser (1974), and others, that in uttering a sentence, the speaker intends or wants to perform a particular illocutionary act and the acts it entails and to have the hearer recognize
this intent. The speaker, that is, is not performing a speech act
without meaning to do so or without knowing that that is what he is
doing. This condition has been called the intent condition.[4] A
closer paraphrase of (1a), then, is (14):

(14) I concede the election, and it is obvious why I
$$\left\{\begin{array}{l}\text{intentionally perform}\\\text{intend to perform}\\\text{have the intention of performing}\\\text{choose to perform}\\\text{mean to perform}\\\text{want to perform}\end{array}\right\}\text{this act,}$$

(a. . . . since I'm 374 votes behind now.)
(b. . . . since I've realized I don't want to be in
politics anymore.)
(c. *. . . since I'm writing my concession speech.)
(d. *. . . since I'm saying that I give up.)

The reason can optionally be expressed, as is shown in the parenthe-
sized clauses of (14a-d). We notice that reasons (a) and (b) are still
acceptable, while (c) and (d) are not.

This paraphrase suggests a structure in which the sentence adverb
is no longer dominating the explicit performative sentence; it now
occurs in the related assertion which expresses the intent condition
on the illocutionary act. This relationship between the adverb and
this assertion also serves to account for the set of sentence adverbs
that can occur in surface performative sentences.

The intent condition must be true for the illocutionary act to go
through. Thus, it can only be dominated by a sentence adverb if the
resulting combination assumes the truth of this condition. But as we
have seen, Schreiber's two classes of adverbs do either assign truth
values to their predications or entail their truth in giving a value
judgment of them.

When we look at the class of modal adverbs, we see that only
subset A listed in (15) can occur with explicit performative sentences.

(15)	A	B	C
	certainly	possibly	allegedly
	clearly	probably	conceivably
	obviously		presumably
	??undoubtedly		evidently
	??unquestionably		apparently

This seems to be because the semantic interpretation of these adverbs is that their associated predications are true. [5] <u>Possibly</u> and <u>probably</u>, however, in subset B do not entail that their predications are true, and a speaker does not say that predications are possibly or only probably true if he knows they are in fact true, according to the rules of conversation (for English, at least). Subset B would also be out for the same reason as subset C. Impressionistically, subset C adverbs assign truth values to their predications on the basis of what seems to be the case (<u>evidently</u>, <u>apparently</u>), or of what it seems logical to believe (<u>presumably</u>, <u>conceivably</u>), or of what someone else says is so (<u>allegedly</u>). None of them assigns truth values on the basis of what the speaker himself knows to be true. But the proposition expressing the intent condition describes a mental state of the speaker--his intentions--which he knows more about than anyone else, so it would be anomalous for a speaker to assert that he is assigning truth values based on evidence other than that of his own feelings.

Turning to the list of evaluative adverbs, we would predict that they would all be acceptable in this sentence type, since they entail the truth of their predication. This seems to be the case for some of them. The sentences in (16), with the evaluative adverbs <u>naturally</u> and <u>understandably</u>, work as expected.

(16a) Naturally I promise to help you pack, since you'll never finish otherwise.

(16b) Understandably I accuse the Duke of Denver, since all the evidence points to him.

For some other evaluatives, however, rather farfetched contexts must be conjured up, and the sentences containing them meet with a considerable range in the judgments that hearers have as to whether they are explicit performatives or not. I have not yet found a satisfactory explanation for this.

My account of this sentence type, then, explains at least for modal adverbs the otherwise unaccounted for fact that only some of the class of sentence adverbs can occur with surface performative sentences.

One possible source for sentences like (1a) would be an underlying conjunction of sentences, roughly like (17).

(17)

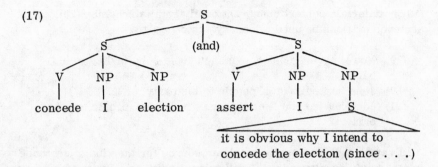

it is obvious why I intend to
concede the election (since . . .)

One conjunct would be the explicit performative act. The second
conjunct would be an assertion in which the speaker asserts the propo-
sition underlying it is $\left\{\begin{array}{l}\text{obvious}\\ \text{understandable}\\ \text{etc.}\end{array}\right\}$ why I intend to perform this
act. [6]

It has been proposed that there is evidence from other sources
that the grammar needs to generate conjoined illocutionary acts;
first, to account for such sentences as (18),

(18a) I swear that this is true and I admit that I previously
perjured myself.

(18b) Hand me the phone, or will Harry be home yet?

and, second, to account for the illocutionary force of nonrestrictive
relative clauses. There are problems with such a source, however,
for this sentence type.

For one thing, a syntactic conjunction would suggest that each
conjunct is of equal weight illocutionarily. But this is not the way we
understand sentences like (1a). Rather, we interpret them as being
primarily concessions or promises or whatever, to which are
attached a secondary assertion which comments on a particular
aspect of the primary act. This disparity in importance would not
be predicted by a conjunction.

Another problem for a syntactic conjunction source is that we
would have to account for really drastic changes in the course of
derivation in order for so elaborate an underlying structure to end
up as the desired surface form.

It might alternatively be proposed that the source for these sentences could be an amalgam of the sort discussed recently in Lakoff
(1974). Roughly, the gist of this proposal is that if in a certain context the logical structure of one sentence is conversationally entailed
by the logical structure of a second sentence, then in that context part
of the second sentence can be amalgamated with the first (if certain
other conditions are met also, of course). If, for example, sentence

(19) in a certain context conversationally entails sentence (20), then
sentence (21) can be used to convey sentence (20).

(19) You'll never guess how many people John invited to his
party.
(20) John invited a lot of people to his party.
(21) John invited you'll never guess how many people to his
party.

It seems that a syntactic amalgam source for the kind of sentence
in (1a) would need to meet the following conditions. We need a type of
sentence which contains a sentence adverb and which can convey indirectly a direct speech act. This direct speech act must also be able
to occur with that sentence adverb and not be too different syntactically
from the indirect act. A sentence like (22), for instance, seems to
meet these conditions.

(22) Obviously I must concede the election.

It has the sentence adverb; it can be used to convey a concession; and
it is relatively close syntactically to sentence (1a). Now if this is to
be the right type of sentence it has to be the case that if the speaker
asserts that he <u>must</u> obviously perform any illocutionary act, this
will convey that illocutionary act (for all those acts that can be in
construction with <u>obviously</u>, etc., as in (1a), since otherwise the
entailing sentence in the amalgam source will not exist). If this is
so, we can propose the mechanism for this type of syntactic amalga-
mation--that is, that everything is deleted under (rather fuzzy)
identity but the adverb, which is then amalgamated with the direct
illocutionary act that the assertion conveyed.
In favour of this suggestion, we can point out that for several
illocutionary acts it has been shown that they can be conveyed by a
sentence in which the speaker asserts that he must perform that act.
The nature of such sentences has been discussed by Fraser (1973).
The illocutionary acts of warning, requesting, and forbidding, for
example, can be conveyed with sentences (23a-c) respectively, which
are from Fraser's paper.

(23a) I must warn you that I will be there.
(23b) I must ask you to speak louder.
(23c) I must forbid you to leave.

However, there are other illocutionary acts which it is not clear that
this sentence type can convey, and this would constitute counterevidence to the amalgam proposal, given that sentence adverbs can

occur with explicit expressions of these acts. Can sentence (24) count as a promise, for example?

(24) I must promise to help you (since I'm your friend).

Furthermore, for the parallel to be proven systematic, it must be that the sentence adverb can occur with both the <u>must</u> sentence and the direct act it conveys. But sentence (24) with <u>obviously</u> still does not convey a promise, while the direct promise with <u>obviously</u> does, as in (25).

(25) Obviously I promise to help you (since I'm your friend).

Conversely, there are illocutionary acts, like informing, which can be expressed indirectly with <u>must</u> and a sentence adverb, as in (26a), but which are not acceptable when directly expressed with a sentence adverb, like (26b).

(26a) Obviously I must inform you that you are fired.
≠(26b) *Obviously I inform you that you are fired.

There is the additional problem that the sentence adverb functions differently in indirect acts with <u>must</u> than it does in direct acts; that is, its meaning is different. For it to have the same function, as one would expect it should, it would presumably have to relate to the intent condition. But it seems that it is impossible to express an illocutionary act indirectly by asserting that, for example, it is obvious why the speaker intends or wants to perform the illocutionary act, as in (27a), which cannot convey (27b).

(27a) It is obvious why I $\left\{\begin{array}{l}\text{want to}\\\text{intend to}\\\text{have the intention to}\\\text{intentionally}\end{array}\right\}$ promise to help you.

≠(27b) Obviously I promise to help you.

(Perhaps this is because there is too great a disparity between what the adverb <u>obviously</u> modifies and the usual way in which indirect illocutionary acts are performed.) Thus the source we would need on semantic grounds for sentence adverbs will not fit into the amalgam paradigm.

It seems to me then that it is probably not possible to find an amalgam source for sentences of the kind we have been looking at, as long as syntactic amalgams are constrained as I understand them to have been to date. Such a source might be maintained, however, if amalgams were generalized in some way, so that the logical structure of the amalgamated material would not have to convey the same meaning (broadly understood) as the logical structure of the sentence into which part of it is to be substituted. Such a solution will, of course, have to deal with one problem it has in common with a syntactic conjunction source: that of discovering the constraints on what can be amalgamated or conjoined. Since this would appear to be largely a pragmatic question in this case, it might also be considered further evidence against a syntactic conjunction source.

In the end, a pragmatic analysis would probably be preferred over a syntactic one, for this sentence type. [7]

In summary, I have attempted to show in this paper: (1) that surface performative sentences with sentence adverbs do not constitute counterevidence to the performative analysis; (2) that an adequate analysis of sentence adverbs must account for the fact that they cannot underlyingly dominate performative sentences because of their meaning, behaviour, and cooccurrence restrictions; (3) that sentence adverbs which occur superficially with performative sentences actually come from an underlying source where they are in construction with the intent condition on illocutionary acts; and (4) that the facts about sentence adverbs are consonant neither with a syntactic conjunction source nor with an amalgam source (as this proposal is presently constrained), but that the final answer will probably lie in the area of pragmatics.

NOTES

1. One class of adverbs which might appear to need consideration is what Schreiber (1972) calls 'style disjuncts', like frankly and reluctantly. He demonstrates that these are surface sentence modifiers, but that they derive from manner adverbs in underlying performative sentences. Manner adverbs would seem to be VP modifiers rather than sentence modifiers; however, it has been argued that in the underlying structure for manner adverbs, the main (surface) sentence is dominated by the predicate source for the manner adverb, as in (i) and (ii), both due to Kuroda (cited in Schreiber 1972), which would be the sources for the surface sentences (iii) and (iv) respectively.

(i)   The manner [John dresses in some manner] is elegant.
(ii) John was happy [John dressed].
(iii) John dresses elegantly.
(iv) John dressed happily.

If these structures are correct, such adverbs would still be problems for the performative analysis. However, this analysis is shown to be wrong by Thomason and Stalnaker's (1973) analysis of adverbs, which sees them as complex predicates on the basis of the nature of the logical relationships among sentences containing such adverbs.

Thus I exclude from discussion such sentences as (v), (vi), and (vii), since their adverbs are style disjuncts.

   (v) Reluctantly I pronounce you man and wife.
  (vi) I urgently beseech you to help me.
 (vii) Frankly, I admit I'm guilty.

2. Two other kinds of sentence modifying adverbs which are not treated here are (a) frequency adverbs, which cannot occur with performative sentences (see (i), which is unacceptable on the performative reading), and (b) discourse, or sentence connecting, adverbs, like (ii), which are to be analysed as units of discourse, rather than as parts of a single sentence, the unit we are considering.

  (i) I frequently promise to help you.
 (ii) Consequently, I find for the defendant.

Another kind of sentence adverb Schreiber mentions is epithet adverbs, of which <u>wisely</u> in (iii) is an example, and (iv) and (v) derivationally related forms.

 (iii) John wisely left.
 (iv) John was wise to leave.
  (v) It was wise of John to leave.

Since Schreiber's article on these forms (cited in Schreiber 1972) is unavailable to me, however, and since performative sentences containing them seem only marginally acceptable, if at all, as in (vi) and (vii), I do not consider them either.

 (vi) *Wisely I resign from this position.
 (vii) ??Stupidly, I accept your terms.

3. It should be noted that this paraphrase does not make the finer distinction between kinds of sentence adverbs that Schreiber makes, but since its purpose is only to distinguish sentence from predicate adverbs, this is not relevant.

4. This condition might be thought of as a refinement or subpart of what Searle calls the 'essential condition' on each type of

illocutionary act: that the utterance count as a performance of the relevant act. Part of this condition must be that the speaker of the utterance has the intention of performing that act, that is, of having his utterance count as that act.

5. I am not sure why unquestionably and undoubtedly are relatively bad, but it may be that if one asserts something is not questionable or not to be doubted, it seems to raise the possibility conversationally that there might indeed be some question, in the same way as asserting Your wife is faithful brings that fact into question, as has been noted elsewhere.

6. The fact that the proposition expressing the intention does not usually appear on the surface as a second conjunct is presumably due to the fact that it is completely redundant if it appears by itself without further modification, given that it is a necessary condition on performing the act.

7. I have recently come across a paper by Patrick Wilson where a concept is introduced which seems relevant to constraining the pragmatic elements involved here. This is the concept of 'situational relevance', or, more specifically, of 'significant situationally relevant information'. The nature of these notions is described briefly as follows: 'The concept of situational relevance . . . is based on [a] definition of logical relevance, on the notion of evidential relevance drawn from inductive logic, on the notions of a personal stock of knowledge and a set of personal concerns, the latter explained in terms of preferences over ranges of alternatives. Situationally relevant items of information are those that answer, or logically help to answer, questions of concern. Significant situationally relevant information is explained in terms of changes of view in relation to questions of concern' (Wilson 1973:457).

While I have not yet worked through the details of this idea, it seems to me that the reason clauses that can be expressed in [Sentence Adverb + Performative] sentences must conform to the requirements for significant situationally relevant information as Wilson defines them. Further, it seems that by the use of the adverb the speaker is indicating that he recognizes the situational significance of certain information to his situation and sees it as compelling his act.

REFERENCES

Davison, Alice. 1973. Words for things people do with words. Papers from the Ninth Regional Meeting. Chicago, Chicago Linguistic Society. 114-22.
Fraser, Bruce. 1971. An examination of the performative analysis. Bloomington, Indiana University Linguistics Club.

Fraser, Bruce. 1973. Responsibility and illocutionary acts. Paper delivered at the 1973 Annual Meeting of the Linguistic Society of America, San Diego, Dec. 28.

Fraser, Bruce. 1974. Review of: Searle's Speech acts. Foundations of Language 11.433-46.

Heringer, James. 1971. Some grammatical correlates of felicity conditions and presuppositions. Ohio State University Working Papers in Linguistics, No. 11, 1-110.

Lakoff, George. 1974. Syntactic amalgams. Papers from the Tenth Regional Meeting. Chicago, Chicago Linguistic Society. 321-44.

Lewis, David. 1970. General semantics. Synthese 22.18-67.

Ross, John Robert. 1970. On declarative sentences. In: Readings in English transformational grammar. Edited by Roderick A. Jacobs and Peter S. Rosenbaum. Waltham, Mass., Ginn. 222-72.

Schreiber, Peter A. 1971. Some constraints on the formation of English sentence adverbs. Linguistic Inquiry 2.83-101.

Schreiber, Peter A. 1972. Style disjuncts and the performative analysis. Linguistic Inquiry 3.321-47.

Searle, John R. 1969. Speech acts. Cambridge, At the University Press.

Thomason, Richmond H. and Robert C. Stalnaker. 1973. A semantic theory of adverbs. Linguistic Inquiry 4.195-220.

Wilson, Patrick. 1973. Situational relevance. Information Storage and Retrieval 9.457-71.

THE PLAYBACK: AN INSTANCE OF VARIATION IN DISCOURSE

MARILYN MERRITT

University of Pennsylvania

This paper is based on naturalistic observations of speech in one type of social context or situation. That social context I identify by the term 'service encounter'. [1]

By a service encounter I mean an instance of face-to-face inter-action between a server who is 'officially posted' in some service area and a customer who is present in that service area, that inter-action being oriented to the satisfaction of the customer's presumed desire for some service and the server's obligation to provide that service. Thus, a typical service encounter is one in which a customer buys something at a store, that transaction being realized as an inter-action between server and customer. If a customer comes into a store or service area to buy something that the store does not sell, or chooses not to buy something that the store does sell, that interaction between server and customer is also a service encounter. Thus a service encounter is roughly equivalent to an encounter that is in some sense 'officially' oriented toward the transaction of service, whether or not such a transaction is actually consummated. [2]

The service encounter can be appropriately categorized as a type of 'speech event'. [3] And the speech that occurs between server and customer can be appropriately categorized as 'discourse'. Further, this discourse, in conjunction with certain nonlinguistic moves (handing over selections, nodding, pointing, handing money, etc.) is ipso facto an instance of coherent discourse--coherence being in some pragmatic sense 'guaranteed' by its observed occurrence in the real world. In the case of service encounters coherence is further guaranteed by the outcome of the transaction itself.

My interest is in this property of coherence--the way utterances link one to another, and the work that is contributed by each to the overall structure of the discourse. To account for the coherence of a segment of discourse is to my way of thinking to come to terms with the pragmatic value of its constituents.

In the case of the service encounter the most prominent structural feature of the discourse is its dialogistic character. That is to say, the discourse proceeds as a sequence of turns:[4] the server has a turn, then the customer, then the server, etc. As each speaker takes his turn he speaks to the other, and thereby performs not only a linguistic act but a social act as well. The nature of the service encounter is such that many of these acts are baldly instrumental: requests, orders, and offers abound. However, not all utterances in the dialog can be easily identified as particular speech acts. To refer to any utterance in the dialog, whether or not labelled as a particular speech act, I use the more neutral term 'move'.[5] Every turn then consists of at least one move.

I have been examining service encounter discourse in a small 'notions' store. The store sells cigarettes, magazines, newspapers, school supplies, cosmetic items, small houseware and hardware items, and other miscellaneous items. Most of the merchandise is displayed openly and the store is basically self-service. In the main, customers bring their selections to the cash register counter, or serving post, to make their purchases, and this is when most of the interaction between server and customer takes place. However, customers often make inquiries about the availability of some item before making a selection. When a customer makes such an inquiry the server does not always answer directly. Rather he may also ask for clarification of the request. For example:[6]

(1) (A-1, 6-14)
    C: Do you have any-uh-eye wash ((or em eye--)) eye
       k-cleanser?
    S: Yeah, we have eye wash. Yeah, d'you mean--for
       reg'lar eye--not contact lenses?
    C: No.//Hunh-unh just for your eyes.
    S: Just just reg'lar eye wash.

In many cases this query action by the server is formally definable in terms of the preceding utterance. It is the playing back of the name of the requested item, with question intonation, and sometimes with a qualifying or interrogative particle. Such a move can be called a 'query playback' or a 'queryback'. For example:

    (2) (A-36, 12-14)
        C: (( )) red ribbon?
        S: Red ribbon?
        C: Yeah.
        S: Yes sir. Ya wanna come with me.

where Red ribbon? is the queryback; and

    (3) (A-52, 12-14)
        C: You don't have any yarn ribbon do you?
        S: Yarn ribbon?
        C: Unh hunh.
        S: No, no yarn ribbon. Just--uh--I forget--for wrapping
            packages?
        C: Unh hunh.
        S: No, we have--what you see over here.

where Yarn ribbon? is the queryback; and

    (4) (A-33, 12-14)
        C: Do you have any stamp pads?--no?
        S: Ink stamp pads?
        C: Right.
        S: Yeah, Yeah. Right here.

where ink stamp pads? is the queryback with a qualifying particle
ink.
    In the notions store there are a few items such as cigarettes and
tobacco which are kept behind the server's counter and must be asked
for just prior to purchase. After the customer makes such an order
or request, a similar kind of queryback move is often employed by
the server. For example:

    (5) (A-15, 12-14)
        C: Two packs of True Greens.
        S: All right. True Greens. Didya say two packs?
        C: Yes.
        S: That's a dollar. Thank you.

where True Greens. Didya say two packs? is a queryback with
interrogative particle Didya say; and

(6) (A-19, 12-14)
    C: Pack o' Vantage.
    S: O. K. Vantage. Blue?
    C: Right.
    S: Fifty cents.__Right. Thank you.

where Vantage. Blue? is a queryback with qualifying particle Blue;
and

(7) (A-7, 12-14) (Here the customer began this request just
    as the server was finishing some sorting out of change.)
    C: C'n I have a pack of Doral ((in a minute)) please?
    S: Doral menthol?
    C: Regular.
    S: Fifty cents.__Five, six, seven, eight, nine and fifty
    change. Thank you.

where Doral menthol? is the queryback with qualifying particle
menthol.
    These verbal moves made by the server might be categorized as
requests for confirmation or requests for further information. The
server's query indicates his understanding or best guess about the
customer's request, and asks for confirmation or correction. It is
oriented to the possible need for error correction, as shown in
example (7), and requires a response by the customer. In (7)
Customer responds Regular; in (6) Right; in (5) Yes; in (4) Right;
in (3) Unh hunh; and in (2) Yeah.
    In examining my data I have found that the server sometimes
responds to a customer's order in a way that easily permits correction by the customer but which does not require a response as
does the query playback. What the server does is to play back the
order or name of the requested item, but without question intonation
or interrogative particle. Such a move can be called an assertive
playback or simply a playback. For example:

(8) (A-45, 12-14)
    C: A carton of Winston // please.
    S: A carton of Winston. O. K.__This's four fifty. --Out of
    ten.
    RING (of cash register)
    S: Four fifty, five, and five is ten.

where the server's A carton of Winston is a playback; and

(9) (A-43, 12-14)
    C: C'n I have a package of True Blue?
    S: True Blue. O. K.__That's uh fifty and ten--sixty cents.__
        Here's your forty change. Thank you.
    RING

where True Blue is an assertive playback; and

(10) (A-47, 12-14)
    C: Could I have a pack of Winstons? (( ))
    S: A pack of Winstons. All right.__And a magazine,
        right?
    C: Unh hunh. Yes.
    S: So it's a dollar fifty cents altogether.
    C: Thank you.
    RING

With the phrase A pack of Winstons in (10), True Blue in (9), and A carton of Winston in (8), the server lets the customer know what his understanding is of the order. Such a display provides an opportunity for the customer to make an error correction if need be, but does not require affirmation. The beauty of the affirmative playback is that it is a move that can be responded to (i. e. error correction can be made) but which need not be responded to.

Thus, both the affirmative playback and the query playback are involved in doing one kind of work: the playback provides an opportunity for the customer to correct any error in the server's interpretation of the customer's request or order (though in the case of the affirmative playback no response is expected if there is no error displayed).

Once I had noticed the way the playback seems to work, I noticed other patterns of response that seem to perform in a similar fashion.

There are at least two points in service encounters that are vulnerable to error correction. One is when the server is receiving a request or order from the customer made either by asking information about the availability or whereabouts of some self-service item, or by placing an order at the serving post. This is what we have been looking at. Another is when the server is costing out the customer's purchases at the serving post, some or all of which the customer may have selected himself. Though in these interactions it is often the server who speaks first, the customer, in bringing his selection(s) to the serving post, has effected a request for service. Thus, when the server speaks he makes a move that fills a structural 'slot' which might be again called 'response to customer's request'.

Here, too, I have found this slot in the discourse sometimes filled by queries and sometimes by assertive moves which are complements to the queries. As the customer's request for self-service items is usually nonverbal these moves are not playbacks, but the parallel in the function of the alternation of the query mode and the assertive mode seems clear. For example:

(11) (B:079, 6-15) (C has some large pieces of drawing board)
    S: (clears throat)Whatta ya got--three?
    C: One, two, three, four.
    S: Four. O.K. A dollar and six tax, a dollar six.

where the server queries <u>Whatta ya got--three?</u>; and

(12) (A-37, 12-14)
    S: Wa ya got? Two papers?
    C: Uhm hum.
    S: New York papers. Thirty cents.

where the server queries <u>Wa ya got? Two papers?</u>; and

(13) (A-34, 12-14)
    S: New York Times?
    C: Yes.
    S: Fifteen.

where the server queries <u>New York Times?</u>; and (14) where the server again queries <u>New York Times?</u> but gets a negative response.

(14) (A-22, 12-14)
    S: New York Times?
    C: No, the uh--I already--I had the New York Times//
        I'm buying just the--heh--just the--
    S: All right. Just a Playboy.
    C: Yeah. heh
    S: O.K. Thank you.

These contrast with (15) and (16) which illustrate the assertive mode:

(15) (A-49, 12-14)
    S: O.K. New York Times. Fifteen.
    RING
    S: That's seventy-five, eighty-five change, right?
    CLOSE DRAWER
    S: Thanks.

(16) (A-10, 12-14)
        S: O. K. Uh--Playboy magazine. Dollar and a half.__
        Right. Thank you.

In examples (11), (12), (13), and (14), the server makes some
form of query to which the customer responds. In (15) and (16) the
server lets the customer know what he assumes is being selected but
goes directly on to cost out the purchases. In (15) the phrase New
York Times and in (16) the phrase Playboy magazine seem to function in the discourse just as the assertive playbacks did in examples
(8), (9), and (10). That is, the server overtly displays his understanding, upon which rests the outcome of some action which he is
about to take. The customer is thereby given the opportunity to
correct any misunderstanding, but is not expected to make a response
if there is no correction. The assertive mode might be thought of as
a kind of 'unofficial' query. It is unofficial in that no response is
required; yet it can count as a query source if a correction is made;
and no response counts as agreement with the server's understanding.

Now, this assertive mode occurs in the server's response slot at
two points: (1) after the customer requests something from behind
the serving post (e. g. cigarettes); and (2) after the server presents
his selections at the serving post for purchase. [7] At the point at which
the customer requests an item from behind the counter there is
another kind of move which sometimes accompanies the query of
assertive mode moves, or fills the slot by itself. These are the
confirmative particles O. K. and All right.

In example (17) O. K. fills the slot by itself:

(17) (A-11, 12-14)
        C: Uh. C'n I have two packs of Vantage Blue?
        S: O. K. (coughing)
        C: And a New York Times.
        S: Dollar fifteen.
        RING

In examples (8) and (9) O. K. accompanies the assertive mode; in
(10) All right accompanies the assertive mode. In example (5) All
right accompanies the query mode, and in (6) O. K. accompanies the
query mode. [8] In (7), the only example of this set with a qualifying
particle (Doral menthol? with menthol as qualifying particle), there
is no accompanying confirmative particle.

My analysis of this is that these moves are basically confirmative
--confirmative of the server's commitment to take the next necessary
action to negotiate the transaction. In the case of the cigarette orders
the next necessary action is for the server actually to get the

cigarettes. However, getting the cigarettes takes a few seconds and creates a lag in the basic rhythm of the turn-taking of the encounter, that rhythm having been set by verbal turn-taking. Thus, the server's saying something affirmative as he begins to get the cigarettes is a way of his beginning to take his turn even though the most relevant part of his turn is the nonverbal action of getting the cigarettes. His verbalizing satisfies what I call a 'place-holding' function in the discourse. [9] The implication of place-holding here is the server's commitment to action. He indicates that he is beginning or about to begin the next necessary action of the transaction. In other words, he thereby confirms the customer's order.

In conclusion, I have shown that though there are differences in the pattern of responses to query playbacks and assertive playbacks, both do essentially the same kind of work: (1) they both orient to a possible need for error correction; and (2) they both confirm the server's intention to satisfy the customer's request.

The methodology I have used here is to collect materials from a single type of speech event and to identify within the event one or more points in its structure. For each point, having identified such a point secondarily identifies whatever follows as filling a particular 'slot'. This methodology has allowed me to observe patterns of variation in the way language is actually used.

In this case the speech event I have been looking at is the service encounter. The points I have been looking at are all describable as 'customer request or order'. The secondarily generated slots are each describable as 'server response to customer's request or order'. This commonality would predict similar patterns of interaction for all three points in the discourse. I have illustrated that for two points at which customer requests or orders occur (the cigarette order and the self-selected purchase), the corresponding server response slots are filled sometimes in a query mode and sometimes in an assertive mode. [10] For both slots this variation has been related to the degree of need for error correction, with parallel functions for the two sets of filler responses.

NOTES

1. The notion of service encounter is one that I have worked with for several years. It is treated in more detail in my forthcoming University of Pennsylvania dissertation. My use of this term is heuristic rather than analytic, the point being to identify some range of recurring activity for investigation.

2. The notion of an encounter is borrowed wholesale from Goffman (1963:88-89): 'When two persons are mutually present and hence engaged together in some degree of unfocused interaction . . . They

can proceed from there to engage one another in focused interaction, the unit of which I shall refer to as a face engagement or an encounter. Face engagements comprise all those instances of two or more participants in a situation joining each other openly in maintaining a single focus of cognitive and visual attention--what is sensed as a single mutual activity, entailing preferential communication rights. As a simple example--and one of the most common--when persons are present together in the same situation they may engage each other in a talk. . . .'

It has been suggested to me that the notion of encounter is not routinely appropriate to describe the interaction between server and customer. For instance, many such interactions are so deritualized as to involve no verbalization or eye contact at all. Such interaction might then be labelled service 'contact' rather than service 'encounter'. My view is that there is not a dichotomy but rather a continuum operating here, and further, that this continuum is not necessarily related in any simple way to other contextual features. In particular, it seems that even the most perfunctory situation can host a fully ritualized encounter. Thus I choose to label the entire continuum 'service encounter'.

3. The notion that some kind of speech-involving activity (speech event) might be considered a viable analytical unit was proposed by Hymes (1962). Hymes' interest in the notion of speech event seems to be oriented primarily to the fact that different societies engender the need for different speech events, reflecting differences between speech communities in the function of language. My use of the term has a different motivation. For me, the notion of speech event provides a unit for observation and analysis within a single speech community (particularly as the notion of speech community when applied to geographically mobile sectors of complex societies tends to become amorphous). It provides a locus for controlled observation of the interaction of situational and linguistic features.

4. This is, of course, a vastly oversimplified model of turn-taking. See Sacks, Schegloff, and Jefferson (1974) for a fuller treatment.

5. I borrow the term 'move' from Goffman (1969:89-90): 'I shall use the word turn to refer to Harry's moment and opportunity for choice, and move to refer to the action he takes consequent on deciding to play his turn now. . . .'

6. The examples used in this paper are transcriptions of tape-recorded service encounters that took place in a single service area during regular business hours. These service encounters were observed (as nonparticipating customer) and taped by the writer; transcription was also done by the writer. No attempt was made to insert into these transcriptions nonverbal cues that were not

recoverable from the tape recording. Conventions for transcription
are essentially borrowed from Gail Jefferson:

(( )) indicates inaudible or uncertain hearing
// indicates that the next speaker is here beginning his turn
    and thus overlaps what follows // of the current speaker
underline indicates heavy stress on that segment
ALL CAPITALS indicates a nonspeech noise.

Following each example number is a parenthetical expression that
codes the whereabouts of the encounter in my data. For example
(A-14, 12-14) indicates tape side A, encounter number 14; December
14 recording.

7. This paper has introduced three 'points'. In addition to the two
just mentioned there is (3), after the customer requests information
about the availability or whereabouts of some self-selectable item.
In the data I have examined thus far the assertive mode playback does
not occur in this server's slot. Thus no analysis is presented here.
At first I thought that this pattern might reflect a differentiation
between those points at which the server's satisfaction of the customer's request was primarily nonverbal (e.g. (1) getting the requested item, and (2) taking and costing out customer-selected items),
and those at which the server's satisfaction is primarily verbal (e.g.
(3) reporting on the availability or whereabouts of some item). But
after reflecting on this it seems more likely that the relevant factor
here is the effect of the assertive mode playback to 'buy time' in the
turn for some to-be-completed server action--whether that action is
nonverbal or not. Thus, I would expect to find some assertive mode
playbacks at point (3) as well as at points (1) and (2). Only point (1)
is analyzed here in detail.

8. For these examples there is another pattern: With the interrogative mode playbacks the confirmative particle precedes the playback; with the assertive mode playbacks the confirmative particle
follows the playback. At this time I am not sure if this pattern holds
for all of my data, nor how such ordering should be interpreted.

9. This place-holding function corresponds to the 'buying time'
effect mentioned in note 8. Though the O.K. and All right of point
(3) do not place-hold a nonverbal next action, I would argue that such
particles do place-hold for the server's activity of costing out the
selected items. This activity is expressed verbally (Fifteen cents,
A dollar and six tax. Dollar six altogether.) but includes the server's
examining items for the price marked or processing his remembrance
of the price for more routine items.

Though the argument for place-holding is most straightforward
in the case of buying time for nonverbal to-be-completed actions,

such as occur at point (1), my feeling is that place-holding is a quite general function.

10. Recall that although three points have been presented in this paper, not all three points exhibited both the query mode and the assertive mode playback. In particular, point (3) 'after the customer requests information about the availability or whereabouts of some customer selectable item' has exhibited (in my data) only the query mode playback. See note 8.

REFERENCES

Goffman, Erving. 1963. Behavior in public places: Notes on the social organization of gatherings. New York, The Free Press of Glencoe.
Goffman, Erving. 1969. Strategic interaction. Philadelphia, University of Pennsylvania Press.
Hymes, Dell. 1962. The ethnography of speaking. In: Anthropology and human behavior. Edited by T. Gladwin and William C. Sturtevant. Washington, D.C., Anthropological Society of Washington. 13-53.
Sacks, Harvey, Emanuel A. Schegloff, and Gail Jefferson. 1974. A simplest systematics for the organization of turn-taking for conversation. Lg. 50.696-735.

BEYOND ETHNOGRAPHY:
A CONVERSATIONAL ANALYSIS OF AUCTIONS

LINDSEY CHURCHILL AND SUSAN GRAY

City University of New York

Introduction. Our topic here is selling by the auction method.
More specifically, we are interested in how the auctioneer attempts
to keep prices up when buyers may legally make any bids whatsoever.
This kind of issue: Who will control? or Who will win the power
struggle?, is a traditional one in sociology, our 'home' field. Yet
most of the work on power has been done on the macrolevel, where
the power of classes, vested interests, and the like, has been
studied. Not many empirical studies of power have been made in
microlevel situations. The auction setting is one such microlevel
situation, and we feel that our analysis will contribute to the understanding of this classical sociological issue.

Our sharpest difference with our sociological colleagues, however,
is not macro- vs. microlevel studies, but the choice of a methodological criterion. We feel that our work--and all sociological work--
must be as definite as possible. To that end we have adopted a criterion of reproduction to guide our methodology. The hard test of
our analysis is whether or not it can reproduce social activities
under study. That, we realize, is a familiar criterion to the modern
linguist. The persons from whom we take inspiration in sociology
are Harvey Sacks and his co-workers, Emanuel Schegloff, Gail
Jefferson, and Roy Turner, among others. We do not assume, however, that we will be successful in our attempt to reproduce social
activities, as Sacks assumes. Rather, we feel that we will know
definitely, or as definitely as possible at the present time, whether
or not the task is accomplishable.

Harold Garfinkel, for example, proposes that the production of social activities by members can never be reduced to rule-following, no matter how elaborate the structure of rules proposed. For him there is an essential vagueness in the production of social activities that makes our proposed task impossible in principle. Nevertheless, we persevere in using a criterion of reproduction because we feel that it is important to know about essential vagueness in a definite way. Our analysis will provide a more definite and detailed answer to how essential vagueness enters into the auction setting, if Garfinkel is correct.

It is this criterion of reproduction that takes us beyond ethnography. Our analysis is descriptive, just as is the ethnographer's analysis. But the reproduction criterion forces a structure into it that ethnography does not have, in most cases. To clarify these points, we turn to a discussion of a classical ethnography of auctions, followed by our own analysis.

A classical ethnography of auctions: On the Block. Robert Clark has recently completed an ethnography of auctions (Clark 1973). Clark did his work in Montana and his analysis has a Western flavor. Specifically, he concentrates on two of the many possible kinds of auctions, livestock auctions and household goods auctions. He proposes that there are three essential features of auctions: trust, trouble, and deals. By 'trust' he refers to the question of how much buyers and sellers can trust an auctioneer to conduct an honest auction, e.g. to represent goods honestly and not use shills to drive prices up. By 'trouble' he refers to the variety of things that buyers can do to 'screw up' the auction, including not knowing how to bid, bidding drunkenly, wanting their money back because the item was 'misrepresented', etc. Clark shows us once again that any social procedure like this one is necessarily simplistic; persons responsible for putting the procedure into practice will have to handle a variety of problems that were not anticipated and therefore not incorporated in the procedure. By 'deals' Clark refers to the fact that buyers want to get 'good deals' on items, and he elaborates some features that distinguish 'good deals' from 'bad deals'.

In general, we find Clark's report informative and helpful. However, Clark cannot answer any of our 'how' questions, the kind that are generated by a criterion of reproduction. When we ask of his report, 'How does the auctioneer create trust in buyers and sellers?' or 'How does the auctioneer handle "trouble"?', we get no answer. The classical method of ethnography is simply not prepared to answer questions like these, which require some kind of more structured reply. Hence, our criterion forces us beyond Clark, to search for analyses unlike anything he presents.

The present study. One of us (Gray) taped twenty auctions conducted in the New York City metropolitan area during the summer of 1974. Gray made an effort to tape as many different kinds of auctions as she could find. Included were jewelry auctions, an art auction, a household goods auction from the 'backyard', a textiles auction, a book auction, a bankruptcy sale auction of the merchandise of a drugstore, and an auction sale of office furniture no longer needed by a business firm. In each case the auctioneer had a financial interest in taking in as much money as possible. As far as we could tell, all of them were working on a percentage basis. In addition, none of the auctions were conducted using an announced policy of 'reserves', i.e. minimum prices for items. (However, an important point in our paper is that auctioneers use 'moral reserves' almost all the time.)

Some of the auctions were taped completely; others were taped only in part. Gray collected, in all, about twenty-five hours of auction talk. The transcripts of the tapes form the corpus of our data for analysis. The transcriptions are merely reasonable ones; they are not at the level of accuracy that, for example, Sacks' transcripts are. However, they are accurate enough for our present purposes.

We spent a long period of time familiarizing ourselves with these auctions, as an ethnographer would. We saw how Clark's three features of trust, trouble, and deals expressed themselves in our materials. This effort resulted in another paper (Gray and Churchill 1974), giving an ethnographic account of how the auctioneer tries to control prices. The following points of that study are relevant here.

First, any bid that a buyer makes is legal, even the smallest. One might suppose that the auctioneer automatically accepts the first bid and counts on further competitive bidding to drive the selling price of the item up. However, consideration of an example shows that more is involved than competitive bidding. Suppose the auctioneer offers a refrigerator for sale, and someone bids a nickel for it. We believe that this bid will be noticed by everyone, auctioneer and buyers, as 'too low'. It is simply not a proper bid for a refrigerator. This example and other evidence in our transcripts lead us to propose the concept, 'range of worth', that prevents the automatic acceptance of any bid from occurring.

We believe that the auctioneer and any interested buyer establish a 'range of worth' for themselves, for each item that is offered for sale (not necessarily consciously, of course). The ranges of worth of different persons need not coincide, though there will be some points of agreement among them. Certain bids will be seen by everyone as too low or too high, clearly below or above everyone's range of worth for that item. Thus, a nickel for a refrigerator is below everyone's range of worth for a refrigerator.

We use the concept of 'range' rather than 'point' or 'estimated value' to reflect the vagueness about the 'real' value of an item in the auction setting. The concept is intended to be 'situated'; the range of worth to which we refer is the one that operates for a given item at that time in that auction. Its range of worth may be different at different times and in different settings, for example, in pricing for retail sale.

The existence of this range allows the auctioneer to characterize bids below the range as immoral and to reject them, if he wishes. Hence, while all bids are legal, some are moral, i. e. in or close to the auctioneer's range of worth, and some are immoral, i. e. well below the lower boundary of the range, fuzzy though that boundary will be.

A second point relevant to our analysis is the following. There are three problems in each item sale that the auctioneer must solve successfully if he is to sell the item at a price well into his range of worth. They are (a) the size of the first bid, (b) the sizes of increments in second and later bids, and (c) the number of successively increasing bids. A low first bid need not bring forth the 'rejection because immoral' response. The auctioneer can, and often does, accept the bid without comment. He then tries to get many successive bids with large increments between them. That is, the auctioneer can 'trade off' between the size of the first bid, and the sizes of increments and/or number of successively increasing bids. For example, it is not at all well known, and probably not legal, but a number of auctioneers in our materials controlled the sizes of increments by not permitting certain legally possible ones. In one auction where the prices were usually below a dollar a unit for large lots of the unit, the auctioneer stated that he would not take an increment of a nickel (though on some items he did). Buyers did not complain in this case, or in the other cases we have noted; they accepted this fiat without comment.

A third point relevant to our analysis is that the auctioneer plays the role of judge as well as adversary of the buyer. The auctioneer is responsible for running a competent, orderly auction. He must prove his competency when describing items, when settling disputes, when handling payments and deposits, and when deciding what to do whenever strange things occur. In fact, his role as judge (including technical expert) plays such a prominent part in the auction that his other role as adversary of the buyer, or representative of the seller, is well hidden. It is this feature that makes the auctioneer look 'classier' than a haggling bazaar merchant. He is not simply a bargaining agent for himself or the seller.

In our other paper we have documented these three general points
--range of worth, the 'trade-off' issue, and auctioneer as judge--
with examples from our transcripts, and we could add further
examples from interviews with buyers, sellers, and auctioneers, if
we wished to collect that kind of testimony. The result looks like an
extension of Clark's ethnography, not differing from it in any essential way. We turn now to what we think is a more definite analysis.

The analysis. With all this build-up we wish we could really
reproduce significant pieces of interaction in the auction. But at
the present time we cannot. However, we make a number of observations that point in that direction, and hope that the reader will be
persuaded of its possibility.

To begin, we have replaced our general question of how the
auctioneer tries to control price levels by the more specific question: how does the auctioneer handle initial bids? That is, we
concentrate on just one of the three problems that the auctioneer
has to solve in each item sale, the size of the initial bid. Our
strategy is to propose pieces of 'machinery' that we believe are
necessary to reproduce the auctioneer's actions at this point. One
final preliminary: we concentrate on the auctioneer's side of the
auctioneer-buyer interaction here. We plan to deal more fully with
the buyer's side at a later time.

The typical sequence of activities that the auctioneer carries out
in an item sale are (a) describing or identifying the item (or lot),
(b) soliciting bids, (c) selling the item, and (d) handling payment for
the item. We are interested in the interaction just after the item
has been described, at the beginning of the bid solicitation.
Operationally, we deal only with the cases where the auctioneer
suggests bids, rather than simply asks for bids. (This practice
occurs very commonly in our materials.) Thus, for now, we rule
out the cases where there is no suggested first bid by the auctioneer.
Hence, we have a 'three-slot' problem: the auctioneer's last suggested bid, followed by some buyer's first bid, followed by the
auctioneer's response to that.

As we view it, these three slots constitute two two-slot pairs,
where the second member of the pair is strongly invited by the first
member of the pair. The 'tie' in the first pair is easy to see. The
pair, Suggestion-Compliance, is similar to the question-answer
pair, and to Schegloff's (1968) summons-answer pair.[3] It is known
to all that some buyer is expected to respond to the auctioneer's
suggested bid. He may not comply, just as he may not 'answer' a
question put to him, but he should respond. It will be 'officially
noticed' if no response is forthcoming from any buyer. It appears
to us that the auctioneer's chant, where he keeps repeating his

suggested bid, functions to prevent silence from occurring when no buyer bids. That is, it operates to keep 'official notice' from happening, since the auctioneer is 'still talking'.

The second pair is less clearly a pairing. To the uninitiated, any bid is as good as any other bid. As mentioned earlier, a naive inference from that is that the auctioneer will think so too, will automatically accept the bid, and begin from that point. However, the auctioneer assumes the right, legal or moral, to refuse any bid, and therefore has to choose to accept a given bid. Thus, the second pair is Bid, followed by Acceptance or Rejection. It is the way in which the auctioneer handles his end of the second pair when he gets an underbid, i.e. noncompliance with his suggestion, that is the goal of our study.

Basically, we believe that the auctioneer's response to a buyer's first bid in this situation will be determined by two ranges of money values. The first is the 'range of worth' for the item, discussed earlier, and the second is the 'range of acceptable first bids'.

Generally, the high end of the range for acceptable first bids overlaps the low end of the range of worth, while the low end is somewhere below the lower boundary of the range of worth. The ranges are related in the following way, in terms of a graph.

(Range of worth)
(Range of acceptable first bids)

0   Money value

Again, we propose a 'range' rather than a 'point', because it is vague as to what constitutes a proper first bid. Since a first bid is only a point at which to begin a series of bids, it has less 'reality' (stability) than even the worth of the item.

We locate the range of acceptable first bids as we do, in relation to the range of worth, for two reasons. (a) The upper boundary, though fuzzy, should be below the upper boundary of the range of worth. That is so because everyone expects to start below the 'real' worth of the item and work up toward it. (b) The lower boundary, again fuzzy, occurs at the point where any lower amounts would be seen as outrageous if offered as bids. For example, a nickel for a refrigerator falls below the range of acceptable first bids. Implicitly, then, the range of acceptable first bids defines a third range that lies below it, that can be called the range of outrageous bids.

We assume that the auctioneer's first suggested bid is ordinarily drawn from the intersection of these ranges, i. e. a value in the low end of the range of worth that is also in the high end of the range of acceptable bids. We have done some computations in the auctions where the auctioneer regularly reports the list price of the item he is selling in his description of the item. One clear case of this occurred when auctioning merchandise in a drugstore. Many of the toys and cosmetic items had list prices put on the wrappers by the retailer. In two auctions like this we found that the auctioneer's first suggested bid averaged 18 percent and 26 percent of list price. We have not done any comparable computations as yet to try to define the lower boundary of the range of acceptable first bids. We estimate (for reasons that will become apparent later) that it is between 5 percent and 10 percent of the list price of the item, if there is one. Obviously, in cases where there is no stable value for the item, such as a list price, both ranges are much more vaguely bounded. For example, second-hand goods like chairs or tools may sell at widely varying prices in second-hand stores and elsewhere, so that the relation of a first suggested bid to a 'real' value is much more vague than in the previous cases.

As with the range of worth, we regard the range of acceptable first bids as 'situated'. It will vary with a number of features of the situation, including the kind of item; the place of the item in the sequence of items sold; the speed with which items must be sold, i. e. the number-of-items to time ratio; and even to the desire by the auctioneer to do favors or otherwise create good will. For example, there may be no lower boundary to the range (and hence no range of outrageous bids) because the auctioneer is willing to give the item away, if necessary, for some other advantage. This is analogous to a 'loss leader' in supermarkets.

A third piece of machinery, a procedure rather than an 'object' like the range of worth, permits us to begin analyzing examples from our materials. We call the procedure the 'sliding scale down' procedure. Technically, this procedure is not necessary to our analysis of the 'three-slot' sequence, if we begin with the auctioneer's last suggested bid. However, it helps to illuminate the working out of the three 'slots', and we include it for that reason.

The auctioneer uses the 'sliding scale down' to move down through his range of acceptable first bids until he receives a first bid from a buyer. For example, if a toy with a list price of $4.98 is offered for sale, the auctioneer may suggest $2.00 as a first bid. If no one responds to that, he typically will 'slide down' to $1.00, then to 50 cents, even to 25 cents, if necessary. The successive suggested bids are almost always approximate (round) numbers, as opposed to precise numbers, in whatever range of values the item falls (see

Churchill 1966). Successive suggested bids are commonly related to each other by halving, i. e. the next suggested bid is one-half of the last suggested bid. In cases where halving a suggested bid does not produce an approximate number, a nearby approximate number may be used. For example, since one-half of $25.00 is $12.50, 'too precise' a number in this procedure, the auctioneer customarily shifts to $10, sometimes to $15. In cases where there are no nearby approximate numbers, he uses a precise one. As an example, one-half of five cents per unit yields two and a half cents per unit. This is 'too precise', but there are no nearby approximate numbers. In this case we have seen the auctioneer move to three cents per unit or to two cents per unit.

Let us now look at some examples from our data. There are two basic possibilities that we distinguish for how a buyer may fill the second slot of the three-slot sequence. He may equal (or in rare cases surpass) the auctioneer's suggested bid, or he may bid under the auctioneer's suggested bid. As noted earlier, our interest is in how the auctioneer handles these possibilities, particularly the cases where he receives an underbid to his last suggested bid. Schematically, we have:

A(Auctioneer): Last suggested bid
B(Buyer): Makes first bid equal   Makes first bid less
to last suggested bid   than last suggested bid
('equal bid' case)   ('underbid' case)
A(Auctioneer): Accepts bid (This   ?
case is of no
particular interest
to us at the moment.)

Examples illustrating the 'equal bid' case are the following:

(1) A: All right, let's go. I can see everybody.
Asst: Go ahead, on the fifty-cent (list price) kitestrings.
A: All right, fifty cents--forty-five kitestrings. All
right, a nickel apiece. I got a nickel. Any more
than a nickel? Who's got his hand up? . . . (LG,
p. 1)

(2) A: . . . Lot fifty-seven: two hundred and ten glass
shelves//--with the hooks.
Asst: With the clips. (i.e. the glass shelves are similar
to the kind commonly found in medicine cabinets.)
. . .
Asst: Two hundred and ten pieces.

A: Of glass.

Asst: With the clips.

A: Quarter apiece--quarter apiece--quarter apiece for
the glass--dime apiece--nickel apiece--a penny
apiece--penny apiece? Penny apiece he says.
(Kan, p. 27)

(3) A: How much for the (artificial Christmas) tree?

B: Bring it out.//Let's see it.

A: Five dollars?

Asst: Here it is.

A: Three dollars for the tree--three dollars--three
dollars for the tree.

Bs: Oohhhhh! (said sarcastically)

A: Three dollars--

Asst: And there's more to it, there's more. (i.e.
ornaments)

Bs: Oohhhhh! (said sarcastically)

A: A dollar for the tree?

Bs: (laughter)

A: (Sold for) A dollar--next lot. (Amo, p. 29)

Example (1) gives the classic case where the auctioneer suggests
a bid and a buyer meets it immediately. Examples (2) and (3) show
two uses of the 'sliding scale down' procedure. Example (2) shows
a four-step scale down, equal to the longest we have in our materials:
25 cents--ten cents--five cents--one cent. Example (3) shows the
mix of approximate and precise steps: $5 (approximate)--$3 (precise)--$1 (probably approximate).

If some buyer meets one of the auctioneer's suggested bids, then,
obviously, the bid is accepted, and the bidding commences from
there. Ordinarily, if there are no further bids, the auctioneer will
sell it to that buyer for the bid he made. In this sense, when the
auctioneer suggests a bid, as opposed to asks for a bid, he will be
willing to sell it for that price. However, we found one auctioneer
who treated the suggested bid only as a starting point, and not as a
selling point. Consider example (4).

(4) A: An antique Rockwood bowl, signed and dated, nineteen
twenty-one. Fifteen dollars on it going once, and
fifteen I have. Seventeen and a half--twenty dollars
bid once--twenty dollars on it twice--Are you through
and finished at twenty? Any advance on twenty? No
advance on twenty? Set it down.

Here, the auctioneer not only doesn't sell the item for the first bid that met his suggestion ($15), but he won't sell it for the third bid that was made, even though he apparently accepted all three bids. And no buyer makes any complaint about his action here.

We turn now to the 'underbid' case. The usefulness of the range of acceptable first bids can now be seen. We believe that the auctioneer will comment on the underbid in some way and often reject it, if it is below his range of acceptable first bids, i. e. in his range of outrageous bids. On the other hand, he will ordinarily accept it without comment if the underbid is still within his range of acceptable first bids.

We present some of the latter examples first, where the auctioneer accepts the underbid without comment.

(5) A: All right, Lot Number six.
   Asst: We're selling four hundred as--four hundred and fifty assorted posters.
   A: All right, that's these on the floor, and that includes the dayglows (a kind of luminescent poster). Right?
   Asst: Right.
   A: Those boxes right there.
   Asst: All five of these boxes.
   A: One, two, three, four, five boxes, including the dayglows. All right, three cents a piece for these--two cents I have--two--two--two--two--two--two--two--two--two--two--two cents--any advance--two cents? Fair warning at two cents . . . (Kan, p. 3)

(6) A: How much for the complete outfit (upholstered furniture)?
   Asst: Genuine corduroy.
   A: Fifty dollars for it--fifty dollars for it--fifty dollars --twenty-five dollars for it--
   B: Ten.
   A: Ten dollars bid--fifteen dollars bid--. . . . (Amo, p. 2)

Example (5) shows a buyer underbidding the acutioneer's first suggested bid; example (6) shows the auctioneer's use of the 'sliding scale down', where a buyer acts as the auctioneer's 'assistant', in the sense that his underbid is (or is close to) what the auctioneer himself would suggest next if he had to move down again. Apparently, neither underbid puts the buyer into the acutioneer's range of outrageous bids. In our materials the underbids in cases of 'accept without comment' are ordinarily no less than 1/4 P, if P is the first suggested bid. In (5), three cents is P, and two cents is 2/3 P, above the 'cutting point' of 1/4 P. In (6), $50 is P, and $10 is 1/5 P, less than 1/4 P. However, recall that the next step in the scale down really should be $12.50, but that is too precise, so $10 is substituted for it. In this sense, $10 equals $12.50, and in effect, $10 is equal to 1/4 P.

We give one more example in this series, one where the auctioneer does comment on the underbid but where the problem seems to rest on the preciseness of the number rather than falling into the auctioneer's range of outrageous bids.

(7) A: All right, how much am I bid for the pool table? Ten
        dollars apiece?
    B: Four.
    A: Give me a round number. What are you? How about
        five? Four--You got five fingers.
    Asst: Five he (the Buyer) says.
    A: Five is bid . . . (LG, p. 6)

Here, the buyer 'failed' his role as auctioneer's assistant. If he had bid $5, rather than $4, we believe that the auctioneer would have accepted his bid without comment, and proceeded from there.

We now turn to the most interesting set of cases, 'underbid' situations where the auctioneer comments on the underbid in one way or another before accepting or rejecting the bid. Consider the following examples where the auctioneer accepts the bid.

(8) Asst: They're a dollar nine to two oh nine (in list price).
    A: All right, twenty cents apiece.
    B: A dime.
    A: Who said a dime? All right. That's a good number.
        Fifteen--Do I hear the twenty now? . . . (LG, p. 11)

(9) A: It's supposed to be a very expensive (movie) screen,
        I'm told. How much? Fifty dollars for it? Fifty
        dollars?
    Asst: Take a look at it. Anyone interested--
    Asst: On the movie screen we're selling.
    A: Twenty-five dollars for the screen.
    B: Five.
    A: Oh, come on. Five dollars? All right. We'll try.
        Five dollars . . . (Amo, p. 28)

(10) A: Lot number twenty-one are twenty-one condominium
         guides (books).
     Asst: All--all/alike.

> A: How much apiece for them? Quarter//--what?
> B: Fifteen. Fifteen.
> A: Fifteen. He goes backwards, good. I got fifteen
>   bid . . . (Rap, p. 1)

In these three cases the auctioneer comments that he notices the lowness of the bid, but he will start from there. The underbid appears to lie toward the lower end of his range of acceptable first bids without being outrageous.

We believe that the auctioneer's 'noticing' comments instruct the buyers about two things: (a) that the auctioneer is not a 'patsy'--he will point out immoral bids, even if they are legal; (b) where the lower boundary to the auctioneer's range of acceptable first bids is, on an item like this one. Hence these comments are part of the auctioneer's overall strategy in the power struggle over prices.

We next present examples where the auctioneer comments more strongly on the underbid, and in several of the cases rejects the bid.

(11) A: Three thousand six hundred and eighty-five pieces
    (posters). A dime apiece--a couple of pennies
    apiece--two cents apiece--two cents apiece--
    no money for it--Kama Sutra is worth it--it's
    beautiful.
Asst: Look at the paper it's on.
A: A couple of pennies apiece--a penny apiece.
B: Half a cent apiece.
A: I hate to sell out for that kind of money. You'll go
    on up to Park Bernet and tell them that I sold Kama
    Sutra prints for half a penny apiece--a penny I have
    --a penny-- . . . (Kan, p. 22)

(12) A: Lot number thirty-two. We're selling a hundred and
    fifteen forms. A hundred and fifteen of them. That
    is just how they look.
Asst: That's right.
A: All right. Except they're not busted. Show them
    another one. That one's busted, John.
Asst: They're hard to take out.
A: All right, don't bother. A hundred and fifteen of
    them--a dime apiece--first man for a dime--
B: Two cents apiece.
A: All right, I'll give you a ride for two cents apiece.
    Two cents apiece I have--two cents-- . . . (Kan,
    p. 16)

(13) A: Three Corningware candles.
Asst: Right here, on the candles.
A: All right, quarter apiece
Asst: (Corning) candles.
B: Try a dime--what the --
A: Dime is gone. (Sold to) BF.
Asst: All right . . .
A: He's heavy on those dimes with me . . .
B: (Laughs) (LG, p. 17)

(14) A: Ten hundred and eighty-eight yards (of cloth). There
it is. How much for it? How much for it? . . .
How? Quarter a yard anybody? Quarter--quarter--
quarter--quarter--quarter--quarter--quarter a yard
--What do you say? Quarter a yard?
B: Dime.
A: That's nice. Leave your name and address (said
sarcastically).
. . .
Consigner: What do they want? That's heavy nylon.
A: I know it. Quarter--Who'll start me? Mike?
Fifteen cents a yard is bid--any more?-- . . .
(Al, p. 11)

(15) A: Twenty-five dollars for it (a poster rolling machine).
There's a motor on there, too, right?
Asst: Right, right.
A: That's no money for it. Twenty-five dollars--
fifteen dollars I got. Is that what you said?
Fifteen dollars I have--
Asst: Come on--no money for it--
A: Fifteen--fifteen--fifteen dollars--sold--(to) RD.
Asst: The man has to steal. (Kan, p. 25)

(16) A: How much for the carpeting? One thousand dollars
for it? One thousand dollars for the carpeting?
How much? Five hundred dollars? Start me off--
I don't care--
B: (Laughs)
A: Any bid on the carpeting?
B: Twenty-five.
A: How much?
B: Twenty-five dollars.
2nd B: What does it go, by the yard, or all the carpeting?
A: The whole--

Asst: All of it--all the carpeting--
A: All the carpeting. Any bid on it?
2nd B: You got a bid on it.
B: I bid twenty-five dollars.
A: Wouldn't sell it for twenty-five.
B: Thirty.
2nd B: Thirty-five dollars.
A: Any bid on it?
3rd B: Seventy-five.
A: Seventy-five dollars is bid for all the carpeting. One
hundred dollars I got bid for all the carpeting-- . . .
(Amo, p. 32)

We have put the examples in rough order of increasing sharpness of
the auctioneer's (or his assistant's) comment on the underbid. In
some of the examples the underbid quite clearly falls in the auctioneer's range of outrageous bids, e.g. (11), where the underbid is 5
percent of the first suggested bid. In other cases it is not so clear
that the underbid is outrageous. It appears that the auctioneer had
started at the bottom of his range of acceptable first bids rather than
at the top. Thus, in (15) $25 must be a bottom price for a poster
rolling machine, and in (13) a quarter must be a low price, according to the auctioneer, for a Corningware candle.
These examples lead us to the following observations.
1. The auctioneer can treat the underbid as the first member of
a number of different kinds of pairs, where the second member is
tied to the first, as in a question-answer pair. In (11) the underbid
is treated as unprofessional; in (12) it is treated as a request for a
favor; in (13) it is treated as an eccentricity of a buyer who likes to
bid 'dimes'; in (14), (15), and probably (16), it is treated as an
attempt to steal. The auctioneer, by making the response that he
does, 'completes' the 'invitation' that he detects in the underbid, to
produce the pair.[1] This class of 'invitations' is an extension of
Sacks' concept of 'correction-invitation'.[2] By attributing a quality
to the underbid, best stated in terms of adjectives such as joking or
playful or immoral or surprising or eccentric or favor-seeking, the
auctioneer turns the underbid into the first member of an 'invitation'
side sequence (see Jefferson 1972). In effect, the underbid provides
the auctioneer with the opportunity to invoke one of a variety of
activities that are done in conversation, by treating the underbid as
the opening move in that activity. The end result of this is, ordinarily, a negative attribution to the underbidder. The virtuosity
with which the auctioneer can 'magically' invoke activities in this
way will help determine whether he or the buyers will control prices

in the auction. This 'hidden weapon' of the auctioneer gives him a tremendous advantage over most buyers, who simply do not know about it until they are subjected to it.

2. We pursue the observations just made in two specific cases, misfires and insults.

(a) By a 'misfire' we refer to a breakdown in the interaction caused by not hearing or not understanding a remark. [3] Remarks that indicate misfires are <u>What did you say?</u> and <u>I don't understand what you mean.</u> We believe that a misfire remark is possible as a first response to any remark, thereby turning it into a 'poorly delivered' or 'poorly framed' remark. As described earlier in this paper (see (16)), the auctioneer then forces the underbidder into a misfire side sequence.

A: Any bid on the carpeting?
B: Twenty-five.
A: How much?
B: Twenty-five dollars.

However, we do not believe that very many of the misfires following underbids were 'natural', in the sense that the auctioneer actually didn't hear or understand at that point. Rather, he uses the misfire 'machinery' to make the buyer repeat his bid, if he wants to. The misfire serves at least two purposes, which put pressure on the underbidder. It draws notice to the underbid; and it is often delivered in a surprised or aggressive tone that conveys the auctioneer's dissatisfaction with it. The buyer must then repeat his 'immoral' bid, thus exposing his 'thieving' character to everyone present.

(b) By 'insults' we refer to the variety of 'stealing' and 'chiseling' remarks that the auctioneer makes in response to underbids. Example (15) shows this phenomenon clearly. In this case the underbid is treated as so immoral that it requires the auctioneer to take notice of it. Thus, what appears to be a 'free' insult of the buyer by the auctioneer is really a sanction for the buyer's insulting underbid, so the auctioneer would have us believe.

(c) The 'sliding scale down' provides the possibility of a very elegant 'insult' strategy by the auctioneer. The possibility occurs when the underbid is the next step down in the auctioneer's sliding scale at that point. That underbid can be treated in one of two ways by the auctioneer: neutrally, as merely 'helping the auctioneer out' to where he was going anyway; or negatively, as 'an immoral bid'. We believe that predicting which alternative will occur is essentially problematic for the buyer.

The problem occurs because the buyer does not know where the auctioneer started in his range of acceptable first bids, nor does he

know when the next step down will put him in the auctioneer's range
of outrageous bids. Worse, the auctioneer may treat the underbid in
either way, no matter how he feels about it. In effect, the auctioneer
can attribute 'stealing' to any underbid. He can make this attribution
seem plausible to everyone, because of his role as judge as well as
adversary. Judges are supposed to be fair and impartial. When they
say a price is too low, it is believed. Compare the auctioneer, for
example, with the bazaar merchant who is haggling with you. The
bazaar merchant will not be able to carry off this attribution of
'stealing' to any underbid of yours nearly as well as will the auctioneer.

This strategic use of conversational activities makes the auctioneer
a formidable conversationalist. For the underbidder the cost of a
'good deal' is not just money; it is suffering a mild form of degradation as well, without being able to do anything about it. [4]

Conclusion. There are a number of other points raised by these
examples that we skip for now. To conclude, we hope that we have
convinced you of the following:

1. There is a real possibility that we can reproduce many
of the 'three-slot' sequences we have just described, though
we have not achieved that here. Certainly, the attempt will
reveal whether or not there are any essential impediments
to the task, as Garfinkel proposes.

2. Essential to that reproduction task are two pieces of
'machinery': the range of worth and the range of acceptable
first bids.

3. If the auctioneer receives an underbid, as we have
defined it here, he may bring in one or more of a number of
activities to deal with it. Most of these activities treat the
buyer in a negative light for having made the underbid.
These activities can be conceived as 'subroutines' in computer language, in the sense that they have regular methods
of production that are independent of the particular conversation into which they are 'imported'.

4. The reproduction task cannot be achieved (if at all)
until the same task is applied to the 'subroutines' like
sanctioning and misfiring. Some progress has been made
on these activities by Sacks and others, but much work still
remains to be done.

5. Finally, to return to our original question, the
auctioneer has one major advantage over most buyers in
the power struggle to control prices. He is simply a more
skilled conversationalist than they are in the activities
needed to resolve disputes over underbids in his favor.

NOTES

1. This is similar to Sacks' analysis of how we hear the mommy in The baby cried. The mommy picked it up. as the mommy of the baby. See Sacks (1972).

2. See, for example, Lindsey Churchill, 'Invitations in Questioning', 1972, unpublished paper, for a discussion of Sacks' concept.

3. See Lindsey Churchill, 'Misfires in Questioning', 1972, unpublished paper, for a discussion of misfires.

4. See Harold Garfinkel, 'Conditions of Successful Degradation Ceremonies', American Journal of Sociology, 61 (1956), for discussion of an analogous phenomenon.

REFERENCES

Churchill, Lindsey. 1966. Notes on everyday quantitative practices. American Sociological Association Meetings, Miami, Fla.

Clark, Robert E. 1973. On the block: An ethnography of auctions. Ann Arbor, Mich., Xerox University Microfilms.

Gray, Susan and Lindsey Churchill. 1974. Ritual insult and business activity: The 'auctioneer' and his audience. October. Unpublished MS.

Jefferson, Gail. 1972. Side sequences. In: Studies in social interaction. Edited by David Sudnow. New York, Free Press.

Sacks, Harvey. 1972. On the analyzability of stories by children. In: Directions in sociolinguistics: The ethnography of communication. Edited by John J. Gumperz and Dell Hymes. New York, Holt, Rinehart and Winston.

Schegloff, Emanuel. 1968. Sequencing in conversational openings. American Anthropologist 70. 1075-1095.

INFORMATION STRUCTURES IN DISCOURSE

CHARLOTTE LINDE

Hunter College, City University of New York

Some of the speaker's morphological and syntactic choices appear
to be influenced by or determined by the nature of the information
which the speaker intends to convey. With some well-known exceptions, information is thought of as being either new in the discourse
and hence new to the hearer, or already mentioned in the discourse
and hence known to the hearer. The subject has generally been analyzed as the position for the placement of old information, while other
constituents of the sentence, which may bear the main stress of the
sentence, have been seen as the position for new information
(Bolinger 1972). Chafe also has noted that in the least marked instances, the old information is carried by the surface subject (Chafe
1970:212). Similarly, the article system is the morphological system
which most directly reflects information status, and all other things
being equal, it is assumed that the definite article is the one appropriate for old information and the indefinite for new information.
Jespersen, for example, states that the definite article 'denotes one
individual (supposed to be more or less familiar to the speaker or
writer)' (Jespersen 1949:421).

If these familiar analyses are correct, they should be successful in
predicting speakers' choice of articles and surface subjects in actual
discourse. In this study, the discourses examined are a group of 72
apartment layout descriptions. They were elicited as part of a survey
of attitudes on urban living, conducted in New York City. The people
interviewed were not told that the interviewer was primarily interested in their language. Analysis of the apartment layout descriptions
has shown that they are clearly a well-defined speech act, in Hymes'
sense, and indeed are so coherent that formal rules can be written to

226

describe the major transitions from real-world information to syntactic patterns (Linde 1974; Linde and Labov 1975).

In the sentences of this data, the subject position is occupied by locative phrases, by the dummy there, by pronouns, and by full noun phrases. It is the full noun phrase subjects which are the most suitable for a study of the informational status of the subject position.

In this body of data, there are 82 sentences which have noun phrase subjects. Of these, over half, 46, express old information, or information which has not been mentioned specifically but whose existence can be assumed from the preceding discourse. These sentences containing old information in the subject position follow the postulated unmarked distribution of information, and appear to have relatively few constraints on the nature of the information of the subject position. Examples of such sentences are (1), (2), and (3).

(1) Then there's a really skinny hallway that same width as the other hallway I described. . . . and then that hallway opens into the kitchen.

(2) And then to the left of the living room are two bedrooms. The two bedrooms are on the same side of the building.

(3) Could you tell me the layout of that apartment? The last apartment was a garden apartment.

Twenty-seven of the 46 sentences containing old information in the subject noun phrases are examples like these, in which the referent of the subject noun phrase has been directly mentioned in the preceding discourse. Similar to these are those sentences containing subject noun phrases which refer to something whose existence is entailed by the preceding discourse. An example is (4).

(4) You come into a small, uh, hallway, and one side leads to the bathroom.

Neither the specific noun phrase nor some synonym for it has appeared before in the discourse, but the existence of its referent can still be treated as known information. That is, if we know that there is a hallway, we know that it has a side. Indeed, objects and their parts are among the clearest examples of such pragmatic entailment. We may consider sentences like (1), (2), and (3), and sentences like (4) to be equivalent. In both, the speaker repeats information whose existence has been previously established in the discourse, either directly or indirectly, and uses the placement in subject position as a link with what has already been said.

However, the remaining 36 sentences with noun phrase subjects appear to contradict the postulated patterning of the information of sentences, since they contain new information in the subject position. Twenty-eight of them introduce new rooms and 8 introduce other new information. These 36 cases represent 44 percent of the sentences with full noun phrase subjects. As usual, the examination of the discourses actually produced by speakers reveals an apparently chaotic situation.

However, when we examine the interaction of the subject position introductions and the choice of article, some order begins to emerge. If the noun phrase subjects have any article, they have the definite article. This is an expected finding. The two should go together: the subject position and the definite article have both been analyzed as appropriate for the same kind of information. We may hypothesize that perhaps speakers are treating the newly introduced information as if it were already known. What this means can be made clearer by an examination of article choice for all introductions.

We will consider the introductions of all the rooms in this body of data, in every position in the sentence. The inquiry will be confined to the introduction of new rooms, since this type of information is physical, discrete, and least open to the question of whether its existence is presupposed by other elements in the discourse. We find that 38 percent of all introductions of rooms are made with the definite article. Table 1 shows the identity of rooms introduced with the definite article.

TABLE 1. Rooms introduced with definite article.

Room	Number of introductions
Kitchen	28
Living room	25
Bathroom	21
Bedroom	20
Dining room	5
Foyer	1

The introduction of rooms with the definite article is not entirely un-conditioned. Most of the rooms introduced with the definite article are major rooms: only six are not. (A major room is defined as a room which an apartment may be expected to have--living room, bedroom, kitchen, and bathroom, although bathroom is a special case. A minor room is defined as a room which an apartment may or may not have--dining room, den, library, study, laundry room, etc.).

Minor rooms constitute 12 percent of all the introductions in this data, but only 6 percent of the introductions with definite articles. Thus, minor rooms are introduced with the definite article only half as often as would be predicted by their overall frequency in the data. In general, speakers use the definite article to introduce rooms which an apartment can be assumed to contain, rooms whose existence in an apartment can to some extent be treated as given. (It should be noted that the minor rooms introduced with the definite article are dining room and foyer. Although neither is a major room, they are the most frequent of the minor rooms. The rarest of the minor rooms-- laundry room, library, etc.--are not introduced with the definite article. However, it is impossible to say that they would never be introduced this way, since they are so rare that the present data is not extensive enough to warrant such a claim.)

The nature of the rooms introduced in subject position is necessarily similar to that of the rooms introduced with the definite article, since there is a great deal of overlap between the two groups. Table 2 shows the rooms which are introduced in subject position.

TABLE 2. Rooms introduced in subject position.

Room	Number of introductions
Bathroom	8
Kitchen	7
Living room	5
Bedroom	4
Room	2
Foyer	1
Dining room	1

Here too, the most unexpected rooms are not introduced in subject position. That is, just as there are no sentences like (5), there are also no sentences like (6) and (7).

(5) At the end is the library.
(6) The laundry room is at the end.
(7) My den is straight ahead.

Introduction of a new noun phrase in subject position appears to be subject to the same conditions as introduction with the definite article: it is found with those rooms whose existence can be assumed.

However, the very notion of introduction with the definite article itself poses a problem. One of the best established patterns of article use is that a new noun phrase is introduced with the indefinite article and is subsequently mentioned with the definite article. That is, simple introduction into a discourse is enough to change information from new to old. Examples of this discourse pattern are (8) from Jespersen, (9) from Sorenson, and (10) and (11) from Stockwell et al.

(8) Once upon a time there lived an old tailor in a village. The old tailor was known all over the village as Old Harry.
(9) Yesterday Anderson kissed a girl with blue eyes. The girl called the police.
(10) I saw a cat in the tree this morning, but when I looked this afternoon, the cat was gone.
(11) A boy and a girl were walking down the street together and the girl was shouting at the boy.

When we examine the articles assigned to information on first and subsequent mention in the data of the present study, we find that not even this well-known pattern is categorical.

The structure of apartment layout descriptions permits us several ways to study this question. These apartment descriptions are most typically in the form of an imaginary tour, with each room and its position mentioned as an imaginary tourer would come to it. A spatial arrangement is thus transformed into a temporal one, which leads to the analysis of apartment layout descriptions as a type of pseudo-narrative. The similarity to true narratives is actually quite close. As true narratives often contain an introductory abstract, so layout descriptions optionally begin with an introductory summary which may enumerate the people living in the apartment, mention its noteworthy features, evaluate its desirability or lack of it, or list the rooms of the apartment.

Apartment descriptions which begin with an enumeration of the rooms of the layout are the clearest places to begin examining the pattern of the distribution of articles. The standard analysis of the article system would predict that speakers would use the indefinite article for mention of the room in the initial summary, and the definite article for subsequent mention in the layout description proper. But in fact speakers do not restrict themselves to this pattern. There are four possibilities: indefinite article in both summary and layout; definite article in both summary and layout; indefinite article in summary followed by definite article in layout; and definite article in summary followed by indefinite article in layout. Speakers produce all but the last of these possibilities. That is, there are sequences like (12), (13), and (14), but none like (15). (Each example contains the relevant portion of the summary followed by the relevant portion of the description.)

(12) It sort of went like this, like a fading highway, with, the living room is a little bit wider . . . You walked into the living room.

(13) It had a living room, a bedroom and kitchen and bathroom. . . . There was a kitchen off the, let's see, corridor, a living room . . .

(14) It had a bedroom, about the size of the living room, a big kitchen that could have been partitioned off into a dining room and kitchen. . . . You entered into a tiny little hallway and the kitchen was off to the left of that. And the bedroom was like, the bathroom was straight at the end of that hall and to the left again was the bedroom.

(15) *It has the big entrance hall, the living room and two bedrooms. . . . You walk into a big entrance hall and straight ahead is a living room, to the left is my kitchen, and in back are two bedrooms.

Table 3 shows the frequency of each case.

TABLE 3. First and subsequent article, summary and description.

		Subsequent article	
		a	the
First	a	10	11
article	the	0	6

It might be argued that the 10 examples of repeated indefinite article are due to error or forgetfulness, the speaker losing track of the fact that he has already introduced the room with the indefinite article and so repeating it in the layout proper. But such forgetfulness does not produce the pattern of first mention with definite article and subsequent mention with indefinite article.

Another possibility open to the speaker is to mention a room more than once in the layout description proper, usually because he needs the second mention of a room as a reference point for a direction, or because he wishes to add further information about the room. Examples are (16), (17), and (18).

(16) To your left was a hallway, leading to a bedroom which
     was like an L-shape. So in other words, you went to
     your left through a hall, . . .
(17) On the right was the kitchen, and off the kitchen, even
     further from the kitchen was my little maid's room.
(18) There's a long hallway which opens into a foyer.
     Now in back of the foyer there's the dining room.

Table 4 shows the frequency of each case.

TABLE 4. First and subsequent article, description proper.

Subsequent article

		a	the
First	a	8	40
article	the	3	25

This table reveals a number of interesting patterns. One striking
feature is the presence of three cases in which a room is introduced
with the definite article and later mentioned with the indefinite article.
These are examples (19), (20), and (21).

(19) You walked into the kitchen and then there's a bathroom
     and a kitchen, a john, a door, you know, in the kitchen
     with a little john there.
(20) It has a long hallway that you walk into and straight
     ahead is the kitchen, there's a door and then from the
     hallway into I mean a big dining room and there's a big
     kitchen off that.
(21) You took a right down this long narrow hallway and on the
     right was the kitchen and off the kitchen even further from
     the kitchen was my little maid's room, and then keeping
     on going down the hall, on the right was a large bedroom
     and directly down the hall straight ahead down the hall
     was another bedroom. It was a dining room, it was
     turned into a bedroom, off a long hall.

This is the one pattern which is unexpected, and therefore it is not
surprising that two and possibly all three of the examples involve
mistakes, networks in which the speaker lost the thread.

Another interesting feature is that this table looks much more like
the pattern predicted by the standard analysis of the function of the
articles. The greatest number of cases use the indefinite article for
first mention and the definite article for second mention. It is

illuminating to compare this pattern in the two kinds of repeated mention. When the two mentions of the room are divided between the summary and the description proper, the expected pattern of indefinite article followed by definite article is no more frequent than the pattern using indefinite articles for both mentions. When the room is mentioned twice in the description proper, the expected pattern is significantly more frequent. [1]

These facts lead to a number of conclusions about the notions 'discourse' and 'new and old information'. These notions are often appealed to in discussions of syntax, but as they are currently used, they do not predict the behavior of speakers. Most discussions of information status assume that information is not known until it is introduced into the discourse, after which it becomes known. The transmission of information of this type is the main point of the discourse. In addition, there is shared knowledge, which is treated in the same way as information which has been introduced into the discourse explicitly. A clear statement of this common position is provided by Chafe (1970:211).

> Now typically, it is the case that the speaker assumes that some of the information he is communicating is new: it is information he is introducing into the hearer's mind for the first time. But typically it is also the case that some of the information in the sentence is not new. Some of it is information which the speaker and hearer already share at the time the sentence is spoken. This shared information constitutes a kind of starting point based on concepts 'already in the air', to which the new information can be related.

There are also further complications--generic noun phrases, parts of known wholes, etc. But in general, this very common conception of information appears to be implicitly based on a theory of discourse which consists of a speaker who knows something, a hearer who does not know it, and a mutual desire for its transfer.

When we actually examine conversation, it is remarkable how few situations like this there really are. There has been much discussion recently about the pragmatics of ordinary conversation--the illocutionary and perlocutionary intentions of speakers in a given social context (Gordon and Lakoff 1971, R. Lakoff 1973, Weiser 1974). However, such discussion has not yet begun to examine in a serious way the problem of information, which is still being cavalierly treated as 'the point of the discourse' or 'what the speaker intends to convey'. It is unclear, for example, how to analyze the informational status or intended force of conversations which fall under

Malinowski's heading of phatic communication, talk for the sake of something being said. These are conversations like the following.

A. Hi, how are you?
B. Fine, and you?
A. Oh, getting along.

A. This bacon is half raw. It's disgusting.
B. Yeah, I like my bacon crisp.

The information of these conversations must be analyzed as being about states of health or tastes in bacon, but clearly the point of the conversation is not to convey this information.

The apartment descriptions are equally hard to fit into a simple binary model of information transfer. The speaker does have information that the hearer does not have: he is describing his own apartment. But the hearer is not entirely ignorant. Although he does not know the details of a particular apartment, he does have a general knowledge of the nature of apartments. He knows that an apartment almost certainly has a bathroom, probably does not have a library, and certainly does not have a moat. It is this partial knowledge of the hearer which complicates the analysis of information and which permits the speaker's variation in choice of article and position of introduction of new rooms. Given the particular communicative task of describing an apartment, either article is appropriate. To introduce a kitchen or a bathroom, the speaker may decide that the room has not been mentioned before and hence is new, and may be introduced with the indefinite article. Or with equal justification, the speaker may decide that the hearer knows that an apartment normally has a bathroom and a kitchen, and hence the rooms are not new information, and may be introduced with the definite article. Both analyses of the status of information are coherent and so both choices of article are made. (It might be argued that the description of an apartment layout is a peculiarly complicated case, more ambiguous than most other types of discourse. But it is my suspicion that, in fact, the apartment description is a relatively simple discourse type, since it deals with the physical relations of objects in the real world, rather than evaluating people and events, or attempting to influence beliefs or behavior.)

In examining the patterning of information in discourse, it is also of greatest importance to clarify what is meant by discourse. In syntactic theory, this term is used to mean any string of sentences in an utterance context. Such phenomena as article choice and pronominalization are analyzed as being at least partially determined by discourse, since they may require reference to preceding sentences. But there

has been little or no attempt to analyze just what a discourse is, or
whether different types of discourses have different effects on the
syntax of the sentences comprising them. In anthropology and sociolinguistics, there has been a more careful attempt to distinguish between different discourse types. Hymes, for example, provides a
taxonomic framework for the identification of speech acts and speech
events (Hymes 1972). But this theoretical orientation has not, as yet,
proceeded to the study of the syntactic effects of the organization of
discourse.

The results of this study show that the two kinds of research must
be united. Phenomena such as article choice cannot be studied over
any connected sequence of sentences. Rather, it is necessary to
know the type of discourse formed by the sentences. Even within a
given discourse type--in this study, apartment descriptions--the
articles are patterned differently depending on whether they appear
in the same section of one discourse or two different sections of the
same discourse. This is direct and compelling evidence that the study
of syntactic variation must rest on careful studies of the organization
of discourse.

NOTES

I would like to thank Frank Anshen, Teresa Labov, and Geoffrey
Nunberg for their helpful comments and suggestions.
1. The difference is statistically significant ($X^2 = 7.18$, $p < .01$).

REFERENCES

Bolinger, Dwight. 1972. Accent is predictable (if you're a mind-
    reader). Language, Vol. 48, Number 3.
Chafe, Wallace. 1970. Meaning and the structure of language.
    Chicago, The University of Chicago Press.
Gordon, David and George Lakoff. 1971. Conversational postulates.
    Papers from the Seventh Regional Meeting. Chicago, Chicago Lin-
    guistic Society.
Hymes, Dell. 1972. Models of the interaction of language and social
    life. In: Directions in sociolinguistics. Edited by John J.
    Gumperz and Dell Hymes. New York, Holt, Rinehart and Winston.
Jespersen, Otto. 1949. A modern English grammar on historical
    principles. London, Allen and Unwin.
Lakoff, Robin. 1973. The logic of politeness: On minding your p's
    and q's. Papers from the Ninth Regional Meeting. Chicago,
    Chicago Linguistic Society.
Linde, Charlotte. 1974. The linguistic encoding of spatial infor-
    mation. Unpublished dissertation, Columbia University.

Linde, Charlotte and William Labov. 1975. Spatial networks as a site for the study of language and thought. Language, Vol. 51, Number 4.

Sorenson, H. S. 1959. The function of the definite article in modern English. English Studies, Vol. 40.

Stockwell, Robert, Paul Schachter, and Barbara Hall Partee. 1973. The major syntactic structures of English. New York, Holt, Rinehart and Winston.

Weiser, Ann. 1974. Deliberate ambiguity. Papers from the Tenth Regional Meeting. Chicago, Chicago Linguistic Society.

HOW COME YOU ASKED HOW COME?

WALT WOLFRAM

Federal City College and
Center for Applied Linguistics

TODD D. WOLFRAM

Woodlin Elementary School

0. Introduction. This paper focuses on one relatively stable conversational frame in which a 'how come' question is asked.[1] The
conversational frame typically takes the following form. (1) As part
of a conversation, an individual is asked how old he/she is (i.e. 'How
old are you?'). (2) The participant responds with a statement indicating his/her age (i.e. 'I'm ___ years old.'). (3) The participant
who asked the original question then asks 'how come' or 'why'. (4)
The participant responds to the 'how come' question in some manner.

The format is relatively simple and, as I indicated, is usually
integrated into a more extended conversation that is taking place between the participants. In other words, the person who is asked the
'how come' question is not aware of the fact that a response to this
question is deliberately being posed for the sake of some type of linguistic or sociolinguistic study.

At this point, you may wonder how come I decided to ask 'how
come' questions of this type. First of all, I must confess, I was
interested in finding out some things about my own language usage
that had been noticed by others. Several of my colleagues who also
qualify as friends have told me that I ask 'how come' questions in
contexts that strike them intuitively as inappropriate. While I may
do this unconsciously to a certain extent, I must admit that I have
utilized such questions in a type of teasing or joking behavior, and

in this regard, I do not consider myself all that unusual. For example, I found myself asking the following question.

(1) Wolfram: Where are you from anyhow?
    Addressee: New York.
    Wolfram: How come?
    Addressee: Because that's where the hospital was located.

So, my first interest, then, was in looking at how I was using such types of questions, whether they were used as a form of joking behavior or simply asked in contexts that others found obtrusive.

There is, however, another reason which promulgated my interest in this type of questioning, and this relates to the types of questions that children sometimes ask. It seems to be a well-known but little studied fact that children, during certain periods of development, are 'full of questions'. Whereas the mere quantity of the questions may be impressive to some observers, there are also cases which stand out to adults as different from the types of questions adults ask each other. Children have, in fact, been known to ask 'how come' or 'why' questions in the type of frame that I set up for this study. From the home of one of my colleagues comes the following exchange:

(2) Father: Well, Judd, in a few more days you'll be five and
            three quarters.
    Judd: How come?
    Father: Well, that's just the way it works out.

A similar anecdote comes from my own home (before my wife knew I was interested in eliciting such questions). A friend was asking my three-year-old son how old he was when the following exchange took place:

(3) Friend of family: How old are you now, Terry?
    Terry: Two and a half.
    Mother: No you're not, you're three.
    Terry: Why?
    Mother: Remember, you had a birthday, so you're now
            three.

The only point that I'm trying to make here is that children do ask questions that fall into the frame that I have set up for my 'how come', so that an investigation of it may lead to some notions of why some of the questions that children ask may strike adults as different from the sorts of questions they feel are appropriate.

While I am concerned here with one simple question frame, I am investigating it within the broader context of question asking. What we are concerned with is the interaction of real life experience with language usage in the determination of question appropriateness. In this regard, we will see that one of the issues that becomes crucial is the distinction between what we might label 'obvious' and 'non-obvious' information. By obvious information here, I am referring to information about the real world that the speaker and hearer can be expected to have access to and each assumes such knowledge on the part of the other. Both speaker and hearer in the conversational set have acquired such knowledge and have the ability to discriminate on this basis. Nonobvious information, on the other hand, does not meet these criteria for one of the participants in the conversational set. On one level, the notion of 'obvious' and 'nonobvious' information seems to relate to the role of language as it interacts with pragmatics. That is, we use our real life experience to determine what is an appropriate and an inappropriate question. There is, however, another dimension that enters into this issue when such matters are related to age differences. What, for example, is the status of children in terms of such information? If such information is, to a certain extent, determined by culture and a child is in the process of being enculturated, it must be expected that a child may be exempt from the constraints of 'obvious' knowledge which are operative for adults. In this regard, then, the relationship of question appropriateness to real life experience may extend beyond pragmatics to ontology. Although we focus upon a particular question frame as a case in point, we are concerned with more general principles about the role of question appropriateness in language usage.

1. Asking 'how come?'. The literal reason that an object is designated to be a specific age is related to the regular divisions that are made in our culture based on the particular calendar that we have adopted. This procedure for measuring age is, of course, accepted by convention in our culture and is not necessarily that which may be accepted in another culture. For example, in some cultures, a different computation system may be devised based on a different division of a calendar. Or, the same calendar may be adopted but the year may be calculated from the inception point of the designated division rather than the completion, so that a baby may be considered to be one year old at birth rather than designating the completion of the first year as the point at which a child is one year old. Obviously, the adoption of a particular calendar system and the method for computation is something that is learned by a child as a part of his enculturation process. Typically, the type of calendar we adopt and the method for computation are accepted by

adults with little question. It is something we simply learn and accept as a part of growing up in our culture.

The traditional acceptance of this measurement of time by regular intervals seems to be an important aspect related to why certain reason questions concerning time strike adults initially as somewhat inappropriate. Thus, we do not often encounter reason questions when an individual states his current age. That is, it seems somewhat strange for a person to ask us 'how come' after telling him what our age is. This, of course, is not to say that all statements of age cannot be questioned in this way. There appear to be certain circumstances in which a 'how come' question with respect to age does not seem nearly as inappropriate.

For example, if one individual tells another individual that his dog is 63 years old, it may be appropriate to ask 'how come'. In this case, however, the reason that a 'how come' question sounds less strange seems to be related to the fact that dogs are not expected to live 63 years according to the conventional calendar adopted for human age measurement. In this case, the apparent appeal to a human equivalency time measurement (i.e. where one calendar year of a human life is roughly equivalent to seven years of a dog's life) calls the conventional calendar for measurement into question based on our real life knowledge of dog life expectancy, so that it appears to be appropriate to ask the 'how come' question. In another case, a person might declare that the Biblical character Methuselah was 900 years old and a person might ask 'How come he was 900 years old?' In this case, it seems somewhat appropriate to ask the 'how come' question since there is an obvious discrepancy between our real life expectations of a human life span and the stated age. But what the individual is really asking about is an account for the discrepancy since we all know that humans do not normally live to be over 900 years old. In this case, a person may explain Methuselah's age in terms of different calendrical calculations, the use of numbers in a figurative sense, or a justification of the literalness of the figure by explaining that God intervened.

A final example of an instance in which it might be appropriate to ask 'how come' to a person's designated age comes from the perennial age of 39 claimed by the late Jack Benny. Given our general knowledge from the real world that tells us that Jack Benny had exceeded the age of 39 by a considerable margin, we might ask 'how come'.

In all the examples just given, the legitimacy or quasi-legitimacy of a 'how come' question with reference to age seems related to the fact that our real world knowledge of age expectancies does not appear to match the designated age. In two of the cases, a dog's age and Methuselah's age, there is an expectation of life span that may call the traditional calendrical convention into question, while the third

case involves a well-known refusal to accept the continuing calculation of age. The important thing in all three cases, however, is
that we need some background information pointing to an apparent
discrepancy in the adoption of the conventional age calculation to
legitimize the question.

2. Real data on 'how come' questions. Now that we have presented some background information on 'how come' questions with
respect to age, let us look at some real data that was obtained from
actually asking this question of individuals after they had specified
their age. Consider the following exchanges:

(4a) FW: How old are you?
     INF: Twenty-six.
     FW: How come?
     INF: (Laughter) I don't know.

(4b) FW: How old are you?
     INF: Twenty-nine.
     FW: How come?
     INF: (Laughter) I don't know, how old should I be?

While the responses from other adults indicate variations we
shall be discussing, these exchanges indicate a very basic point.
Even though the exchange usually took place within the framework
of a more extended legitimate conversation, the question was in-
variably responded to by adults in a way that indicated it was not considered a sincere request concerning the reason for a person's age
(i.e. it violated a felicity condition for questions). This, I believe,
is related to the fact that the informants assumed that I knew the convention for calculating age in our society as a part of my background
knowledge. I could certainly not be asking for such obvious information as a sincere question. In most cases, this was indicated by
laughter, as if I had intended it to be a type of joke and the adult did
not typically respond with a literal reason.

What is it that makes people laugh at this question? As a beginning
point, we may say that it seems funny because the information being
requested seems so obvious to the person who is being asked the
question at the same time that a nonobvious reading of the question
may not immediately come to mind. In this regard, it is instructive
to note that there is a type of joking or riddling behavior in our
society which plays on obvious information analogous to this. Riddles
like 'Why did the chicken cross the road?' (to get to the other side)
or 'Why do firemen wear red suspenders?' (to hold their pants up)
seem to employ an analogous frame. The hearer recognizes that

certain information may be so implicitly obvious that it is ruled out
of consideration as a possible answer. A similar reference to obvious information comes from an interview with the ex-professional
quarterback for the San Francisco Forty-Niners, John Brodie, as it
was quoted by Sports Illustrated in its section entitled 'They Said It':

(5) Reporter: How come such an expensive quarterback like
you holds the football for place kicks?
John Brodie: If I didn't, the ball would fall over.

Admittedly, there are cases where the appeal to obvious information
may be used sarcastically, so that it is sometimes difficult to determine whether the respondent intends it to be an 'obvious information
joke' or a way of evading the nonobvious response to the question (or
a subtle combination of both). Thus, I am unsure of the intent of an
unemployed linguist whom I happened to meet on the way to the
Washington Linguistics Club one evening. As a regular attendant of
such meetings it was fairly obvious that he was on his way to the meeting when I asked him 'What are you doing now?' with the intent of
finding out whether he had found a job yet. His reply was 'Right now,
I'm walking to the Washington Linguistics Club'.

More obvious sarcasm is found in the response of a person who
has lost something when another person asks 'Where did you lose
it?' and he replies 'If I knew where I lost it, I would have found it'.
In this case, the nonobvious reading must interpret 'where' to refer
to general rather than specific location, but the respondent chooses
to interpret it as a 'stupid question' because of a potential interpretation which is out of order with the situation encountered in the real
world. The main point here is that there is a type of joking behavior
which may veer into sarcasm in which the distinction between obvious
and nonobvious information plays an important part.

The difference between these examples and the one with 'how
come' is that the play on obvious information is found in the reply of
the former and in the question of the 'how come' example. This
difference may, in fact, be the thing that sets it apart from the mere
traditional type of 'obvious information' joke or riddle. The possible
interpretation of this type of verbal encounter as a type of joking behavior is reinforced by the types of responses some informants give
to the question. It seems appropriate, for example, to interpret it
as a type of joking behavior which is deserving of an extension. We
thus get the following:

(6) FW: How old are you?
     INF: Twenty-four.
     FW: How come?
     INF: How come? (Laughter) How come, what do you
          mean how come?
     FW: How come?
     INF: How come? Because twenty-four years ago my
          parents worked something out.

In this response, we see that the informant accepted the fact that
it was a question asking for obvious information, and responded to it
with further obvious information which may be interpreted as an extension of the 'obvious' theme. This seems to be one type of option
which a person can give besides laughter and a terminating response
of 'I don't know'. (The response 'I don't know' may reasonably be
interpreted as a failure to read any legitimate reason beyond the
obvious information intent of the question, i. e. 'I don't know any
reason besides the obvious one'.)

There are some informants, however, who attempt to read this
question in terms of some aspect of nonobvious information. Typically, this is read as one where a discrepancy between the actual
age and the apparent age is indicated. This is shown in the following
examples.

(7a) FW: How old are you?
      INF: Twenty-eight.
      FW: How come?
      INF: How come? (Laughter)
      FW: Yeah, how come?
      INF: You mean why I'm not older? I'm a genius.

(7b) FW: How old are you?
      INF: Twenty-seven.
      FW: How come?
      INF: I'll be twenty-eight soon.
      FW: How come you're twenty-seven.
      INF: I don't know, my husband did it to me?
      FW: Your husband did what to you?
      INF: He made me this old.

It should be noted that these examples are analogous to the types
of legitimate uses of 'how come' questions where the designated age
does not appear to live up to the real life expectancies of age spans.
In these cases, the general principle for legitimizing the question on
the basis of accepted background knowledge of age spans is applied

to a particular case in order to legitimize the question, even though there may be no previous general information (as a part of our real world knowledge) to suggest that there is a discrepancy between designated and apparent age. While people who tend to interpret 'how come' as a seemingly legitimate question appear to be less likely to accept it as joking behavior (i.e. they are less likely to laugh), it is not necessarily mutually exclusive with the 'obvious' information reading of the question, indicating that they may be recognizing both readings.

2.1 Adult to child. In the previous discussion, I have only mentioned cases where I, as an adult, ask another adult the 'how come' question concerning his or her stated age. Now let us turn to children and see how they respond to this question. For my purposes here, I will consider children to be age six and under, although I think ultimately the classification will be flexible with respect to chronological age and more related to developmental stages with respect to how children relate to certain types of 'obvious' information. One aspect of children's responses comes out immediately when the responses of children are compared with those of adults-- they don't think the question is very funny. That is, they do not seem to accept it as a form of joking behavior playing on obvious information. In none of the 25 exchanges that I have had with children did any of them initially laugh at the question. They seem to accept it as a legitimate question which deserves a serious answer of some type. Most predominantly, this answer is given in terms of a literal justification of their cumulative years or their present age as established by their most recent birthday. The following examples are typical:

(8a) FW: How old are you?
      INF: Five.
      FW: How come?
      INF: Cause I had five birthdays.

(8b) FW: How old are you?
      INF: Five.
      FW: How come?
      INF: Cause my birthday was last week.

While the occasion of various birthdays seems to be the most common literal response to the question, this is not the only criterion that can be given, as the following examples indicate.

(9a) FW: How old are you?
INF: Six.
FW: How come?
INF: Because I'm in kindergarten.

(9b) FW: How old are you?
INF: Four.
FW: How come?
INF: Cause I'm this big (motions with hands his approximate height).

(9c) FW: How old are you?
INF: Three.
FW: How come?
INF: Cause I go to Sunday School.

(9d) FW: How old are you?
INF: Five.
FW: How come?
INF: Cause my tooth is out (points to missing tooth).

While none of the above examples gives a direct reference to age, it is still observed that the children have given what we might call a 'criterion-based response' (i. e. a basis which justifies their present age) and can readily be seen as an extension of the birthday criterion that other children gave. The statement that a child is six because he goes to kindergarten is related to the fact that children of this age level are found in kindergarten. And the three-year-old who stated that he goes to Sunday School is using as a criterion the fact that children are permitted to enter Sunday School when they reach their third birthday. So we see that the principle guiding the children's responses is really quite similar although the realization of the criterion-based response may be somewhat different from child to child.

There is another type of response by children we should look at briefly because it differs somewhat from the ones that we have just presented. This is the response indicating that the question was interpreted to mean something like 'why aren't you older than the age you are'. We thus get the following.

(10a) FW: How old are you?
INF: Four and three-quarters.
FW: How come?
INF: Cause I have a birthday coming up soon.

    (10b) FW: How old are you?
            INF: Four and one-half.
            FW: How come?
            INF: I'm gonna have a birthday soon.

While there are certain analogies between these children's responses and the adults' responses where the question was interpreted in terms of a discrepancy between designated and apparent age, there seem to be essential differences. Children's interpretations appear to be restricted to the immediately successive age rather than a designated and generic apparent age discrepancy.

Interestingly enough, the child's answer of this sort seem to be more typical (although not exclusively) when a child specifies fractions of an age as opposed to whole integers. In this regard, it is instructive to note that age fractions are usually given only by children and adolescents, and, in most cases, are apparently motivated by the desire to achieve the next age level. This motivation, then, may be the reason that the 'how come' question is interpreted to refer to the next successive age.

I must confess that there were several examples in my corpus where children six and under did not know how to answer the question, as typified by the following:

    (11) FW: How old are you?
          INF: Six.
          FW: How come?
          INF: Um, that's a hard question to answer. (Shrugs
                 shoulders, indicating he doesn't know.)

These sorts of responses were, to my surprise, much less frequent than I had actually expected. Whereas I cannot explain all such cases, it may be that some children are reacting more as older children would (cf. Section 2.2), or they may be thrown off by their status relationship to me as an adult asking the question. While such cases do occasionally occur for one reason or another, their relative infrequency is striking. It is noteworthy to mention that none of the children six and under who did not answer the question laughed as if it were intended as some type of joke.

2.2 Adult to pre-adolescents. So far, I have spoken of only two groups' responses, adults and children six years old and under. There is also a group of children between seven and twelve years of age on which I have tested this question. Interestingly enough, pre-adolescents seem to respond in a way which is somewhat different from both children and adults. On the one hand, the children

typically did not laugh as an initial reaction to the question (I got a
couple of smiles), as if I were deliberately engaging in some form
of joking behavior with them. More typically, they looked puzzled,
as if they were not sure whether it was a legitimate criterion-based
question. Unlike the children six and under, they rejected the
criterion-based responses in terms of birthdays (e. g. 'I had eleven
birthdays' or 'I just had a birthday'). Instead, there was a tendency
to simply state the fact without any attempt to justify it. The following example illustrates this.

(12a) FW: How old are you?
       INF: Twelve.
       FW: How come?
       INF: Because I just am.

(12b) FW: How old are you?
       INF: Twelve.
       FW: How come?
       INF: How come? Because that's my age.

They seem to be caught between the adult interpretation of the question which allows for interpretation as a joke on obvious information
or the apparent age and designated age discrepancy, and child interpretation in terms of a criterion-based reason. In other words, they
are now at a level where they recognize that it is not legitimate to
ask questions concerning obvious information. The intermediate
level in which they are caught is exemplified by the hesitancies in
the following examples:

(13a) FW: How old are you?
       INF: Ten.
       FW: How come?
       INF: Because I was--I don't know.
    Third party: (seven-year-old girl) Because she was
                 born ten years ago.

(13b) FW: How old are you?
       INF: Eleven.
       FW: How come?
       INF: Because I was born--I can't help it if I was born.

There does appear, however, to be one way in which pre-
adolescents can legitimize the question as a criterion-based one;
namely, by interpreting it as a matter of calculation from the date
of birth to the present time. We thus get:

(14a) FW: How old are you?
      INF: Eleven.
      FW: How come?
      INF: Because I was born in 1962.

(14b) FW: How old are you?
      INF: Seven.
      FW: How come?
      INF: Cause I was born in 1966.

This sort of response seems to escape some of the 'obviousness' of a criterion-based answer such as 'I had eleven birthdays', while still retaining the criterion base. This response may be interpreted as not quite so obvious, requiring the type of arithmetic ability which might be 'nontrivial' to the pre-adolescent. Without a criterion-based interpretation that escapes the simplicity of simple counting, the question seems to be quite puzzling to the pre-adolescent who is caught between the child and adult world. One twelve-year-old youngster who happened to be present when I was asking a five-year-old how come she was five seemed to be an adequate spokesman for the pre-adolescent group when he said the following (incidentally, the five-year-old child answered the question in the typical fashion we noted earlier for her group):

(15) 12-year-old boy: That's dumb to ask her why she's five.
      FW: How come?
      12-year-old boy: It's just dumb.
      FW: How come it's just dumb?
      12-year-old boy: It just is.

The lack of option as a type of joking behavior and the inappropriateness of answering it with the type of criterion-based response that seems relatively natural for the younger child obviously makes this question most problematic for the pre-adolescent.

2.3 The child fieldworker. In the previous discussion, I think that I have demonstrated that children, pre-adolescents, and adults respond to the 'how come' question relating to obvious information in different ways. At this point in my study, however, I had a nagging suspicion that the responses by the children and pre-adolescents may have been due to a status relationship between the children and the adult fieldworker. Could it be that the different responses were simply a function of the adult-child status relationship? In other words, maybe the children really thought it was a strange question but felt an obligation to respond because I was an adult. In order to find out what influence this status relationship might have had in the data reported here, I therefore trained my six-year-old son Todd to ask this question in various contexts. My son turned out to be an excellent fieldworker, who could learn to ask the question as a normal part of the conversation without giving away the fact that the frame was being purposely structured into the conversation.

With respect to other children, the responses turned out to be quite similar to the responses that I obtained when I served as the fieldworker. We thus get the following responses from children when they are asked the 'how come' question from one of their peers.

(16a) Child FW: How old are you?
    INF: Five.
    Child FW: How come?
    INF: Cause I had five birthdays.

(16b) Child FW: How old are you?
    Inf: Six.
    Child FW: How come?
    INF: Cause I was born six years ago.

We see that these sorts of responses, which typify the responses from his peers, are the same types of responses that I obtained as the adult fieldworker involved in the exchange. A simple justification for age is given in terms of the number of birthdays, or the most recent birthdays.

Similarly, pre-adolescents responded in a way which matched that of the pre-adolescents when the question was asked by an adult. In some cases, there was the same hesitancy that I had experienced from members of this group, while others legitimized it by interpreting the question as a criterion-based one based on an arithmetical calculation more appropriate for their age level.

(17a) Child FW: How old are you?
    INF: Seven and a half.
    Child FW: How come?
    INF: Because I was--I don't know--I just am.

(17b) Child FW: How old are you?
    INF: Eleven.
    Child FW: How come?
    INF: Cause I was born in '63.

The responses of this group and the children informants leads us to the conclusion that there is a real age-grading or developmental aspect to the interpretation. That is, the differences I obtained from the groups were not simply a function of the fact that I, as an adult, was asking the question of children.

There is, however, a difference observed with a child fieldworker when we look at the exchanges between adults and a child. We previously saw that a major tendency of adults was to react to the question as a type of joking behavior (i. e. an extension of an 'obvious information joke'). This, however, does not appear to be the dominant response on the part of adults when a child asks the question. (In only one case out of ten did an adult laugh at the question and the reason for his laughter is questionable.) More typically, responses are given that indicate that the adult will accept this as a legitimate question from a child. One type of response encountered was the more sophisticated type of criterion-based interpretation that we encountered among some pre-adolescents. We thus get:

(18) Child FW: How old are you, Uncle Jerry?
INF: Thirty-seven, I think.
Child FW: How come?
INF: Cause I was born in 1936.

There are also cases where adults respond in terms of the obviousness of the question, along the same lines that some pre-adolescents did. They did not, however, appear to accept it as a type of joking behavior on the part of the child.

(19) Child FW: How old are you, Grandmom?
INF: Why do you want to know that for?
Child FW: I just do.
INF: Sixty-two.
Child FW: How come?
INF: Cause that's when I was born.

Or, an adult may interpret the question as legitimate by extending the reading beyond the realm of obvious information. In these cases, it seems to be interpreted something like 'How did you ever get to be so old?'

(20a) Child FW: How old are you?
INF: I'm about four times older than you, forty-two.
Child FW: How come?
INF: The years just fly by so fast, they're like birds the way they fly.

(20b) Child FW: How old are you?
       INF: Thirty-seven.
       Child FW: How come?
       INF: I don't know why I'm so old, do you know why I'm
             so old?
       Child FW: No.

While the cultural reasons for this sort of extension may be interesting (given how adults and children differ in terms of their outlook
on age), the important aspect of these adult responses is that the
question asked by a child was considered to be deserving of some
type of legitimate or quasi-legitimate response. We may suggest
that the responses by the adults typify a certain cultural regard for
the necessity of answering a child who asks a question. It is, however, interesting to note the difference between these responses by
adults to the child fieldworker and the qualification that children give
for their age. The information considered obvious by the adult is
eliminated from consideration even though this is how children
typically respond. In this regard, it might be interesting to compare how adults responsible for child rearing respond to such questions by their child as opposed to the adults who served as informants
in this study. Although I have only several examples of parents
actually being asked such a question by their children (cf. example
(3)), it may certainly be the case that the question would be answered
differently by an adult in a child-rearing relationship, but this will
have to await more data. What we have evidence for here is the important difference between the response of adults when a child asks
the question and when an adult asks the question. Interestingly enough,
in several cases where I later asked the adult informants what they
thought of the question by the child, they said that it seemed a little
silly, but that they felt obligated to answer it because the child de-
served an answer when asking a question.

3. Conclusion. In the previous sections, the responses of several
different groups have been examined in the context of one simple question frame. It has been seen that children, pre-adolescents, and
adults tend to interpret the question in different ways, and I have suggested why this might be the case. It has also been seen that the age
of the person asking the question may alter its reading for the adults.
    Ultimately, I would like to look at this question in terms of the
broader framework of language and pragmatics. As a part of such
real life experiences, one may say that there is an important distinction between what may be called 'obvious' and 'nonobvious' information. Questions for which one of the readings may involve obvious
information would appear automatically to reject this reading unless

it is considered acceptable as a type of joking behavior related to the
notion of obvious information. It is, of course, important to note
that the distinction between obvious and nonobvious information is
determined by the particular culture, although the basic distinction
appears to be a good candidate for a universal of language as it relates to pragmatics. Thus, one culture may not consider the rationale
for an individual's age to be a matter of obvious information, whereas
another culture (in the absence of birth certificates, conventional
attention paid to calculating age by a particular calendrical system,
etc.) may consider it as nonobvious information. On the other hand,
another culture may consider certain types of information that we
classify as nonobvious to be obvious information.

Because of the peculiar experiences of children in acquiring the
expertise to discriminate between obvious and nonobvious information,
I would also like to maintain that they are, in some sense, exempt
from the norms of questioning that are operative among adults. That
is, it may be all right for a child to ask an obvious information question while adults would have to avoid it. In this regard, I would like
to suggest that the use of obvious information as a type of riddle or
joking behavior may be beyond the capabilities of children because of
their real world experiences. I am now convinced that children who
tell obvious information jokes (e.g. 'Why did the chicken cross the
road?') really may not understand why it is a joke. They may tell it
because an older person related it to them as a joke, but I really
don't think they understand why it is funny. In other words, this type
of verbal exchange is a joke for a child because someone classified
it as a joke, but the reason that it is funny escapes him. I have long
held this suspicion about some of the jokes that children tell, but the
bit of information I have uncovered in this study now gives me a
principled basis for making this claim.

Before concluding, I should mention something about the type of
methodology that was utilized in this investigation. Essentially, I
have used what I considered to be a questionable verbal exchange as
a basis for making decisions about what can and cannot be subjected
to a reason question. In a sense, this appears to be a sociolinguistic
analogue to the determination of grammatical and ungrammatical sentences that has been utilized to great advantage in linguistics for
some time now. The main difference, however, is that instead of
simply asking people how they would react to such a question, I have
placed them in a real life situation in which they were forced to react
in some way. This seems to be more appropriate for certain types
of verbal exchanges, and I think it is more reliable than asking people
to intuit in terms of certain questionable hypothetical sociolinguistic
occasions. Adding the dimension of child fieldworkers allows one to
observe an important difference in terms of an age variable that

would be difficult to hypothesize about in the absence of such a technique. While I may be wrong in some of my conclusions, and need more quantitative data to be certain of others, the study is readily replicable for anyone who questions my conclusions.

Utilizing this methodology, I must admit, has had two deleterious effects. One is that people whom I have told about this study have become suspicious whenever I ask a 'how come' question. This is compounded by the fact that I have, as mentioned earlier, a tendency to ask 'how come' questions that people consider inappropriate as a part of my peculiar style of verbal exchange. The second effect is that people have been giving me some of my own medicine and have been asking me strange sorts of 'how come' questions so that I don't know whether they're serious or not. Both of these I can learn to live with if I can get some more good data.

In a series of lectures given by Charles Fillmore (1973:15), he is drawn to a particular problem of deixis which he feels might be resolved by an experiment in which he walks around with a dirty face to see whether people are willing to talk about it. As it turns out, he is unable to resolve his problem because he is 'naturally . . . unwilling to do that'. While I can certainly not argue with someone else's desire to avoid certain social inconveniences for the sake of ferreting out interesting linguistic facts, it would appear that a willingness to talk with a certain degree of 'sociolinguistic smudge' on our faces may be the price we have to pay in order to get at some of the most interesting problems in the area. Smudged faces may be the coming thing in sociolinguistics.

NOTE

1. The precise relationship of how come to why is still in some dispute. Bolinger (1970:66) notes that how come is a reduction of how comes it that which asks about something previously established, but why is neutral in this respect. Zwicky and Zwicky (1973:926) observe that how come and what for divide the semantic domain of why on the basis of a cause/purpose distinction. In most cases, it appears that why is interchangeable with how come, although there are several grammatical frames (e.g. responses to commands, which are not factual) in which they operate differently (cf. Bolinger 1970:67). These differences, however, do not appear crucial to the questions I am investigating here.

I am not concerned here with the whole range of how come questions which are considered appropriate reason or cause requests. That is, they meet the type of conditions for appropriate questions elaborated by Lakoff (1973).

REFERENCES

Bolinger, Dwight. 1970. The lexical value of it. Working Papers in Linguistics, University of Hawaii, Vol. 2, No. 8.

Fillmore, Charles F. 1971. Lectures on deixis. Unpublished manuscript, Linguistics Department, University of California, Berkeley.

Lakoff, Robin. 1973. Questionable answers and answerable questions. In: Issues in linguistics: Papers in honor of Henry and Renée Kahane. Urbana, University of Illinois Press.

Zwicky, Arnold M. and Ann D. Zwicky. 1973. How come and what for. In: Issues in linguistics: Papers in honor of Henry and Renée Kahane. Urbana, University of Illinois Press.

THE UNIVERSALITY
OF CONVERSATIONAL IMPLICATURES

ELINOR O. KEENAN

University of Southern California

In the past several years, linguists interested in the interpretation
of whole utterances have made use of a number of concepts developed
by philosophers--concepts such as speech act, illocutionary force,
and performative. More recently, some linguists (Gordon and Lakoff
1971, Lakoff 1973, Heringer 1972, among others) have shown interest
in philosophical ideas concerning the organization of conversation. In
particular, there has been a great deal of discussion centering around
ideas of Paul Grice as set forth in lectures entitled 'Logic and Conversation' (1975). In developing such notions, philosophers probably reflect on conversational conduct as it operates in their own society.
The qualification is not explicit, however, and principles of conversational procedure are presented as universal in application. In this
paper, I examine the validity of this assumption, focusing on the work
of Grice, in particular on his notion of conversational maxim and conversational implicature. I examine these concepts in regard to a non-
Western society, that of the plateau area of Madagascar.[1]

Conversational maxim and conversational implicature. In Lecture 2
of 'Logic and Conversation', Grice presents the idea that certain inferences we make from utterances arise from our expectations concerning everyday conversational behavior. There is a certain code of
behavior we expect interlocutors to follow. We expect them to conform to certain 'conversational maxims'. One such maxim is 'Be
relevant'. That is, interlocutors are expected to make their utterances relevant to the topic or direction of the conversation at hand.
When interlocutor A makes a comment or asks a question, he expects

his conversational partner to attend to that remark and respond in a relevant manner, and he makes certain inferences based on this expectation. For example, if A says, 'The football match is cancelled', and B responds, 'There is an energy crisis', A, assuming that B is following normal conversational practice and has addressed his remark to the topic proposed, may interpret B's utterance as providing a reason why the football match is cancelled. Another way of putting this is to say that in the wake of A's utterance, B's utterance implies that the energy crisis is in some way related to the cancelling of the football match. Implications based on our expectation of normal conversational conduct are referred to as 'conversational implicatures' in Grice's analysis. They contrast with implications based on the truth conditions of utterances. That is, the notion 'conversationally implies' is contrasted with the notion 'logically implies'. We say that certain utterances 'logically imply' others just in case the truth of these utterances guarantees the truth of the others. For example, if an utterance A: 'All public events require an admissions fee' is true and an utterance B: 'Football matches are public events' is true, then Q: 'Football matches require an admissions fee' is true. That is, A and B logically imply Q. The implication does not depend on conversational procedure.

One characteristic of logical implication as used in standard logic (not various modal logics) is that it is not culture-dependent or situation-dependent. The implications hold wherever individuals agree on the conventional meanings of the logical words (e. g. all, not, some, and, if-then, etc.). The same cannot be said for conversational implicatures. It is an empirical question as to whether in all societies and in all situations, independent observers agree on the conversational implicature of a given utterance, since the implicature depends on how the utterer is expected to behave with respect to conversational maxims, and these may vary situationally and cross-culturally.

Conversational maxim: Be informative. In this section, I focus on one particular maxim suggested by Grice as basic to the exchange of utterances in conversation. Grice suggests that participants in a conversation are expected to make their utterances as informative as required by the exchange at hand. The maxim as it stands is not helpful, for it can never be violated. The constraint 'required by the exchange' can be stretched to justify the kind or amount of information in each given case. For example, a speaker may provide information that intentionally confuses or misleads the hearer, but one could include the speaker's intention to deceive as part of the definition of the exchange. The speaker, conforming to the requirements of the exchange so defined, would not be violating the maxim: 'Be informative'.

Likewise, one can build into the definition of the situation, intentions of speakers to provide no information or to allude subtly to certain information (Albert 1964). The speaker in each case would be conforming to the requirements of the exchange as defined by himself or by social convention.

When Grice later illustrates the maxim (1975:45), he presents a more precise interpretation: interlocutors are expected to meet the informational needs of their interactional partner(s). That is, if a speaker has access to the information required by the hearer, then he is expected to communicate that information to the hearer. This is, in part, what it means to 'cooperate' (Grice 1975:45) in talk. The maxim thus leads one to expect that when one interlocutor requests specific information, the conversational partner will provide that information, insofar as possible. The verbal response to such a request may conversationally imply what the utterer knows about the material requested. Thus, for example, if speaker A asks 'Where is your mother?' and B responds 'She is either in the house or at the market', then B's utterance conversationally implies that he does not know specifically where his mother is located. He knows only that she is located in one of two places. If speaker B in fact does know at which of the two locations one could find his mother, he has misled the co-present interlocutor and so violated the maxim.

Almost as soon as one presents this interpretation, members of this society[2] can offer cases in which interlocutors do not abide by the maxim. One does not conform to the maxim if to do so would be indiscreet, impolite, unethical, and so on. Grice might argue that interlocutors generally expect the maxim to hold in social interactions. This contention is supported by the social fact that underspecification of information usually implies that the speaker is not able to offer more specific information. At times, however, conforming to the maxim may 'clash' with other interactional maxims (Grice 1975:49); in certain situations, other maxims may take precedence, leading the speaker to violate the maxim 'Be informative'.

In testing this maxim cross-culturally, one does not expect to find that in some societies the maxim always holds and in some societies the maxim never holds. It is improbable, for example, that there is some society in which being informative is categorically inappropriate. Differences between societies, if there are any, are more likely to be differences in specification of domains in which the maxim is expected to hold and differences in the degree to which members are expected to conform to this maxim (Dell Hymes: personal communication). In some societies, meeting the informational needs of a conversational partner may be an unmarked or routine behavior. In other societies, meeting another's informational needs may be an atypical or marked behavior. Let us consider the way in which this

principle operates in Malagasy society, first, with respect to its
markedness and secondly, with respect to its domains of application.

Conversational practice in Madagascar. To what extent does the
maxim 'Be informative' hold for interlocutors in Malagasy society?
Despite certain clashes with other maxims, are members generally
expected to satisfy the informational needs of co-conversationalists?
No. Interlocutors regularly violate this maxim. They regularly provide less information than is required by their conversational partner,
even though they have access to the necessary information. If A asks
B 'Where is your mother?' and B responds 'She is either in the house
or at the market', B's utterance is not usually taken to imply that B is
unable to provide more specific information needed by the hearer.
The implicature is not made, because the expectation that speakers
will satisfy informational needs is not a basic norm.

There are two reasons for this. The first is related to the status
of new information in this society. New information is a rare com-
modity. Villages are composed of groups of kinsmen whose genealogical backgrounds and family lives are public knowledge. Their day-to-
day activities are shaped to a large extent by the yearly agricultural
cycle. Almost every activity of a personal nature (bathing, play,
courtship, etc.) takes place under public gaze. Information that is
not already available to the public is highly sought after. If one
manages to gain access to new information, one is reluctant to reveal it. As long as it is known that one has that information and others
do not have it, one has some prestige.

When one member of the community requests specific information
from another, the addressee is usually reluctant to part with that information for this reason. It is unlikely, therefore, that the informational needs of the requester will be immediately satisfied. In
fact, interlocutors are generally aware of the reluctance to give up
requested information. They expect the response of the addressee to
be less than satisfactory. Normally, if the information requested is
not immediately provided, the two interlocutors enter into a series of
exchanges whereby the one tries to eke out the new information from
the other.

A second and perhaps more significant motivation for revealing
less information than would satisfy the addressee is the fear of committing oneself explicitly to some particular claim. Individuals
regularly avoid making explicit statements about beliefs and activities. They do not want to be responsible for the information communicated. For example, if someone asks 'Who broke the cup?',
hardly any speaker would want to be the one to specify the culprit.
Such a statement may have unforeseen unpleasant consequences for
the speaker and his family, and he alone would have to shoulder the

tsiny 'guilt' for uttering such a claim. Only if the individual is assured that his statement will not bring tsiny will he make the statement.

Even if someone were caught in the act of doing something wrong, one could not directly point at this person to dishonor him directly. One must use special expressions or go about it in a roundabout way. But if by chance there are people who demand that this wrong-doer be pointed out directly, then the speaker must say directly in his talk who the person is. But because he must speak directly, then the speaker must ask the people to lift all tsiny from him. If there is someone in the audience who wants to know more, who does not understand, then he may respond during a break in the talk:

It is not clear to us, sir. It is hard to distinguish the domestic cat from the wild cat. They are the same whether calico or yellow or grey. And if it is the wild cat who steals the chicken, we cannot tell him from the others. The wild cat steals the chicken but the domestic cat gets its tail cut off. So point directly to the wild cat.

It is not only to past events that individuals are reluctant to make explicit reference. There is a clear tendency to avoid making a specific commitment to some future event. Thus, if a member of household X asks a member of household Y when the turning of the ancestral bones is to take place, he will likely get an answer such as 'I am not certain' or 'In a bit' or 'Around September', but no precise date will be specified even if such a date has been set. Individuals do not wish to commit themselves publicly to a precise date until they are absolutely certain the event will take place at that time. They may suffer tremendous loss of face if the event does not take place as specified. They will be guilty of premature or faulty judgment. Consequently, those outside the family are told details of time and place only at the last moment.

This same fear of committing oneself to some future event taking place leads one to hold back certain information when warning, advising, and giving directions. Thus, if speaker A asks speaker B 'How does one open this door?', speaker B may respond with the instruction 'If one doesn't open it from the inside, the door won't open'. That is, speaker B tells speaker A that if he doesn't do X, then Y will not take place. He is not making the stronger commitment and stating that if A does do X, then Y will take place: if you open it from the inside, the door will open. Again the speaker is unwilling to commit himself to the stronger statement, as he cannot guarantee that the action will take place as instructed. He makes a weaker statement using the double negative 'If not X, then not Y'. The

double negative is used in response to many questions seeking information. Thus, when I once asked an elderly woman when I might find
her brother at home, she gave me this answer, 'If you don't come
after five, you won't find him'. She did not say that if I did come after
five, I would find him. She simply told me what would lead to my not
finding this man. In both of these situations, the speaker has not
made his contribution sufficiently informative to meet the purposes of
the interlocutor.

The hesitation to make explicit statements concerning the actions
and beliefs of individuals affects a wide range of speech behaviors.
One finds, for example, that speakers regularly avoid identifying
individuals in their utterances. Many villagers feel that in identifying
an individual, they may bring his identity to the attention of unfriendly
forces. Someone in the world of the living or dead may overhear the
utterance and take note of the individual referenced. Something unpleasant may befall the individual as a consequence of this specification. The tsiny would rest with the utterer. Consequently, terms
of personal reference that specify individuals as distinct from other
members of the community are avoided in favor of terms that do not
make this distinction. For example, speakers generally avoid referring to individuals by the personal name given to them at birth. This
practice is a virtual taboo in the case where the individual referenced
is a child. It is felt, for example, that such a practice can lead to
malevolent ancestral forces taking the child away from the living.
Every effort is therefore made to obscure the child's identity and
to make the child as unattractive to these ancestral forces as possible. Normally, after an official Malagasy name is given to the child,
a second name is given as well. This name is usually a term referring to some unpleasant item--for example, a small child may be
called 'Garbage Girl' or 'Garbage Boy', 'Dung Heap', 'Dwarf', 'Dog
Face', 'Red Face', and so on. Furthermore, this name is usually
shared by a number of children. When a speaker refers to a child as
'Dwarf', he could be talking about any of several children. The
addressee is to identify the referent from other cues. In highly
missionized areas and in areas where children regularly attend
school, a third name is given. This name is a French Christian
name--Suzanne, Jean, Marie, Philippe, and so on. This name,
however, operates in much the same way that the Malagasy nickname
does. Like the nickname, the French name is usually adopted by
several children in a village. Thus, a village could have half a dozen
boys named Jean and several girls with the name Marie. When one
speaks of individuals using these names one is not marking out one
individual as distinct from others.

The sensitivity towards one's personal name decreases as one
grows older. However, even when one is an adult, one does not like

one's name to be casually handled. There remains a strong feeling
that unfavorable events that befall an individual are associated with
the meddling of malevolent forces. It is not unusual for an adult to
change his name following some unpleasant circumstance. In fact,
in the past, name-changing was a frequent occurrence (six or seven
times in a lifetime). At present a national law exists that limits to
three the number of name changes per person.

If one avoids the use of personal names, what are the preferred
alternatives of personal reference? One alternative is to refer to
the individual by some generalized animate noun. A noun referring
to some social category of which the referent is a member is used.
For example, members of a village may refer to one another as
olona 'person', zazavavy 'girl', zazalahy 'boy', ray aman-dreny
'elder', and so on. Thus, a mother once asked her son Mbola mator y
ve ny olona? 'Is the person still sleeping?' in reference to her husband. And another mother once asked her daughter to fetch ny
kulatin'ny olona 'the person's pants', where 'person' referred to the
daughter's sister. Likewise, a young boy once said to me, Misy
zazavavy ho avy 'There is a girl who is coming' and 'girl' referred
to the boy's sister.

This use of personal reference is clearly distinct from the use of
personal reference in our society. 2 When someone in our society
says There is a girl coming, I see a girl, or I see a person, the
hearer infers that the speaker is not intimately associated with the
referent. In fact, Grice brings up this precise usage (1975:56, 57)
as an example of a conversational implicature that may hold in all
contexts. He states:

> Anyone who uses a sentence of the form 'X is meeting a woman
> this evening' would normally implicate that the person to be met
> was someone other than X's wife, mother, sister, or perhaps
> even close platonic friend. . . . The implicature is present
> because the speaker has failed to be specific in a way in which
> he might have been expected to be specific, with the consequence
> that it is likely to be assumed that he is not in a position to be
> specific.

In this society, we ordinarily distinguish in speech individuals with
whom we have an intimate relationship from others with whom we do
not share this kind of relationship. We expect speakers to note in
their utterance intimate relationships such as kin ties, friendship
ties, and so on. We infer from the absence of such specification
that such ties do not hold between speaker and referent. However,
the same cannot be said of speakers and hearers in Malagasy society.
When someone in a Malagasy village says I see a person, those

listening do not infer that the speaker is not closely associated with the referent. Such a format is simply a conventionalized mode of personal reference. It is a way of referring to an individual without bringing harm to him or shame to the speaker himself.

This difference in conversational implicature is seen in the other alternatives of personal reference as well. For example, a second mode of personal reference that is preferred is the use of agent nouns. Thus, a speaker may refer to a closely associated person as 'cow watcher' or 'house builder' or 'teacher' or 'student', etc. A woman could refer to her husband as 'cow watcher', as in the utterance The cow watcher is coming. Or a young boy could refer to his father as a 'house builder', as in the utterance The house builder is hungry. Normally, in our society, speakers do not refer to intimate relationships in this manner. If a young child were to utter this same sentence in our society, we would infer that no special relationship held between the child and referent.

Another preferred mode of personal reference is the use of the indefinite pronoun someone. No lexical item corresponding to this term actually exists in Malagasy. The indefinite is implied but not specified in the utterance. For example, the utterance Misy mitady translates literally as 'There is looking'. However, it is loosely understood as 'There is someone looking'. Again, the suppressed indefinite is used to refer to those intimately related to the speaker as well as to those remotely known to the speaker. Thus, a speaker may be speaking of his brother or wife or close friend in the utterance cited. In our society, however, a speaker who says There is someone looking implicates that he does not know who that someone is.

It is clear from these examples that speakers regularly mask the exact identity of individuals in their utterances. If they must specify an individual, they do so in the least specific sense. In fact, if at all possible, they try to omit any reference to individuals in their utterances. The deletion is made possible by a careful selection of verb voice. In Malagasy, there exist three voices in which a speaker may couch his utterance. Like Indo-European languages, Malagasy has an active voice in which the performer of an action is the subject of the sentence. For example:

Nanasa ny vilia tamin'ny savony iBozy.[3]
washed the dishes with the soap Bozy
'Bozy washed the dishes with the soap.'

Secondly, like Indo-European languages, Malagasy has a passive voice in which the object of the active sentence is made the superficial subject. For example, it is possible to take the direct object ny vilia 'the dishes' and make it the subject of a passive sentence:

Nosasan-iBozy tamin'ny savony <u>ny vilia</u>.
Washed-by-Bozy with the soap the dishes.
'The dishes were washed by Bozy with the soap.'

Furthermore, in the passive voice, it is possible to delete the personal agent of the action entirely. For example:

Nosasana tamin'ny savony <u>ny vilia</u>.
Washed with the soap the dishes.
'The dishes were washed with the soap.'

Given the prevalent attitude towards personal reference, it is not surprising that passive sentences are preferred over the active form. Passive sentences allow the speaker to omit certain critical information, namely, individual agents of actions. Active sentences do not provide this option.

The option of deleting the personal agent is available in yet another voice, the circumstantial. In this voice, some circumstance of the action taking place is made the superficial subject. For example, the time or place of an action, the instrument with which an action is carried out--any such complement may be made the subject. Thus in the sentence given, it is possible to take the instrument with which the action is carried out, <u>ny savony</u> 'the soap' and make it the subject of a circumstantial sentence:

Nanasan'iBozy ny vilia <u>ny savony</u>.
Washed-with-by-Bozy the dishes the soap.
'The soap was washed-with the dishes by Bozy.'

It is possible to restate this sentence with the personal agent deleted:

Nanasana ny vilia <u>ny savony</u>.
Washed-with the dishes the soap
'The soap was washed-with the dishes.'

Whenever speakers wish to avoid specifying individual agents of actions and whenever it is grammatically possible, the passive and circumstantial voices are used.

This preference for passive and circumstantial forms is not well understood by local Europeans. Most grammars of Malagasy written for Europeans begin with an explanation of the active voice. Somewhere around the middle follows a description of the passive form. The last pages may make mention of the circumstantial voice. Many of the grammars are written by Europeans who have assumed that the active voice plays the same role in Malagasy as it does in Indo-

European languages. Consequently, many European residents learn only the active sentence form. Malagasy villagers who come into contact with these Europeans find their speech offensive and much too direct. European speech is generally stereotyped as brusque and impolite. It is clear that in many cases Malagasy speakers provide less information than a European speaker would provide. If a European knows the name of an individual, or the time or place for an event to take place, he normally specifies this in his utterance. A Malagasy speaker normally does not specify these things. The expectations of interlocutors, then, differ in the two societies. And consequently, conversational implicatures differ in these societies.

Situational constraints on the maxim. It would be misleading to conclude that the maxim 'Be informative' does not operate at all in a Malagasy community. We would not be justified in proposing the contrary maxim 'Be uninformative' as a local axiom. Members of this speech community do not regularly expect that interlocutors will withhold necessary information. Rather, it is simply that they do not have the contrary expectation that in general interlocutors will satisfy one another's informational needs.

One can point to certain features of the speech situation that do influence the direction of one's expectation. The expectation that a speaker will observe such a norm varies according to context. Three dimensions of the speech situation influence adherence to or abandonment of the maxim.

(1) The significance of the information communicated. A speaker is more likely to withhold information when that information is significant than when it is not significant. Significance has to do first with the independent access of the hearer to the information. Information which the hearer can easily obtain independently of the speaker is not significant. For example, a pot of rice cooking on a fire is open to inspection by any member of the community. Information relevant to its cooking can easily be obtained and hence such information is not significant. Its relative insignificance means that it is likely to be discussed openly and explicitly. If someone asks, Is the rice cooked?, a straightforward response is likely to be provided. That is, it is likely that members of the community will follow the maxim 'Be informative'.

Information to which the hearer has no independent access becomes thereby more significant. For example, if only two members of a village of fifty inhabitants go to market one day, then those two alone have information relating to market events that day. Possessing significant information, they may well be reluctant to impart details to those who do not have it. If some member of the community asks

a returning villager, What's new at the market?, he is likely to get
an informationally unsatisfactory response. For example, one is
likely to respond There is nothing new or There were many people
(there are always many people at the market). In this context, then,
the maxim is likely to be disregarded.

A second dimension of significance has to do with the consequences
of imparting information. If imparting certain information may in-
cur unpleasant consequences for speaker or referent, then that information is significant. For example, any information whose communication may bring tsiny 'guilt' to the speaker and henatra 'shame'
to the speaker's family is significant. Information relating to the
misdeeds of individuals falls into this category. Consequently,
speakers are generally reluctant to speak openly on such a topic.
If certain information is not likely to lead to unpleasant consequences,
then that information can be considered relatively insignificant.
When communicating this latter kind of information, interlocutors
tend to be more open and specific. When the utterance precludes
the possibility of tsiny, then the speaker is more likely to satisfy
the informational needs of the addressee.

(2) The interpersonal relationship obtaining between interlocutors.
Speakers are more likely to satisfy the informational needs of the
hearer if speaker and hearer stand in some socially close relationship
with one another than if they are not familiar with each other. Those
who are close kinsmen and neighbors (havana) are more likely to provide explicit information to one another than would distant kinsmen
(havan-davitra) or strangers (vahiny). Thus, for example, a havana
of the speaker is more likely to satisfy the question Where is your
mother? than someone who stands in a vahiny relation to the speaker.
(This is not to say that it is likely that the havana will answer explicitly, only that the probability of his doing so is greater than if the
addressee were a vahiny.)

Havana are tied by a network of moral and social bonds. They are
ritually and economically obligated to one another in a way vahiny are
not. It is felt that havana can be more trusted than vahiny. Thus,
there is a feeling of mutual mistrust among villages in regional
cooperative enterprises, because these organizations include vahiny
as well as havana. For this reason among others, cooperative
enterprises have not been successful. One verbal expression of the
attitude is the reluctance of an interlocutor to meet the informational
needs of a co-present vahiny. Speakers are reluctant to specify details of agents and activities, because they are not certain what the
hearer will do with the information. The speaker cannot guarantee
that the hearer will not use that information to damage the reputation
of speaker or referent. This difference in attitude influences the use

of personal reference terminology. Interlocutors are more likely to
use terms that distinguish individuals (e.g. personal names) if
speaker, addressee, and referent stand in a havana relationship
than if a vahiny relationship obtains between any two. The tendency
to mask the identity of the referent (general animate nouns, agent
nouns, indefinite pronouns) increases as the social distance between
interlocutors (and referent) increases. Speakers are careful that
they do not bring the identity of an individual to the attention of those
they mistrust.

(3) The sex of the speaker. The conversational principle 'Make
your contribution informative' is more likely to be upheld by women
than by men. Women are more likely to satisfy the informational
needs of hearers. They are more likely to reveal details of events
of the past or future. This behavior is not, however, well regarded
by members of the speech community. Both men and women say
that women have a lavalela 'a long tongue'. This long tongue may
reveal things which should not have been revealed. Statements which
women make may offend others and bring shame and loss of face to
the family. In general, women are not trusted to communicate information in formal social situations. They are never recruited as
principal spokesmen to represent the family on ritual occasions.
These occasions require careful speech, speech which will not offend
or bring tsiny 'guilt' to the family. Men pride themselves on their
ability to speak cautiously and inoffensively. They feel that they
alone can be speechmakers. The status of speechmaker is highly
regarded in the community. Men who are good speechmakers are
considered tena ray-amn-dreny 'high elders, knowledgeable individuals'. Men, then, strive to achieve this position. To be recruited, a man must use language in the manner demanded of ora-
torical situations. That is, he must use language that does not
injure the reputation of any individual.

Women are excluded from this respected position, and their style
of speaking is not motivated by the possibility that they might qualify
for it. In this sense, they have less to lose by speaking explicitly
and offensively. In fact, they often have something to gain by speaking in a less than ideal manner. They are able to make accusations
(e.g. to answer the question Who broke the cup?), to gossip, to
criticize others. In short, they are able to gain considerable power
from the fact that they are able to hold others accountable for their
actions.

In Malagasy society, then, the same utterance may have different
conversational implicatures, depending on whether the speaker is a
man or a woman. For example, in response to an information question When are you going to market?, a response such as Either today

or tomorrow may be interpreted differently depending on the sex of the speaker (as well as on other features of the nonlinguistic environment). If the speaker is a woman, the response may conversationally implicate that the speaker does not have further knowledge of the matter at hand, for a woman may be expected to answer the question fully if she has the information desired. This is not the case with a man.

Grice tantalizes the ethnographer with the possibility of an etic grid for conversation. However, no ethnographer can be happy with the paradigm as expressed in Grice (1975:48). The conversational maxims are not presented as working hypotheses but as social facts: 'It is just a well-recognized empirical fact that people do behave in these ways, they have learnt to do so in childhood and have not lost the habit of doing so.' Serious research into conversational practice has only recently gotten underway. At best we have restricted analyses of certain dimensions of conversation (illocutionary force, sequencing, situated meaning, etc.). It is difficult for those with experience in the analysis of conversation to accept Grice's proposal by fiat.

But Grice does offer a framework in which the conversational principles of different speech communities can be compared. We can, in theory, take any one maxim and note when it does and does not hold. The motivation for its use or abuse may reveal values and orientations that separate one society from another and that separate social groups (e. g. men, women, kinsmen, strangers) within a single society.

More importantly, Grice's paradigm orients us to pursue the stronger goal of assessing universal conversational principles. Many of those carrying out research in language use are ethnographers. Their work by tradition focuses on speech interaction in a particular ethnographic area. The value of Grice's proposal is that it provides a point of departure for these ethnographers to pool their observations. That is, it invites ethnographers to propose stronger hypotheses related to general principles of conversation.

NOTES

1. From June, 1970 to September, 1970 I carried out anthropological fieldwork in a small village in Vakinankaratra, Madagascar. This research was supported by the National Institute for Mental Health.

2. Western European, academic society.

3. Underscore in the examples indicates subject of sentence.

REFERENCES

Albert, Ethel M. 1964. 'Rhetoric', 'logic' and 'poetics' in Burundi: Cultural patterning of speech behavior. American Anthropologist 66.6, Pt. 2, 35–54.

Gordon, David and George Lakoff. 1971. Conversational postulates. In: Papers from the Seventh Regional Meeting. Chicago, Chicago Linguistic Society. 63–84.

Grice, H. Paul. 1975. Logic and conversation. In: Syntax and semantics: Speech acts, Vol. 3. Edited by Peter Cole and Jerry L. Morgan. New York, Academic Press. 41–58.

Heringer, James T. 1972. Some grammatical correlates of felicity conditions and presuppositions. Ohio State University Working Papers in Linguistics, No. 11:1–110. Columbus, Ohio, Ohio State University Department of Linguistics.

Lakoff, George. 1973. Fuzzy grammar and the performance/competence terminology game. In: Papers from the Ninth Regional Meeting. Chicago, Chicago Linguistic Society. 271–291.

THE HOWS AND WHYS OF PERSIAN STYLE: A PRAGMATIC APPROACH

WILLIAM O. BEEMAN

Brown University

1.0 Introduction. A decade ago social anthropologists were admonished by Edmund R. Leach (1961) to stop 'butterfly collecting'--that is, to stop the mere description and classification of social systems, and get on with the business of trying to formulate the general principles of operation of social systems. Although formal linguistics in general has been struggling with the problem of general principles of operation in the study of syntax, I feel that it might be well for those of us engaged in the study of variation in language to pay some attention to Leach's admonition.

As Leach implies (1961:2-3), mere descriptivism is in a sense tautological. 'It merely reasserts something you know already in a slightly different form'. With regard to the study of variation in language this means that once variation is discovered and characterized, the increasingly sophisticated formulation of 'rules' and typologies to express that variation is an exercise in the construction of ever more exacting tautology.

There is nothing intrinsically wrong with this kind of exercise, but I fear that in concerning ourselves with it exclusively we will eschew the possibility of dealing with the really central question in the study of linguistic variation, namely: 'Why this particular variation and not another, varying in this particular way and not another, in this particular context and not another?'

2.0 A pragmatic approach to language. As a basis for a first attack on this general problem, I would like to introduce a few observations about communication in general derived from the pragmatic writings of Charles Sanders Peirce (1955). Peirce has not been dealt with sufficiently in either the study of language or the study of society, although his ideas are extremely seminal for both.

It is not well understood that Peircean pragmatism encompasses at once a theory of sign phenomena and a theory of phenomenology. He further demonstrates how the latter encompasses the former in the well-known statement: 'Consider what effects, that might conceivably have practical bearings, we conceive the object of our conception to have. Then our conception of these effects is the whole of our conception of the object'.

For Peirce, all phenomena consist of three elements which are the results of human capacities of perception: firstness, or the essential nature of phenomena--their quality as abstracted from instances of their occurrence; secondness, or the manifestation of phenomena in concrete reality; and thirdness, or the ways that the relationship between the essential quality of phenomena and its manifestation are interpreted. [1]

Peirce's basic statement of pragmatism, cited earlier in this section, cannot be properly understood unless we realize that the process of the conception of the effects of an object involves a process of interpretation, which itself involves either existential relationships between phenomena manifestations and what they import for the person engaging in conception, or convention which is governed by common social agreement, which I regard as a cultural variable.

The beauty of Peirce's system is that it can be used to analyze any object of our conception, even abstractions, such as the concept of 'language'. In a pragmatic sense, then, what can be done with the phenomena of language in terms of analysis depends directly on one's pragmatic conception of language itself.

There has been a recent and important shift taking place in the study of language, and this too can be treated according to a Peircean trichotomy, delineating assumptions about (1) the essential nature of language, (2) the ways in which that nature is manifested, and (3) the ways in which language is interpreted or understood.

The 'old paradigm' declares that (a) language is a cognitive system separable from other forms of human action; (b) units in language are distinguished solely by differences in their characteristics, so that distinctive features are interchangeable with the parameters of formal paradigms; and (c) the relationship between actual linguistic forms and the ways that they are understood is arbitrary.

The 'new paradigm' declares that (a) language cannot be conceptually separated from the context of its occurrence; (b) the units of language are distinguished by the differences in the characteristics of their context of appearance; and (c) the relationship between particular linguistic forms and the ways that they are understood is explicable and understandable, in terms of its pragmatics both in synchronic and diachronic perspective.

It is really this final point, first brought to my attention by Paul Friedrich (1972), which I aim at explicating. To assume that a relationship is arbitrary is simply another way of saying that one cannot deal with it or refuse to deal with it. The question as to whether one can account for the reasons that a particular variation in language occurs in a particular way is inexplicable if one feels that the two or more units resulting when a variation is noted are distinguished solely by qualities which are perceivable in their form. When it is understood that the essential qualities of the variation imply pragmatically the requirements for their interpretation, then the relationship between form and meaning is no longer arbitrary.

The approach I advocate here is not only pragmatic, but must be of necessity ethnographic, for one must be able not only to understand the language forms and their variation, but also the 'cultural logic' by which language behavior in general is interpreted. If verbal behavior is inseparable from the concepts of its occurrence, as I have maintained, then the relationship between the constraints on nonverbal action and the constraints on verbal action should be similar, for similar circumstances.

3.0 The study of Persian variation. I now wish to examine several selected instances of variation in Persian in illustration of the explanatory approach I have just outlined. Material for this study is derived from my own continuing research on Iranian speech style (Beeman 1972, 1974), and from the observations of other researchers in this field such as Hodge (1957), Boyle (1952), Vahidian (1342/1963), Newton et al. (n.d.) and Jazayery (1970). In this series of explanations, I first present examples of variation occurring in Persian speech, then a characterization of the situations in which these variations occur. Finally, I suggest reasons why the particular variations occur (and not others), and why variation occurs in the way that it does.

3.1 The sounds of speech. The essential quality of speech from a phenomenological point of view is characterized in a description of the sound system of language. This corresponds to a Peircean 'firstness'. In standard Persian there is a great deal of variation within the sound system of speech as it is differentially produced in varying sociocultural contexts. Some of this variation might properly be considered morphophonemic in nature; however, several purely phonetic shifts do occur in the language. The most common of these shifts is the reduction of sounds in some contexts which occur in others. It is this type of variation which I consider here.

3.1.1 Reductions. There are three principal sound reductions operative in Persian: (1) deletion of /h/ and /'/ in all but word initial position; (2) neutralization of /r/; and (3) deletion of final elements within consonant clusters. All of these variations are context sensitive.

3.1.1.1 Reduction of /h/ and /'/. Tendencies in speech style lead to the deletion of both /h/ and /'/ in all positions except phrase initially. The following examples serve to illustrate realizations of these two sounds in different styles:

(1a) /da'i/ 'maternal uncle' [da'í] → [daí]
(1b) /mo'omen/ 'pious' [mo:'mén] → [mo:mén]
(1c) /mo'æssese/ 'institute' [mo:'æssesé] → [mo:æssesé]
(1d) /ræ'd/ 'thunder' [ræ'd] → [ræd]

(2a) /sægha/ 'dogs' [sæghá:] → [sægá]
(2b) /mahi/ 'fish' [mahí] → [ma:í]
(2c) /sobh/ 'morning' [sobh] → [sob]

3.1.1.2 Deletion of /r/. /r/ is deleted postconsonantally and word finally in some styles. The tendency for deletion is so strong as to extend beyond morpheme boundaries. Examples (3a) and (3b) demonstrate the deletion of postconsonantal /r/ and the retention of postvocalic /r/ in the addition of the objectivizing particle /-ra/. Examples (4a) and (4b) demonstrate normal postconsonantal deletion of /r/ in final position. Examples (5a), (5b), and (5c) show the deletion of word final /r/

(3a) /sægra didæm/ 'I saw the dog' [sæghá: di: dæm] → [sægo didæm]
(3b) /gorbera didæm/ 'I saw the cat' [gorbéra: di:dæm] → [gorbéro didæm]
(4a) /sæbr/ 'patience' [sæbr] → [sæb]
(4b) /æsr/ 'evening' ['æsr] → ['æs]
(5a) /digær/ 'other, more' [di:gaér] → [digé]
(5b) /næxeir/ 'no' (emph.) [næxeír] → [næxé]
(5c) /četor/ 'how' [četór] → [četó]

3.1.1.3 The reduction of final consonant clusters. There is a general tendency in Persian to reduce word final consonant clusters to a single consonant. However, this reduction does not proceed according to a simple rule. At times the second element in the consonant cluster is deleted, and at other times it is not. The following

examples illustrate. Examples (6a) to (6f) show the deletion of the
second element in the cluster. Examples (7a), (7b), and (7c) show
the retention of both elements.

(6a) /abr/ 'cloud'   [æbr] → [æeb]
(6b) /sætl/ 'pail'   [sætl] → [sæt]
(6c) /sæxt/ 'difficult'   [sæxt] → [sæx]
(6d) /dust/ 'fruit'   [duːst] → [dus]
(6e) /cæšm/ 'eye'   [cæšm] → [cæš]
(6f) /jæmb/ 'next to'   [jæmb] → [jæm]
(7a) /zærd/ 'gold'   [zærd] → [zærd]
(7b) /vaqf/ 'religious bequest' [væqf] → [væxf]
(7c) /šæms/ 'sun'   [šæms] → [šæms]

If one examines the sounds which are preserved in final consonant
clusters vs. the sounds which there is a tendency to reduce in varying speech styles of Persian, one sees that affricates (/f, v, s, z, š, ž,
ɉ, x, h/) have the greatest tendency to be retained as the second element in a consonant cluster. Stops are retained in about half of all
possible combinations, and liquids and nasals (/r, l, m, n/) are nearly
always deleted when they occur in second position in a consonant
cluster (cf. Beeman 1974). Looking at deletion from the standpoint
of the first element in the consonant cluster, the greatest tendency for
deletion in a final consonant cluster occurs when the first consonant
is a fricative, and the greatest tendency for retention occurs when the
first consonant is a liquid or nasal. Thus, the following relationships
can be set up between sound elements in final consonant clusters.

TABLE 1. Deletion tendencies in final consonant clusters.

Tendency to be deleted as second element in consonant cluster:	Tendency to be associated with deletion of second element when serving as first element in consonant cluster:	
highest	liquids/nasals (+sonorant)	fricatives (+strident)
second	stops (+plosive)	stops (+plosive)
lowest	fricatives (+strident)	liquids/nasals (+sonorant)

3.1.2 Situations in which reductions occur. The tendency to delete particular sounds in Persian is associated with several differentiated social dimensions. In a highly seminal article dealing with
language choice among individuals who had learned Hebrew as a
second language in Israel, Herman (1968) suggests that three principal complexes of factors influence the choice of one or another alternative language that a person may choose to employ: (1) the background of the individuals involved in interaction, (2) the personal
needs of the individual, (3) the immediate situation in which interaction occurs. It is striking that this schema also serves well in
characterizing the complexes of factors that are associated with the
deletion/retention of the sound elements in Persian cited earlier in
this paper.

As in Herman's study, in Iran one may speak of the controlling
tendencies in a given situation of verbal interaction in terms of (1)
the controlling social ethic, (2) the controlling individual expressional ethic, and (3) the controlling arena of activity. I am going to
describe each of these briefly.

In Iranian society, considerations of perceptual relationships to
others in terms of hierarchies of unequal relationships and complexes
of equality relationships are highly active in governing individual
interaction behavior. Furthermore, correct marking of these differences or similarities in human interaction is an activity which con-
sumes immense amounts of time and energy in any social situation in
Iran. The system of ta'ārof in Iranian interaction, which one might
gloss in English as 'ritual courtesy' provides a tool for the constant
assessment of the qualitative nature of the social differences that
exist between members of any particular constellation of individuals
who find themselves in a particular arena of interaction at any one
time (cf. Loeb 1969; Beeman 1972). Because inequality is relative
to shifting constellations of individuals, hierarchical relationships
require constant testing and thus an overdetermined communicational
system for that testing. Equality relationships have, on the other
hand, no need of being tested. They embody an ethic of absolute
sacrifice, and absolute understanding between individuals involved in
them.

These two dimensions constitute a social ethic when they are projected onto particular situations of interaction. To see how perceptions of human relations and principles which are operative in human
interaction can be generalized to perceptions of interaction contexts
can be seen in the phenomenon of 'dressing for an occasion'. The
interactions one anticipates in some specifiable future context cause
one to consider how he will identify that context, and what he should
do about his outward appearance (and his mode of communication)

to meet the principles of interaction and environment operative in that context.

In the Iranian situation, then, the perception of symmetry and asymmetry between oneself and other actors constitutes the basic core of the social ethic underlying immediate interaction situations. The pragmatic communicative reflex of that core is overdetermined communication within situations which one perceives as embodying asymmetrical relations within which one must find his own place, and underdetermined communication within situations which one perceives as embodying symmetrical relationships which demand openness, sacrifice, and absolute understanding.

The individual expressional ethic concerns a person's feeling about his ability to operate within different contexts--the degree of 'freedom' he feels in personal expression in interaction. Being able to deal freely with people and say whatever one wishes is expected in situations involving symmetrical relationships. This same behavior in situations involving asymmetry in social relations is labeled pejoratively as por-rou'i 'brashness, audacity', literally, 'full-face'. In asymmetrical situations one is expected to be cognizant of the status of perceptual superiors, and restrict one's behavior. The expectation in this situation is for one to behave with humility, reticence, and bashfulness. A person who behaves this way even in situations where it is not expected is labeled in a slightly pejorative manner as kæm-rou, literally, 'little-face'. The communicative ethics concerning personal freedom in expression depend on an individual's being able to perceive social situations correctly. A person who is reticent and formal with his same-age, same-sex cousins in private would be behaving in an odd manner. Those individuals with whom he was interacting would interpret his expressions as expressions of anger. Likewise, a person who is por-rou is liable to be chastened for his behavior by persons who hold actual power over him: his parents, employers, or political superiors.

Restricted expression in asymmetrical relational situations means paradoxically that the codes of expression must be highly overdetermined and redundant in order for understanding to take place at all. In the Iranian royal court on state occasions, very little goes on other than exact formulaic ritual greeting reinforced by body gestures which replicate the elaborated language. In private with an old schoolmate, body postures are totally relaxed, almost amorphous, as individuals sprawl on a carpeted floor and speak with expressions which may be incomprehensible to anyone but the two individuals involved because of the extreme communality of understanding that both share.

The immediate situation impinges on behavior as it is defined as birun 'outer' or andarun 'inner'. These two concepts are extremely

meaningful and potent in Persian, corresponding as they do to the
sufistic concepts of zāher and bāṭæn (cf. Beeman 1974; Bateson et al.
1974), the external and internal aspects of one's own individual
nature. [2] Traditionally, the inner andaruni was the most private
secluded area of a man's residence--the women's quarters. The
biruni was the place of public reception. These are not just physical
locations, but states of mind as well. The Tehrani family going on a
picnic takes its andarun with it to the outdoors by bringing carpets,
cooking utensils, a samovar, and all the accoutrements of home. A
person traveling to another town will have innumerable locations
available to him where he can be in an andarun--where he can put on
pajamas, take off his street clothing, nap, and eat around a family
dinner cloth. Usually, this is in the home of friends or relatives;
thus it becomes vital that at least one set of social considerations in
marriage be assurance of the fact that members of one family can
indeed become admittees to the andarun of the other family.

Whether a situation is defined as more birun or andarun affects the
social relations between individuals. Two brothers sprawled on the
floor when alone in a room will pull themselves to a cross-legged
sitting position when their father or an uncle enters the room. A
son addresses his mother more respectfully in public and in the
presence of her brothers than in private. Two intimate friends
defer to each other politely when with others in a public restaurant
over, say, a place to sit, but feel free to seat themselves anywhere
when alone together. This is due in part to the ethic governing
symmetrical interpersonal relationships mentioned earlier, where
individuals are expected to protect the interests of their friends and
intimates. The proverbial Persian admonition: zaher-ra hefz kon
'protect the external (appearances)' extends to one's symmetrically
related intimates. Thus one demonstrates to others that one's
brother, cousin, companion, or crony is a person worthy of respect.

One also must protect one's own external appearances. Ostenta-
tion, fine dressing, and fine manners are the hallmark of Iranian
social relations. One never understates one's own social position in
situations which one defines as birun. Thus behavior in general in
birun situations as opposed to andarun situations is overly determined, overstated, and highly redundant.

The three dimensions combine to form interlinked semantic dimensions along which various kinds of appropriate behavior can be
arranged. It may be useful to think of the basic pattern in interaction
consisting of a correspondence between the three dimensions I have
mentioned: (1) the controlling social ethic--asymmetrical vs.
symmetrical social relational prescriptions, (2) the controlling individual ethic of behavior--restricted vs. free expression in social
interaction, and (3) the controlling arena of activity--birun or 'outside'

situations vs. andarun or 'inside' situations. Arranged schematically, the three dimensions appear in Table 2.

TABLE 2. Three dimensions controlling social interaction.

social ethic	asymmetrical → symmetrical
individual ethic	restricted expression → free expression
arena of activity	outside (birun) → inside (andarun)

The sound reductions mentioned in this section correspond directly to this schema. The tendency for /h/ and /'/ to be deleted, the tendency for /r/ to be deleted, and the tendency for final consonant clusters to be reduced all increase as (1) the social ethic being invoked tends to be that of symmetrical social relationships rather than asymmetrical social relationships, (2) the individual engages in free as opposed to restricted expression, and (3) the arena of activity is perceived as more 'inside' than 'outside'.

3.1.3 Sound variation and the pragmatics of interaction. The foregoing provides an account of the variation and its context of occurrence, but our stated purpose in this discussion is to go somewhat beyond this and attempt an explanation of the reasons why these particular variations occur and why they occur in the way that they do.

In order to attempt an explanation of the reasons why particular sounds are deleted in some social contexts, it is necessary to have a little more information about the sounds in question and their role within the Persian language.

Any explanation of these phenomena at this point is bound to be speculative to a degree. One attempt to account for the variation exhibited here hinges on formulating an account of how sounds in language are conceived and perceived by speakers, and dealt with in the pragmatics of conversational interaction.

3.1.3.1 Redundancy in language and sound reduction. An important and interesting study of sound distribution in Persian was completed by Jiři Krámský (1948) some twenty-five years ago. In this study, Krámský, in an extensive computational survey, investigated the frequency of participation of classes of sounds in positioning in monosyllabic words in Persian.

In Krámský's study we see that the consonant which has the most frequent participation in final position for all Persian words is /r/. Indeed, /r/ has the greatest participation of all consonants in all positions. Returning to our earlier description of variation, we see that /r/ is the only consonant which is reduced not only in consonant cluster, but also intervocalically, and as an initial consonant following internal phrase juncture, the latter property which it shares with /h/ and /'/.

From Krámský's study it can be determined that fricative consonants dominate in participation in final consonant clusters as a class over other consonant classes. However, individual members of the fricative class have the lowest degree of participation in consonant clusters. Liquids and nasals exhibit opposite characteristics, having low frequency of participation as a class in consonant clusters, but also having low information content as a class due to high individual participation in consonant clusters. This information is summarized in Table 3.

TABLE 3. Distribution of Persian consonantal phonemes in final consonant clusters (after Krámský 1948) (S=228).

	1st member	2nd member
+ plosive	59 (21.5%) 9.83/member	70 (30.7%) 11.83/member
+ strident	96 (42.1%) 8.72/member	93 (40.8%) 8.82/member
+ sonorant	73 (32.5%) 14.6/member	65 (28.5%) 13.00/member

Comparing Table 3 with Table 1, one could hypothesize the following:

    1. If a consonant in a cluster is to be deleted, it will be the final consonant.

    2. The probability of a final consonant being deleted increases as a function of the information carried by the class of sounds participating in the cluster, as in Table 4.

The pattern which we set up for consonant deletion in consonant clusters works very well for the case of /r/, which, as mentioned earlier, has the highest participation of any sound element in Persian, according to Krámský. According to the foregoing schema, one would predict its deletion in a wider variety of situations due to its low information content, which is in fact the case.

TABLE 4. Probability of deletion of second element in final
consonant cluster.

		Information carried by second element		
		+ strident high	+ plosive medium	+ sonorant low
Information carried by first element	high + strident	low	high	high
	medium + plosive	medium	medium	high
	low + sonorant	low	medium	low

/h/ presents a much more interesting case. Krámský lists /h/
as a fricative in his investigation. However, /h/ does not behave
like other fricatives in its deletion pattern. In point of fact, its
deletion pattern resembles that of /'/ much more than that of
/f, v, s, z, etc./ Both /h/ and /'/ are associated with vowel length
and accent in their usage, which is retained when the sounds are
deleted.

(8a) /soja'/ 'courageous'   [soja'] → [soja:]
(8b) /bæd/ 'bad'   [bæd] → [bæed]
(8c) /bæ'd/ 'afterwards'   [bæ:'d] → [bæ:d]
(8d) /ræfte'id/ 'you (pl.) went'   [ræfte:'id] → [ræfte:id]
(9a) /mah/ 'moon'   [mah] → [ma:]
(9b) /ruh/ 'face'   [ruh] → [ru:]
(9c) /sægha/ 'dogs'   [sægha:] → [sæga]

Vowel length has not been discussed in this paper, but in general,
the range of variation in vowel length shifts in Persian as follows:

/a: i: u: ⟶   /a   i   u
 æ   e   o/   æ   e   o/

Thus, presence of either /h/ or /'/ in one stylistic pole is associated with the vowel preceding it being marked in terms of the vowel
system for that particular style, i.e. tending towards shortening of
the normally long vowels /a:/, /i:/, and /u:/, and lengthening the
short vowels /æ/, /e/, and /o/ at one stylistic pole; this results in

the lengthening of both sets of vowels, thus causing them to be like-wise marked at the other end of the opposite stylistic pole where vowel length does not occur as a regular feature. For examples of this see items (8a), (8b), and (8c), and (9a) and (9b).

Examples (8d) and (9c) give situations where /h/ and /'/ are associated with the only suffixes in Persian with initial consonants, which are accented. The accents are retained at both stylistic poles as the characteristic of the particles in question even as /h/ and /'/ are deleted.

In the first instance, then, /h/ and /'/ are redundant particles with respect to the marked nature of vowel length and accentuation that accompany them. The contrastive vowel length is retained at both ends of the stylistic pole and the redundant /h/ and /'/ are dropped. In the second instance, the accents characteristic of the two suffixes are retained as the distinguishing characteristic of those particles, and the redundant /h/ and /'/ are again deleted.

3.1.3.2 Redundancy in interaction and sound reduction. What I now mean to suggest is that there is a definite relationship between the pragmatic nature of the contexts in which sound deletions occur in Persian, and (1) the types of sounds that are deleted, and (2) the pattern of their deletion. In general, in contexts where individuals assume the social ethic associated with asymmetrical relationships with others, where they feel the imperative for restricted expression, and where they feel that they are in a context which is defined as 'outside' rather than 'inside', their behavior is more over-determined, more redundant, and more overstated. This is one of the ways that individuals have of signalling to others what kind of situation they feel themselves to be in, and what kind of behavior they will be engaging in during that situation. Situations where symmetrical relations determine the social ethic, where personal expression is free, and where the situation is felt to be more 'inside' than 'outside' demand behavior which is in general less determined, less redundant, and more understated. This is not to be thought of as an absence of the behavioral elaboration occurring at the other situational pole, but rather as a positive set of actions which indi-viduals use to demonstrate that they are in a symmetrical relational, freely expressive, or 'internal' situation to other persons who par-ticipate in that situation.

Linguistic behavior in such situations should follow the general pragmatic principles that obtain for all behavior in such situations. That is, it should be more redundant and overdetermined at one pole, and less redundant and less determined at the other pole. In fact, I have given some indications that this is the case. In the instance of sound deletions, it is the most redundant elements with the least information content that have the greater probability of being deleted in contexts where a general reduction in redundancy is required as a concomitant of the action that can be carried out in those contexts.

4.0 Conclusion. The data given here is suggestive rather than conclusive, but I sincerely hope that it has been suggestive enough to encourage other persons to seek to formulate true explanations of variation phenomena in language rather than limiting themselves to simple problems of description.

NOTES

Research on which this paper is based was carried out partially under a grant from the Wenner-Gren Foundation for Anthropological Research, whose help is gratefully acknowledged. Institutional support during my stay in Iran was granted both by the Institute for Social Studies and Research of the University of Tehran and Pahlavi University, to which I am likewise grateful.
1. Unfortunately, space does not permit a complete discussion of Peirce's theory of signs in which these three levels of cognitive perception are applied in defining both the nature of sign phenomena and their application in the phenomenological world. Justus Buchler's edition of Peirce's writings contains a good excerpt of most of those articles which are important for the present discussion.
2. Note the following quatrain by Khayyam:

Guyand marâ ke mei-parastam hastam
Guyand mara 'âref o mastam hastam
Dar zâheram negâh besyârí makon
Kandar bâtan čunânke hastam hastam

They say of me how wine's great friend I am
They say of me how wise and drunk I am
Don't look too hard at my external state
Internally, that which I am I am

REFERENCES

Bateson, Mary Catherine, J. W. Clinton, J. B. M. Kassarjian, H. Safavi, and M. Soraya. 1974. Safa-yi Batin, A study of a set of Iranian ideal character types. Psychology and Middle Eastern studies. Edited by Norman Itzkowitz and L. Carl Brown. Princeton, N. J.: Princeton University Press.

Beeman, William O. 1971. Interaction semantics: A preliminary approach to the observational study of meaning. M. A. thesis, Department of Anthropology, University of Chicago.

Beeman, William. 1972. Stylistic strategies in Iranian interaction. Paper presented at the 71st Annual Meeting of the American Anthropological Association, Toronto, November 29–December 3.

Beeman, William O. 1973. Is there an Iranian national character? A sociolinguistic approach. Paper presented at the Seventh Annual Meeting of the Middle East Studies Association, Milwaukee, November.

Beeman, William O. 1974. The meaning of stylistic variation in Iranian interaction. Ph. D. dissertation, Department of Anthropology, University of Chicago.

Boyle, J. A. 1952. Notes on the colloquial language of Persia as recorded in certain recent writings. Bulletin of the School of Oriental and African Studies 14. 451–462.

Friedrich, Paul. 1972. On the notion of arbitrariness in language. Unpublished MS.

Herman, Simon R. 1968. Explorations in the social psychology of language choice. In: Readings in the sociology of language. Edited by Joshua A. Fishman. The Hague, Mouton. 412–511.

Hodge, Carleton T. 1957. Some aspects of Persian style. Lg. 33. 355–69.

Jazayery, M. A. 1970. Observations on stylistic variation in Persian. Actes du Xe Congrès International des Linguistes. Vol. III. Bucharest. Editions de l'Académie de la République Socialiste de Roumaine. 447–457.

Krámský, Jiří. 1948. A phonological analysis of Persian monosyllables. Archiv. Orientální 16. 103–134.

Leach, Edmund R. 1961. Rethinking anthropology. London: University of London, Athlone Press.

Loeb, Laurence D. 1969. Mechanisms of rank maintenance and social mobility among Shirazi Jews (Iran). Paper presented at the 68th Annual Meetings of the American Anthropological Association, New Orleans.

Newton, John et al. n. d. Notes on ta'arof and polite language in Persian. Tehran, American Peace Corps.

Peirce, Charles Sanders. 1955. The philosophy of Peirce, selected writings. Edited by Justus Buchler. London, Routledge and Kegan Paul.

Vahidian, Taqi. 1342/1963. Dastur-e Zabān-e 'Āmiāneh-ye Fārsi (Grammar of colloquial Persian). Mashhad, Iran, Ketāb Forushi-ye Bāstān.

SEMANTIC SYSTEMS, DISCOURSE STRUCTURES, AND THE ECOLOGY OF LANGUAGE

JOEL SHERZER

University of Texas at Austin

Two current dominant concerns of sociolinguistics are the analysis of linguistic variation and the analysis of discourse. This paper focuses on the second concern, though it suggests one type of relationship existing between both of them.

The search for rules and principles of discourse requires combinations of insights and techniques from various disciplines--philosophy, linguistics, anthropology, sociology, and literary criticism, among them. One of the major recent contributions of philosophy and linguistics has been the extension and abstraction of the domain for formal description--from surface structures to deep structures; from sentences to speech acts and events; from inner- and inter-sentential relations to extra-sentential presuppositions. This has involved an increasing recognition that analysis of what is said requires analysis of what is not said. Social interactionists have focused attention on the ways language is used to do social work in everyday interaction; one interesting way they have gone about this is by looking at natural speech in terms of interchanges or utterance pairs.

I want to discuss here a different kind of discourse organization principle--one relating semantic or lexical systems and discourse structure. My primary example will be drawn from research among the Cuna Indians of San Blas, Panama. But I think the example raises questions that go beyond the Cuna, perhaps beyond the South American Tropical Forest, to societies such as our own.

The Cuna example is <u>kapur ikar</u> 'the way of the hot pepper', a curing chant[1] used against high fever. I will discuss the structure of a large portion of the chant which involves the projection or playing out of a lexical taxonomy (types of kapur 'hot pepper') onto a parallelistic verse pattern. A complete understanding of kapur ikar requires analyzing it in relation to Cuna ethnography of speaking in general.

Kapur ikar 'the way of the hot pepper', like other Cuna curing chants, is performed by the 'knower' of the chant to wooden suar mimmi 'stick dolls', typically placed under the hammock of the patient. Although the chant is for the benefit of the sick person, the addressees are the stick dolls. The chant is performed in a language the stick dolls understand; and after hearing the chant, it is they who will go about doing the curing. One characteristic of Cuna curing chants is that they are extremely long, often lasting several hours at a time. In addition to phonological, morphological, and syntactic features distinguishing the suar mimmi 'stick doll' language from colloquial Cuna, there are special lexical items used in the chants, lexical items which are often particular to single chants or even versions of them. These lexical items refer to the sick person, the chanter, the hammock, and to various objects relating to the disease and its cure. In the case of the kapur ikar 'the way of the hot pepper', one predominant lexical specialization is the proliferation of names for types of kapur 'hot pepper' in the suar mimmi language. It is believed that mentioning or naming objects like kapur in their own language is an important aspect of controlling and directing them.

There are various versions of kapur ikar, corresponding to various schools, various teachers, and students of this chant in San Blas and in the nearby Darien jungle, also inhabited by Cuna. Each of these versions describes the disease, the sick person, his relatives, etc. for the stick dolls. And each must also name the types of kapur 'hot pepper'. In one of the versions I have recorded, 53 different types of kapur are named. These types of kapur are not named randomly, but rather in systematic fashion, from both a semantic point of view and within the chant itself. The naming of the kapur takes place within a long portion of the chant in which a particular pattern, with some slight variation, is repeated 53 times. In each repetition a different type of kapur is named. The resulting discourse structure makes explicit the semantic taxonomy of kapur used by the performer of the chant. The taxonomy is shown in Figure 1, where a, b, c, etc. are the types of kapur 'hot pepper' and x, y, z, etc. are subtypes, usually named for colors.

This semantic taxonomy--types of kapur 'hot pepper'--is plugged into a parallelistic pattern of the chant structure in a systematic way, namely, by beginning at the top, moving down for each type and subtype until it is completed, and then moving on. Thus, first kapur itself, then a, then x under a, then y under a, then z under a, then q under a, then b, then x under b, then y under b, etc. (Some variation and switching are possible. [2]) The verse pattern is as follows:

in the north
name of kapur
name of type of kapur
name of subtype of kapur
is named
the flowers are perceived
the leaves are perceived
the stems are perceived
the seeds are perceived

FIGURE 1. Semantic taxonomy of kapur.

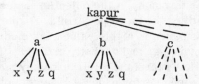

This example, as presented so far, represents an instance of a
relationship between what anthropologists call 'ethnoscience' and
what literary critics call 'poetics'. In essence it is an elaboration
of what Roman Jakobson has called the poetic function or principle
in language--the projection of a paradigmatic axis onto a syntagmatic
axis. Here the paradigmatic consists of the lexical taxonomy--types
of kapur 'hot pepper'; the syntagmatic consists of the parallelistic
verse pattern.

The example raises further questions with regard to Cuna language
and society. These questions can be grouped in two related categories
--linguistic variation and ethnography of speaking. With regard to
linguistic variation, the taxonomy of kapur 'hot pepper' used in kapur
ikar 'the way of the hot pepper' is different from that used in everyday
colloquial Cuna in two ways. The labels are different. The kapur
'hot pepper' labels used in the chant are those of the suar mimmi
'stick doll' language. Furthermore, the taxonomy seems to be more
elaborate than that used in everyday speech. I have not yet carried
out a systematic study of lexical variation among the Cuna. But preliminary investigation seems to indicate that in the area of medicinal-
curing plants and animals there is considerable variation--not only
between everyday language and ritual language, but also among the
different types of ritual and ceremonial language themselves--that of
chiefs, medicine men, various chant 'knowers', puberty rites
specialists, etc. (For a general discussion of Cuna linguistic
varieties, see Sherzer 1975.) Some of this variation involves the
fullness or completeness of taxonomies such as those for kapur, i.e.

whether x, y, z, etc. are present or not. [3] But there may also be variation in the organizational structure of the semantic field as a whole. [4] It is quite probable, then, that the elaborate taxonomy of kapur discussed here does not exist in the Cuna language independent of its use in kapur ikar. Rather, the full taxonomy is both drawn on for the chant and actually defined in the performance of the chant. [5]

A related question raised by 'the way of the hot pepper' has to do with Cuna ethnography of speaking in general. Cuna medicinal and related chants involve the use of verbal means to control such objects as plants and animals. An important aspect of this control is the naming of the object in the appropriate linguistic variety (thus showing knowledge of its origin). What better way to do this than systematically to go through the taxonomy of the object(s) in question--the more and the fuller, the better, the more powerful. Furthermore, for the Cuna, length of performance is highly valued, as medicinally effective, rhetorically convincing, and verbally artistic. The combination of a parallelistic pattern and a full taxonomy makes possible the production of very long performances. I might note also that such systematic use of a taxonomy provides a mnemonic memorization device valuable in a nonliterate society. Finally, an important aspect of Cuna ethnography of speaking is the existence of various special linguistic varieties, whose primary manifestation is lexical. Thus the elaboration of types of kapur 'hot pepper' is a striking expression and manifestation of one such linguistic variety and a performer's knowledge of it.

Before leaving the Cuna, let me suggest that I strongly suspect that the principle I have just discussed in kapur ikar is also at work in others within the rich set of Cuna ritual and ceremonial genres and that it might be fruitful to look at other Tropical Forest groups from this perspective as well.

I have argued here, on the basis of a single and perhaps special example, for the importance of looking at discourse from the perspective of the projection of paradigmatic systems (semantic or otherwise) onto syntagmatic patterns. A corollary is that uses of speech or discourse structures actually serve to define or elaborate certain linguistic subsystems. I would like to use the term 'ecology of language' to label this situation, i. e. the fact that subsystems of language are resources or potentials that are (1) projected onto discourse structures and (2) defined in full only in the context of their use.

Let me now briefly present some other examples. First, a famous English ballad, 'The Gallows Tree,' this version recorded in Indiana. It is as follows (from Brewster 1940:125-127):

1.   'Slack your rope, hangs-a-man;
      O slack it for a while;
  I think I see my father coming,
      Riding many a mile.

2.   'O Father, have you brought me gold,
      Or have you paid my fee?
  Or have you come to see me hanging
      On the gallows tree?'

3.   'I have not brought you gold;
      I have not paid your fee,
  But I have come to see you hanging
      On the gallows tree.'

4.   'Slack your rope, hangs-a-man;
      O slack it for a while;
  I think I see my mother coming,
      Riding many a mile.

5.   'O Mother, have you brought me gold,
      Or have you paid my fee?
  Or have you come to see me hanging
      On the gallows tree?'

6.   'I have not brought you gold;
      I have not paid your fee,
  But I have come to see you hanging
      On the gallows tree.'

7.   'Slack your rope, hangs-a-man;
      O slack it for a while;
  I think I see my brother coming,
      Riding many a mile.

8.   'O Brother, have you brought me gold,
      Or have you paid my fee?
  Or have you come to see me hanging
      On the gallows tree?'

9.   'I have not brought you gold;
      I have not paid your fee,
  But I have come to see you hanging
      On the gallows tree.'

10. 'Slack your rope, hangs-a-man;
    O slack it for a while;
  I think I see my sister coming,
    Riding many a mile.

11. 'O Sister, have you brought me gold,
    Or have you paid my fee?
  Or have you come to see me hanging
    On the gallows tree?'

12. 'I have not brought you gold;
    I have not paid your fee,
  But I have come to see you hanging
    On the gallows tree.'

13. 'Slack you rope, hangs-a-man;
    O slack it for a while;
  I think I see my lover coming,
    Riding many a mile.

14. 'O Lover, have you brought me gold,
    Or have you paid my fee?
  Or have you come to see me hanging
    On the gallows tree?'

15. 'Yes, I have brought you gold;
    Yes, I have paid your fee,
  Nor have I come to see you hanging
    On the gallows tree.'

The structure of this ballad involves the projection of a simple paradigm onto a parallelistic verse pattern. The paradigm is the set of kin or relative terms. The 'lover' can be viewed as either a marked member of such a set or else not a member of the set at all, as shown in Figure 2.

FIGURE 2. Taxonomy of kin terms in the ballad 'The Gallows Tree.'

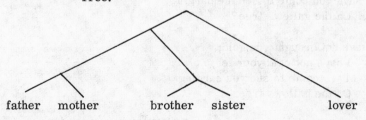

father   mother   brother   sister   lover

In any case, the rhetorical effect of the ballad depends on the placement of the lover last, in the final verse-trio, together, of course,
with the shifts from negative to positive and positive to negative
(another paradigm) in the final verse.

Children's rhymes and language games often provide examples of
the principle I am discussing here, as well as often illustrating playing with the principle as part of the process of language and speech
learning. Thus Sanches and Kirshenblatt-Gimblett, in their paper on
children's speech play, cite a well-known jump-rope rhyme (from
Withers 1948:141):

I went downtown
To see Mrs. Brown
She gave me a nickel
To buy a pickle.
The pickle was sour,
She gave me a flower.
The flower was dead,
She gave me a thread.
The thread was thin,
She gave me a pin.
The pin was sharp,
She gave me a harp.
The harp began to sing,
'Minnie and a minnie and a ha ha ha.'

What is interesting here is that the phonic-rhyming cohesion seems in
excess as compared with the concomitant lack of complete semantic
congruity. That we feel this to be the case argues for the existence
of some kind of semantic paradigm underlying coherent discourse.
Children who perform this rhyme are often probably as aware of the
semantic incongruities as we are and enjoy the rhyme as language
play. Adults also enjoy such play and interplay with the projection of
phonic and semantic paradigms onto syntagmatic structures, as is
shown by this dialogue between Vladimir and Estragon in Samuel
Beckett's Waiting for Godot (1954:48):

Vladimir: Moron!
Estragon: Vermin!
Vladimir: Abortion!
Estragon: Morpion!
Vladimir: Sewer-rat!
Estragon: Curate!
Vladimir: Cretin!
Estragon: Crritic![6]

From adults again, and from another part of the world, there is the intriguing example of Rotinese (in Indonesia) ritual language, as described by Fox (1975). Rotinese ritual language consists of pairs of lines whose parallelism is based on lexical sets (dyadic sets). The pairs of words in each set manifest various kinds of semantic relationship, reinforced by their use in the parallelistic verse structure. One way in which members of dyadic sets can be related is the following: one member is from an eastern Rotinese dialect and one from a western Rotinese dialect. This is an excellent example of what I have called here linguistic ecology, in that various types of lexical relationship, including dialect differences, are drawn on in the creation of ritual language. Rotinese ritual language thus seems to define dialect differences as one kind of lexical-semantic relationship. Furthermore, Fox's description strongly suggests that one of the reasons that Rotinese dialect differences (often rather slight) have persisted is because of their important role in the formation of dyadic sets, crucial to the ritual language.

One might object at this point that all of my examples have been drawn from a particular class of discourse--formal, ceremonial, ritual, literary, relatively fixed, single-speaker. This is true to a degree. The examples do, though, manifest considerable variety within such a class; and such styles of speaking or types of discourse are well worth studying in and for themselves. In addition, I propose --more as a question at this point than as a definitive claim--that systematic rules of projection of linguistic paradigms or subsystems onto syntagmatic structures may well be worth studying in more spontaneous, casual, natural speech. This would mean focusing on the use of the poetic principle (in Jakobson's sense) in everyday speech (not the same thing as studying the poetry of everyday speech). [7]

My final example, then, is from the opposite end of the formal-casual continuum in speech. It results from an exercise I have been giving students in classes for several years. 'In the course of any verbal interaction, with any others, in any way, request repetition of the speaker.' [8] The result is a quite spontaneous, casual, unrehearsed, two-participant speech event, with the structure in Figure 3, where A and B are the participants, 0 the original utterance, (?) the request for repetition, and R the repetition. [9]

FIGURE 3. Repetition discourse structure.

A: 0
B: (?)
A: R

The problem (and here I use problem in the sense of Schegloff and Sacks (1973)) for A (actually for A and B together) is to say in R what he thinks B 'missed' in 0 so that he can get back into the verbal interaction that B 'interrupted'. Though R is sometimes an identical repetition of 0, it often is not. In fact, 0's relationship to R often manifests the existence of particular linguistic subsystems shared by the speech community(ies) of which A and B are members, or particular personal understandings shared by A and B alone. To reformulate this example in the terms I have been using here to discuss other examples, Figure 3 is a discourse structure onto which are projected (must be projected in order for this discourse structure to be 'solved', completed properly) miniparadigms of various kinds. These paradigms may be phonetic, as when R differs from 0 in that R is louder or slower, or the vowels of R are longer or the consonants more aspirated (on the table: on the THAABLE). Or 0 may be in slang and R in a more standard form (or vice-versa --notice here that I am talking about A-B definitions of slang). Or 0 and R might be rough paraphrases of one another (paraphrase here being understood as A and B agreeing, obviously not consciously, to treat R as in some way equivalent to 0, or as a clarification, explanation, etc. of 0 so that they can get on with their discourse business). Or 0 is an imperative form and R is a more polite form of a command. (Open the window: would you open the window.) Or, as in examples from language use in the Chicano community in Austin, Texas, [10] 0 might be in English and R in Spanish (Where are you going?: ¿Dónde vas?). Or other pairs of linguistic varieties A and B share 0 and R (again from the Chicano community in Austin: limpiamos la yarda, you know: limpiamos el solar, you know). (Or 0 is in a local dialect of Arabic and R is classical Arabic.) These 'potential' mini-paradigms, projectable onto the simple discourse structure, can be represented as in Figure 4.

FIGURE 4. 'Mini-paradigms' potentially projectable onto the discourse structure in Figure 3.

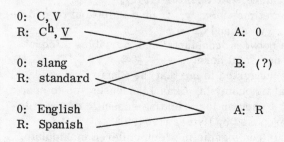

0: C, V
R: C^h, V   A: 0

0: slang
R: standard   B: (?)

0: English
R: Spanish   A: R

etc.

I use the term 'potential' here (for the paradigms on the left side of the arrows) to stress what I have been calling the ecological aspect of these paradigms--the fact that they exist as linguistic resources in a particular speech community (or just in the shared speech of A and B) and can be, and in fact are, drawn on when needed, as in the case reported here--quite spontaneously, when asked to repeat.

This example from spontaneous speech is particularly interesting precisely because it involves a very common discourse pattern-- something we all do often, every day (repeat what we say at the request of others), which taps or, actually, sets in motion a wide range of linguistic paradigms or subsystems, by projecting them onto the simple discourse pattern.

In this paper, I have investigated one basic principle of discourse in a variety of different manifestations. This principle is the projection of paradigmatic systems of language onto syntagmatic discourse structures. I think my examples suggest several areas or questions for future research: (1) to look more carefully, fully, and formally at the full range of principles by which paradigmatic systems get projected onto syntagmatic discourse structures--from conversational genres to more formal ways of speaking; (2) to ask how this principle of discourse is related to other basic principles of discourse (notions of textual cohesion as discussed by Bellert, Halliday, and others; conversational implicature; adjacency pairs; etc.); and (3) to ask what kinds of linguistic variation (phonological, lexical, grammatical, etc.), in what kinds of speech communities and groups within speech communities, become evident and are exploited and manipulated in the process of discourse organization.

NOTES

Research among the Cuna Indians was supported by NSF grant USDP GU1598 to the University of Texas and an NIMH small grant.
1. I use the term 'chant' for what the Cuna call ikar or 'way'. For a much fuller discussion of the place of Cuna curing chants in Cuna ethnography of speaking, see Sherzer (1975).
2. For example, sometimes an x, y, z, or q is left out or ordering is reversed among x, y, z, and q.
3. Kay's distinction between 'constants' and 'variables', 'core' and 'periphery', might be useful here.
4. Brian Stross has suggested to me that the Cuna ritual specialists are botanical taxonomists, Cuna Linnaeuses, so to speak.
5. Such an approach to semantics, relating semantic contrast to usage in context, was proposed by Hymes (1964:4-5).
6. An interesting children's game in which children manipulate, display, and compete in competence in the projection of lexical

taxonomies is <u>Categories</u>, performed by groups of children in a round. I am indebted to Richard Bauman and others involved in his project on children's folklore for discussions concerning the relationship between children's folklore and the ideas raised in this paper.

7. I owe this observation to Dina Sherzer.

8. In the terminology of Merritt (this volume), this would be a request for 'playback'.

9. Notice that 0 can involve a wide range of speech acts and events--declarative statements, questions, commands, narration, etc.

10. These examples are drawn from the ongoing research of Lucía Elías-Olivares into varieties of language use in East Austin.

REFERENCES

Bauman, R., and J. Sherzer, eds. 1975. Explorations in the ethnography of speaking. Cambridge and New York, Cambridge University Press.

Beckett, S. 1954. Waiting for Godot. New York, Grove Press.

Brewster, P. G., ed. 1940. Ballads and songs of Indiana. Bloomington, Ind., Indiana University Press.

Fox, James. 1975. Our ancestors spoke in pairs: Rotinese views of language, dialect, and code. In: Explorations in the ethnography of speaking. Edited by R. Bauman and J. Sherzer. Cambridge and New York, Cambridge University Press.

Hymes, D. H. 1964. A perspective for linguistic anthropology. In: Horizons of anthropology. Edited by Sol Tax. Chicago, Aldine. 92-107.

Jakobson, R. 1960. Concluding statement: Linguistics and poetics. In: Style in language. Edited by T. A. Sebeok. Cambridge, Mass., MIT Press.

Kay, P. 1976. Constants and variables of English kinship semantics. [This volume, 294-311.]

Merritt, M. 1976. The playback: An illustration of the need for the study of discourse. [This volume, 198-208.]

Sanches, M., and B. Kirshenblatt-Gimblett. n.d. Children's traditional speech play and child language. In: Speech play. Edited by B. Kirshenblatt-Gimblett. Philadelphia: University of Pennsylvania Press. 65-110.

Schegloff, E. A., and H. Sacks. 1973. Opening up closings. Semiotica 8. 289-327.

Sherzer, J. 1975. Namakke, sunmakke, kormakke: Three types of Cuna events. In: Explorations in the ethnography of speaking. Edited by R. Bauman and J. Sherzer. Cambridge and New York, Cambridge University Press.

Withers, C. 1948. A rocket in my pocket. New York, Holt.

CONSTANTS AND VARIABLES
OF ENGLISH KINSHIP SEMANTICS

PAUL KAY

University of California

I have argued elsewhere (Kay 1973a) that the basic, invariant core
of the system of kinship semantics of all dialects and varieties of English consists of five binary predicates: SELF, PARENT (the relation
of parents to children), SIBLING, NUNCLE (the relation of aunts and
uncles to nieces and nephews), and COUSIN. In addition, the singulary
predicates MALE and FEMALE are of course involved, but these are
not specific to kinship and have no specialized meaning in kinship contexts.[1] The five basic predicates are in turn defined by formulae of
Grafik, a universal kinship algebra (Atkins 1972a, b; forthcoming).
The few technical aspects of Grafik that are of concern here are
briefly and informally explained as follows.[2]

Any consanguineal relation can be thought of as a tracing of con-
secutive child-of and parent-of links from one of the related persons
up to a common ancestor and then down from the common ancestor to
the other person. We use 'Q' to stand for child-of and 'P' to stand for
parent-of. Since our focus is on the kin relations themselves rather
than on particular individuals, we do not proceed in terms of a particular ego and alter, but rather express the relation independently of
ego-alter direction. Specifically, we normally express generationally
asymmetric relations in the direction senior-to-junior; for examples
in the form of Grafik employed here, 'Pat is the child of Leslie' is
expressed by the same formula as 'Leslie is the parent of Pat':
'PARENT (Leslie, Pat)'. (For discussion of the substantive motivation for this approach, see Kay 1973a, especially note 6.)[3] By
convention, the 'child-of' part of the tracing is always written first.
Thus, the relation diagrammed in conventional form in Figure 1(a)

which is called in my dialect 'first cousin once removed', is given the Grafik representation of Figure 1(b), and corresponds to the English phase of Figure 1(c).

FIGURE 1. 'First cousin once removed'.

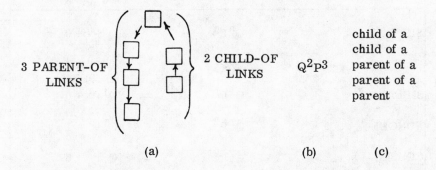

3 PARENT-OF LINKS

2 CHILD-OF LINKS

Q^2P^3

child of a
child of a
parent of a
parent of a
parent

(a)   (b)   (c)

Since by convention the number of child-of links is always smaller than or equal to the number of parent-of links, the exponent on P may be expressed as the sum of the exponent on Q and a (possibly zero) residuum. Thus, in Figure 1, the exponent on Q represents the length of the shorter branch, ascending to the common ancestor (i. e. 2), and the exponent on P may be expressed as the sum of this number and the residuum (i. e. 2 + 1). This way of splitting things up is not arbitrary. The number of links in the shorter chain corresponds to 'degree of collaterality' in the sense of Lounsbury (1956:168n) (which in turn corresponds to the notion of collateral distance attested for modern Chinese; see Atkins 1972a:17ff., 1972c). The residuum, the number of links by which the longer chain exceeds the shorter, is the generational separation of the relation, in this case unity. Following Atkins (1972a) we use 'ν' (Greek nu) for Lounsbury's 'degree of collaterality' (= Atkins' 'collateral removal' 1972c:19) and 'δ' (Greek delta) for generational distance. In general, a consanguineal relation may be expressed in terms of the two parameters collateral removal ν and generational distance δ, as in (1).

(1) $Q^\nu P^{\nu+\delta}$

When $\delta = 0$, we have a 'same generation' of 'zero generation' relation.[4] Equipped with these preliminaries we may express the semantic structures underlying the basic predicates of English kinship (Table 1).

TABLE 1. Basic predicates of English kinship terminology and
their Grafik representations in compact and expanded
form.

Basic predicate	Compact form	Expanded form $\nu \; \nu \quad \delta$
SELF	$Q^0 P^0$	$Q^0 P^0 + 0$
PARENT	$Q^0 P^1$	$Q^0 P^0 + 1$
SIBLING	$Q^1 P^1$	$Q^1 P^1 + 0$
NUNCLE	$Q^1 P^2$	$Q^1 P^1 + 1$
COUSIN	$Q^2 P^2$	$Q^2 P^2 + 0$

It can be seen in Table 1 that--ignoring the singulary sex predicates MALE and FEMALE, which are peripheral to the logic of the
system--there is just one primitive predicate necessary to model
all English consanguineal relations, PARENT-OF ('P'). CHILD-OF
('Q') may, of course, be defined as the converse of PARENT-OF
(Kay 1973a, Atkins 1972a; forthcoming). In order to extend the analysis to affinal relations as well, we need add only the primitive
SPOUSE-OF, written 'M' for marriage. Atkins (1972b:1) has given
a general formula for the semantic representation of the English
noun phrase my relative. This is easily converted to the definition
of the English predicate, or deep morpheme (Talmy 1972; Kay 1972b,
note 3) BE-RELATED-TO, [5] where M, Q, P, ν, δ, and ϕ are defined as already indicated and u, v are variables taking the values
zero or one.

(2) BE-RELATED-TO = df $(M^u Q^v P^{v+\delta} M^v)^\phi$ $(u \leq v)$

The relations shown in Table 1 are, to my knowledge, present in
all dialects and varieties of English. Upon these relations are based
the definitions of the terms father, mother, sister, brother, son,
daughter, uncle, aunt, niece, nephew, and cousin (Kay 1973a: Table 2).
These facts are constants of English kinship semantics. They appear to constitute the semantic core of a system that has remained
stable over centuries and across continents and gives every evidence
of remaining so for the foreseeable future. Attention is now directed
to the meanings of certain bound morphemes that combine with the
basic terms just listed to produce morphologically complex kinterms.

It is in this area that interpersonal variation is found, although there is much here also that is constant across dialects. Among these data some general patterns regarding the distribution of constant and variable features may be observed: (1) the fewer the linguistic implications of a feature, i. e. the less a change in this feature entails adjustments elsewhere in the system, the more likely it is to vary among speakers; (2) some variable features have clear sociogeographical correlates, although most do not. [6]

The four classes of superficial morphemes with which we are concerned are (1) great, grand, (2) -in-lâw (not to be confused with the noun ín-làw(s) (Kay 1973a: note 4), (3) the expression by marriage and the uses of the nuncle and nibling terms to refer to relatives by marriage, and (4) first, second, . . . and once removed, twice removed, . . . as applied to cousin. The semantic representations underlying all of these forms involve the use of predicate modifiers (Kay 1973a). I will express the relationships in the form of 'rules' employing arrows. One may, and I prefer to, think of these 'rules' as supplied with inessential 'X-' and '-Y' end-variables (Postal 1971: 106-110) on both sides of the arrow and to interpret them as transformations in the accepted sense (insofar as there is one). I give partial justification for this weak preference elsewhere (Kay 1973a: note 6). I have, however, no compelling arguments for this preference and one may equally well consider these 'rules' as rules of semantic interpretation or projection if one prefers an interpretivist semantics, or as meaning postulates in either a generative or interpretive semantic framework. In fact, I can find no outstanding arguments to be made for unequivocally classifying the generalizations encompassed in these 'rules' into any particular part of any extant grammatical theory, and thus regard them merely as empirical generalizations that offer interesting challenges to existing grammatical theories. From now on, I am going to discuss these matters in the terminology of generative semantics, i. e. in a way that assumes underlying syntactic structures and semantic representations to be the same. In so doing, I commit myself to this assumption to the extent that it provides at present the most convenient vocabulary for talking about the facts I have to discuss.

Atkins' standard Grafik conventions use the symbols u, v for variables whose values range over $\{o, 1\}$; h, k for variables ranging over the natural numbers; and ϕ for a variable with the values $\{-1, +1\}$. The rules that follow are adapted from the 'b' versions of the rules in Kay (1973b). They have been simplified in superficial form here by incorporating the side restrictions into the main body of the rule, as urged by Atkins (personal communication), and by dropping inessential (syntactic) variables, in the sense of Postal (1971:106-110). This makes the parallel with the defining expressions of Atkins (1972b) much more apparent. There are also some minor substantive changes.

great, grand
(3) $Q^{up^{u}+2+h} \rightarrow$ GREAT $Q^{up^{u}+1+h}$

The way this rule operates is discussed in detail in Kay (1973a) and is, in fact, the only rule discussed in detail there. I repeat here only some observations regarding variation in lexical insertion rules that operate after the application of rule (3). Repeated application of rule (3) eventuates in one of two results: a sequence of (h-1) GREAT's followed by $Q^{0}P^{1}$, or a sequence of (h-1) GREAT's followed by $Q^{1}P^{2}$. $Q^{0}P^{1}$ is replaced by PARENT and $Q^{1}P^{2}$ by NUNCLE. In either case, all dialects replace all but the last instance of the deep morpheme GREAT by the surface morpheme great. In the case of PARENT, all dialects replace the last instance of GREAT with grand. In the case of NUNCLE, dialects differ, some speaking of great uncles and grand nephews, some of great uncles and great nephews, etc. There does not seem to be any particular correlation between these usages and social geography that I can discover. Some idiolects may optionally delete all instances of great before any nuncle term, yielding uncle as an optional variant for great uncle (or grand uncle), great great uncle, etc. In some idiolects this may be obligatory. Again, I am aware of no regional or social predictors of these variant usages; Casson (1973:190) refers to the dialect he reports, which has optional reduction of great uncle, great great uncle, . . . to uncle, as 'my own dialect of American English (Southside Chicago)', which suggests that he considers his own usage to be shared throughout the area indicated. Whether this areal homogeneity has been observed by Casson or is merely assumed is difficult to judge.

-in-law
(4) $(M^{u}Q^{w}PM)^{\phi} \rightarrow Q^{w}P$ IN-LAW $(u \le w)$ inclusive dialect
$(u = 0)$ exclusive dialect

The inclusive dialect is, I believe, the more recent usage; spouse's siblings' spouses are considered siblings in law; for example, a man's wife's brother's wife is considered his sister-in-law. A personal anecdote may illustrate the lack of geographical correlation with dialect. My wife and I were raised 150 miles apart (Laurel, Miss., and New Orleans, La., respectively). Soon after marrying, I had occasion to refer to my wife's sister's husband as my brother-in-law (inclusive dialect). My wife corrected this usage saying that brother-in-law cannot be used that way, and I accepted this, supposing I had just learned English wrong in that respect. More than ten years later

I heard my mother use the term brother-in-law in a context that appeared to require the inclusive dialect interpretation. Questioning revealed that she had always used the inclusive dialect, which explains where I had gotten that usage. Since that time I have asked many Americans about their usage of brother-in-law/sister-in-law and found no geographical or apparent social correlation with the inclusive/exclusive dialect difference. An interesting aspect of the story is that it was possible for me to go for more than ten years without running across evidence in naturally occurring speech which demonstrated clearly that a large proportion of the speakers I was in contact with used the inclusive dialect that I had been raised on and had abandoned. One may conjecture that the inclusive dialect is newer and is part of a number of changes gradually creeping into the English system which reflect a tendency to think of the world of kinship as a series of sentimentally connected spouse pairs or nuclear family groups rather than as a series of individuals connected by specific ties of blood and law (Schneider 1968). This is purely a conjecture, but there are other changes taking place in the system, discussed further on, which are also explained if this conjecture is correct.

uncle by marriage, aunt by marriage, niece by marriage, nephew by marriage

(5) $MQ^1P^2 \rightarrow Q^1P^2$ BY-MARRIAGE

Rule (5) accounts for the 'affinal' senses of the nuncle terms by means of a later rule which simply deletes the deep morpheme BY-MARRIAGE, obligatorily in some dialects and optionally in others. Again, the variation does not seem to have any social or geographical correlation or significance. Rule (5), incidentally, shows that terms such as uncle are not polysemous (cf. Casson 1973) and do not require disjunctive definitions (D'Andrade 1970) in any interesting sense of those terms, both of which have generally been used by anthropological linguists in a way that presupposes a single structural level of syntax.

It may not be concluded from this, however, that Q^1P^2 and MQ^1P^2 (or Q^1P^2-BY-MARRIAGE) are distinct in underlying structure in the sense that this term is ordinarily used by generative semanticists. As McCawley (to appear) correctly points out, the usual test for ambiguity (nonidentity of underlying structure) versus vagueness shows that a term like uncle is vague not only between the meanings 'mother's brother' and 'father's brother' but equally between either of these and 'mother's sister's husband' or 'father's sister's husband'. A sentence such as (6a), for example, may be correctly used to describe the facts given in (6b).

(6a) One of my uncles is bald and so is one of Harry's.

(6b) My mother's brother is bald and Harry's father's
sister's husband is bald.

If these were all the relevant facts, we should conclude that rules
like (5) were either meaning postulates or interpretive rules (or perhaps some kind of new pretransformational rule that operates before
the level of 'underlying' structure is reached), but certainly not
ordinary transformations. McCawley appears to conclude that the
matter is as simple as testing for ambiguity versus vagueness and
so finds that terms such as uncle are vague as between 'mother's
brother', 'father's brother', 'mother's sister's husband', and 'father's
sister's husband'. This, in turn, predicts that 'the semantic structure of "x is y's maternal uncle" will simply be "x is related to y
through y's mother" conjoined with "x is y's uncle"' (McCawley to
appear:4-33). But unfortunately, the latter is not true; 'x is y's
maternal uncle' cannot be used appropriately when x is in fact y's
mother's sister's husband. In general, maternal and paternal can
cooccur with only underlying Q^1P^2, but not with underlying MQ^1P^2
(or Q^1P^2 BY-MARRIAGE). One's mother's sister's husband may
not be referred to as his maternal uncle. (It could be that the difference here is truly a dialect difference between McCawley and myself,
but that seems unlikely. In any case, my dialect is shared by everyone with whom I have discussed the problem who has maternal-/
paternal- at all; and the facts of this dialect will need explaining.) It
appears that, contra McCawley, the difference between consanguineal
and 'affinal' nuncles shows itself to be a structural one both semantically and syntactically, while this is not the case for the nuncles on
the father's side versus those on the mother's side. Just how this
fact is to be incorporated into linguistic theory I am unfortunately not
able to say. It seems, moreover, that what is at issue is not just an
isolated fact but rather the linguistic status to be accorded 'rules'
such as (3), (4), and (5) and those of a similar nature discussed
further on and in Kay (1973a). [7]

Cousin. The most complex and interesting area of dialect variation in English kinship terminology arises in the methods of counting
(or not counting) cousins. As far as I have been able to determine,
most, but not all, speakers in North America and the British Isles
belong to one of three major groups of dialects: (a) those who do not
count cousins in any way, either restricting cousin to first cousins or
using cousin both for first cousin (Q^2P^2) and also for any consanguineal relative (optionally that relative's spouse also) more distantly
related than nuncles or niblings ($Q^{2+h}P^{2+h+k}$ or $MQ^{2+h}P^{2+h+k}$); (b)

those who count cousins according to rule (7); (c) those who count cousins according to rule (8).

(7) $(Q^{2+h}P^{2+h+k})^{\phi} \rightarrow \underline{(h+1)}TH\ Q^2P^2\ \underline{k}\ \text{TIMES-REMOVED}$

(8) $(Q^{2+h}P^{2+h+k})^{\phi} \rightarrow \underline{(2h+k+1)}TH\ Q^2P^2$

The way rules (7) and (8) work is illustrated in Figure 2.

FIGURE 2.   Illustration of operation of rules (7) and (8).

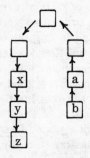

Pair of individuals	Values of h and k	Name of relation under rule (7)	under rule (8)
(a, x)	h=0 k=0	first cousin	first cousin
(a, y)	h=0 k=1	first cousin once removed	second cousin
(a, z)	h=0 k=2	first cousin twice removed	third cousin
(b, y)	h=1 k=0	second cousin	third cousin
(b, z)	h=1 k=1	second cousin once removed	fourth cousin

By rule (7) the children of siblings are first cousins, the children of first cousins are second cousins, and so on. The number of TIMES-REMOVED k is, of course, just the generational separation (i. e. δ, the number by which the exponent on P exceeds the exponent on Q); the number of the cousin (i. e. first, second, etc.) is $\nu-1$, one less than the collateral removal of the relation, since SIBLING inhabits the first degree of collateral removal.

Rule (8) dispenses with the notion of removal and may be a historical simplification of the former dialect. I should hasten to add that I have no direct evidence for this conjecture, which is based principally on the fact that the second dialect is simpler and the system in general seems to be moving toward simplification and attenuation of the classification of more distant relatives. [8] According to rule (8), first cousins are defined in the same way as in rule (7), i. e.

Q^2P^2, and each link in each branch leading up to or down from a first cousin relation adds unity to the number of the cousin. Dialects (7) and (8) are the only fully productive ways of counting cousins in English that I have come across, excluding asymmetric dialects--about which more later on. Both are present in both Britain and North America and show, from my unsystematic sampling, no obvious regional or social correlates within these areas. I would guess that intensive investigation would uncover both of these dialects in other English-speaking areas such as Australia, New Zealand, and South Africa, but I have not performed such an investigation. [9]

I now discuss a few dialects of cousin terminology, which I provisionally class as 'minor', in order to give the reader some idea of the range of variation existing in English. The first family of dialects is known to me only from New Zealand and appears to be widespread there, thus violating the general tendency of variable kinship classification to show no correlation with geographical variables. [10] In the first subdialect of this family, first cousin refers to the relation Q^2P^2 (as in all dialects of English), second cousin designates Q^2P^3 (the relation designated first cousin once removed in the dialect (7) which I hypothesize to be the oldest), and all more distantly related consanguineals are designated forty-second cousin [sic]. Third cousin is recognized as a minority variant usage for forty-second cousin. [11] The second subdialect of this dialect uses the same surface forms, but with slightly different meanings. First cousin, of course, means Q^2P^2. Second cousin, however, designates not first cousin once removed, Q^2P^3, but the relation called in the hypothesized original dialect (7) second cousin, Q^3P^3. Forty-second cousin (or again, alternately, third cousin) designates any consanguineal relation more distant than Q^3P^3. This, of course, leaves the first cousins once removed unaccounted for. These are referred to with asymmetric, complex expressions depending on the direction of seniority; one's parent's first cousins are called a father's (mother's) cousin and one's first cousin's children are called cousin's child (son, daughter).

The final dialect to be considered is that of a man from Indianapolis, Indiana and another from Princeton, New Jersey. This dialect is entirely asymmetric, using parent's cousin, grandparent's cousin, etc., when counting upward from ego to the first cousin pair and adding one cousin-unit for each link downward from that pair. First cousin, of course, refers to Q^2P^2, as in all dialects. The child of one's first cousin is called one's second cousin, the child of this person is one's third cousin, etc. One's parent's first cousin is called parent's cousin, one's grandparent's first cousin is called grandparent's cousin, etc. One speaks of a cousin of any type only for a relative of same or lower generation than the propositus. Hence, when there are links both ascending to and descending from the first cousin pair, one must use the relevant ancestral term followed by the appropriately modified cousin term, e. g. my grandfather's second cousin. In the relation diagrammed in Figure 3, x refers to y as his grandfather's third cousin and y refers to x as her grandmother's fourth cousin.

FIGURE 3.   Illustration of a dialect of English cousin terminology.

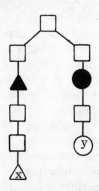

The (Indianapolis) informant for this dialect is quite explicit about the conceptual asymmetry of the notion 'cousin' for him. He says, 'For me, cousin contains a feature "same or younger" [? = same or lower generation].' When I explained to him the operation of the dialects of cousin terminology which I have called major in (7) and (8), he said that they seem silly to him in that, say, a seventh cousin could be several generations above as well as several generations below one. This man's dialect seems quite as bizarre to me as mine, rule (7), does to him, and yet we had previously talked together at length without discovering any semantic differences in our dialects and very likely could have continued to do so virtually indefinitely had I not specifically interviewed him about his cousin terminology. It would seem that with respect to things that people hardly ever talk about any more, such as distant cousins, idiolects may diverge radically without speakers becoming aware of the divergence.[12]

In a very general way, social events seem to be influencing English kinship semantics. The fragmentation of lineage and extended family systems, the reduction to the nuclear family as the only kinship group of any importance, and the loss of important ties between relatives who do not share any nuclear family memberships have led to a general attenuation of fine-grained reckoning of distant relatives. But the particular ways of achieving reduction of the (hypothesized) original system seem to appear in particular families and even particular individuals rather than following lines of geographical, class,

or ethnic cleavage. If my hypothesis is correct that the inclusive
dialect for sibling's-in-law is newer than the exclusive dialect, it
forms an interesting exception to the generalization that newer
terminologies are inevitably reductions of older ones. But it is an
exception that confirms, nevertheless, the two major points (a) that
change is due principally to a social shift to the nuclear family as
the only important kin group throughout most of the English-speaking
world (I exclude consideration of peasant communities for which I
have no data), and (b) that the linguistic changes apparently stemming
from these globally present social forces appear to take place
capriciously so far as sociogeographical subdivisions within the
society are concerned and are best thought of as representing logical
possibilities inherent in the basic system. A closely related view is
expressed by Wallace (1970:844): 'It would appear, furthermore,
that the [American kinship] system is determined in its structure by
its own grammar and thus is related only in the most general way to
variations in customs of kinship behavior'. (I am indebted to John
Atkins for calling Wallace's perspicacious comment to my attention.)
Carden has shown that variable phenomena comparable to those we
have considered at the level of semantics operate also at levels more
traditionally considered syntactic and further, that many of these
phenomena, like those discussed here, show no social or geographical correlation. He assigns such phenomena to 'random dialects',
which term he contrasts with social and geographical dialects, and
proposes

> Any fully satisfactory analysis of a system of randomly distri-
> buted dialects must offer an explanation of how the language
> learners could have constructed different grammars from the
> same data. In other words, the grammars of randomly distri-
> buted dialects should differ only on points that are under-
> determined by the data likely to be available to the language
> learner (Carden 1972:8).

This is substantially the conclusion to which one is forced by independent consideration of semantic data such as those considered here.
    This kind of variation seems to reflect more directly the structural
possibilities inherent in the language than it does social forces such
as emulation of prestigious speakers (Labov 1966:482ff; 1973:84ff).
This unperceived variation cannot serve 'to symbolize the differing
social entities which members may assume' (Blom and Gumperz
1972:421). Finally, if one compares the absence of correlation of
linguistic with social (including geographical) variables found here
for semantic data to the strong sociolinguistic correlations by such
workers as Labov and Gumperz, correlations which appear to

increase in strength with the precision of phonetic detail, one is led
to suspect that the degree of correlation to social variables may
differ on different linguistic levels: the closer to sound, the
greater the extent of social determination of linguistic variation.

Semantics appears to offer different possibilities for mechanisms
of variation and change than does phonology. Whereas all phonetic
habits become rapidly apparent in a small sample of speech, people
can easily maintain different semantic systems and communicate
with each other over long periods of time without becoming aware of
the differences, as long as the differences are in semantic areas
that are infrequently focused on in conversation. That is, some
things are infrequently talked about while there are no such things
as speech sounds infrequently heard or phonological processes
(Stampe 1972) infrequently employed. The English kinship system
appears to have remained remarkably stable over a long time and a
wide geographical area with respect to those central relations and
relatives that everyone continues to talk about. In areas where
people no longer talk about their relatives much any more, great
variation, unpredictable from social factors, is found. [13]

NOTES

1. In this paper I am not concerned with the singulary sex predicates, for the treatment of which see Kay (1973a).

2. For a rigorous presentation of Grafik, see Atkins (1972a, b;
forthcoming); for substantive motivation, see these references and
also Kay (1973a, b).

3. It is occasionally necessary to distinguish in the expression
for the relation itself between a kin relation and its converse (often
called its 'reciprocal' in the anthropological literature). If the converse of a relation R holds between two individuals a, b, in that order,
there are two common ways to express this fact in logic: one is to
permute the argument expressions and write '$R(b, a)$' (or in another
familiar notation 'bRa'), while the second is to alter the symbol expressing the relation and write '$R^{-1}(a, b)$' (alternatively '$aR^{-1}b$'). The
major empirical motivation for distinguishing a relation from its converse in the study of kinship is not, as might be supposed, to provide
distinct underlying semantic representations for such pairs of English words as parent, child which, I believe, may tentatively be considered to derive from a single underlying predicate PARENT-OF
with an argument-permuting transformation (perhaps ultimately re-
latable to passive) operating in the derivation of sentences containing
the morpheme child in superficial structure (Kay 1973a:note 6;
1973b:86ff). Rather, we usually distinguish a kin relation from its
converse so that we may speak of the relation formed by the union of

a relation R and its converse R^{-1}. An example is the relation
sibling-in-law which (in some dialects) is the union of the relation
sibling's spouse and its converse spouse's sibling. In Grafik the
union of a relation R and its converse is designated 'R^ϕ'; i. e.
R^ϕ = df R or R^{-1}.

4. The type of composition of relations involved is not the familiar
relative product but Atkins (1972b) geneaproduct, which has the important additional property that all nodes in the chain are necessarily
distinct (so long as the chain does not contain the identity relation
SELF [P^o, Q^o, M^o]).

5. Atkins' preference for defining the noun phrase my relative
rather than a corresponding predicate would appear to derive from
the emphasis upon superficial structure dictated by the influence of
structural linguistics in anthropological semantics (Kay 1973b).
This seems to complicate matters unnecessarily as the definiens of
(2) is a proper part of the definiens Atkins gives for my relative.
That is, Atkins' definition of my relative is, in fact, built out of the
predicate expression $(M^u Q^\nu P^{\nu+\delta} M^\nu)^\phi$ by the addition of logical
machinery which converts a predicate expression to a special type
of term, suggesting that my relative is, in fact, semantically more
complex than BE-RELATED-TO.

Recent work (e.g. Bach 1968; McCawley 1970) has also produced
a body of evidence and argument of a purely syntactic kind to the
effect that all superficial nouns may be derived from underlying
predicates, singulary or n-ary, and these arguments would appear to
apply with particular force to relational nouns--many of which are
explicitly deverbal in English (e.g. employer, employee < employ).
In many languages (e.g. Seneca) the derivation of kinterms with
superficial nominal properties from verb roots is quite obvious and
explicit (Kay 1973b). Since kinterms are relational nouns par
excellence, if the hypothesis that semantic structure is the same
as underlying syntactic structure is even remotely correct, then we
would predict that kinterms will be derived from underlying verbal
morphemes universally. (Often the source appears to be a conjunction of sentences with a binary and a singulary predicate. Thus,
John's father may come from something like the surface form one who
is parent to John and who is male).

My notation differs trivially from Atkins' in employing the letter Q
for CHILD-OF where he uses a backwards capital 'P'. The absence
of an exponent on a relation symbol 'R' means the same as 'R^1'; or
'R^{+1}' in particular P = P^1, Q = Q^1, M = M^1.

6. The kind of linguistic variation dealt with here differs in
several respects from that considered by workers such as Bickerton,
Gumperz, Labov, Sankoff, and others who have dealt either with
recordings of natural conversations or interviews conducted in

situations which simulate as closely as possible the relevant social conditions of natural conversations. I deal in this paper with acceptability judgments, not with spontaneous speech, thus with reception rather than production and with deliberate rather than spontaneous responses. The kind of variation that Labov and others have treated in the form of variable rules does not arise in this context, since what are taken for data here are judgments by the subject that are invariant for him over time. This method has the weakness of ruling out of the analysis the informant's answers to many of the questions the linguist would like to put to him and about him; it has the counterbalancing advantage of restricting the data in a principled way to portions of people's idiolects which are relatively invariant and hence subject to methods of analysis of conventional kinds.

Of course, if one assumes that a theory of language must be a theory of what speakers actually say, as contrasted, for example, to what they can understand, what they think they say, what they think they ought to say, what they think others say, etc., then unedited recordings of candid conversations are the only linguistic data. I think Chomsky's objections to the view that linguistic theory should be a theory of corpora of actual speech data are fundamentally sound, and one may note the cogency of these objections--which need not be rehearsed here--without adopting any particular version of the distinction between linguistic competence and other factors influencing speech performances. On the other hand, the assumption that carefully considered acceptability judgments, whether those of the linguist himself or of others, furnish direct and error-free access to underlying 'linguistic competence', is not self-evident, though it is frequently taken to be so. Some good results have been achieved using both kinds of data and deriving justification from both kinds of epistemological dogma. Scientists as a rule do better when doing science than when arguing epistemology, and linguists are probably no exception.

I do not wish here to enter an epistemological debate, but only to point out that in speaking of 'variability' I am speaking of variation in the kind of acceptability-judgment data that generative linguists usually work with (e.g. Carden 1970, 1972, 1973), rather than in the sort of live-speech data encountered by those workers sometimes identified as variation theorists or sociolinguists. Discussions of 'linguistic variation' do not always distinguish as carefully as they might these two distinct sorts of data.

7. It might be thought that the difficulties just presented could be avoided by returning to the traditional notion that the semantic content of a lexical item consists of an unstructured set of features (Chomsky 1965:214), but I believe the semantic arguments presented against this view in Kay (1973a) are conclusive. More strictly

syntactic arguments can be adduced, notably in specifying the selection conditions relevant to the lexical insertion of such modifying adjectives as distant or remote as in distant cousin, distant relative, remote ancestor, remote connection (the latter mostly in non-North American dialects of English). If the semantic structure of any underlying consanguineal relation is given by an expression of the form $Q^i P^j$, then the additional part of the semantic structure of the compound expressions with distant, remote, etc., may be naturally represented as roughly 'i+j is a big number'; the semantic problem of specifying their meaning is thus reduced to the general (albeit unsolved) problem of specifying what is meant by the expression big (number). If, however, the meanings of kinship terms are thought to consist of unstructured sets of features, there seems no way of representing what is meant by distant, remote, close, etc. without adding to the componential analysis an ad hoc feature of 'distance' which plays no role other than providing an out for this embarrassment, and which will anyway have to be defined in some form equivalent to the '$Q^i P^j$' notation. Moreover, such a tactic would require positing different definitions for all terms that take such modifiers (e.g. cousin, relative, ancestor) in dialects which differ only by the presence in one of such a modifier, hardly a desirable consequence.

8. Indirect evidence is given by the fact that both the Oxford and Webster's dictionaries give information on cousin consonant with rule (7), while the New Random House Dictionary gives information compatible with rule (8). Webster's also mentions rule (8) type usage preceded by the words 'though these are often called . . .' I am indebted to William Geoghegan for pointing out these facts to me.

9. John Atkins (personal communication) has informed me of another productive cousin dialect lacking 'removed', which, he says, is 'very, very common--more common in my parts of the country I'm sure (Michigan, Philadelphia, Pacific Northwest) than (8) . . . there are [as in (8)] no 'removed's' and every cousin is a (h+k+1)th cousin. This simply incorporates the k (which is really delta) in with the h+1 . . . It simplifies (7) in the obvious way: by coalescing the two relevant kinds of removal distinguished by (7), i.e. generational removal and collateral removal, into one kind, where the "coalescence" is simply addition'. That is, integral (nonremoved) cousins are counted as in (7); the steps of removal are added to the 'cousin number'. For example, a second cousin once removed is a third cousin; a fifth cousin twice removed is a seventh cousin, and so on.

10. But even this exception is subject to qualification. See note 11.

11. I have a report of <u>thirty-second cousin</u> [sic] from two areas of Northeastern United States meaning 'any cousin more distantly related than a second cousin' but without clear indication of homogeneity between informants on what <u>second cousin</u> means.

12. Robert Randall has pointed out to me that the fully productive cousin dialects can be cross-classified according to whether they are or are not symmetric (contain 'reciprocal' usage) and whether or not they contain the concept of 'removal', i. e. generational separation. (By 'fully productive' I mean in this context dialects which provide for the enumeration of an indefinitely large number of cousin relations: <u>first</u>, <u>second</u>, <u>third</u>, . . .). Dialects (7) and (8) and the one mentioned in note 9 are, of course, symmetrical, the former employing 'removal' and the latter two not. The dialect just described is asymmetric and does not contain removal. Randall has discovered an informant (from England) who exemplifies the final logical possibility, an asymmetric dialect with removal. The way this dialect works is illustrated in Figure 3. For this dialect, in Figure 3 person y refers to person x as her <u>third cousin once removed</u>, as would a speaker of dialect (7), but, asymmetrically, person x refers to person y as his <u>fourth cousin once removed</u>. There are two ways in which the logic behind this usage can be conceived: (1) ego calculates, as in dialect (7), the number of his same generation cousin who is either an ancestor or descendant of alter; the number of steps (up or down) between alter and this (real or hypothetical) person is the removal number; (2) the number of steps from ego to a member of the ancestral sibling pair is the number of the cousin, and the generational separation of ego and alter is the removal number.

13. I am indebted to William Geoghegan and Robert Randall for informative discussions regarding these data as well as the general subject of variation in kinship semantics. Randall's unpublished work (n. d.) has been a major impetus for my interest in the subject. I also thank John Atkins for criticism of an earlier version and for many ideas on the subject of kinship in general.

REFERENCES

Atkins, John R. 1972. GRAFIK definitions of English kinterms. Ms.
Atkins, John R. 1974a. On the fundamental consanguineal members and their structural basis. American Ethnologist 1:1-31.
Atkins, John R. 1974b. Consanguineal distance measures: A mathematical analysis. In: Mathematical models of social and cognitive structures. Edited by Paul Ballonoff. University of Illinois Press.
Atkins, John R. 1974c. GRAFIK: A general relational algebra for investigating kinship. In: Genealogical mathematics. Edited by Paul Ballonoff. The Hague: Mouton.

Bach, Emmon. 1968. Nouns and noun phrases. In: Universals in linguistic theory. Edited by E. Bach and R. T. Harms. New York, Holt, Rinehart and Winston.

Blom, Jan-Petter and John J. Gumperz. 1972. Social meaning in linguistic structures: Code-switching in Norway. In: Directions in sociolinguistics. Edited by John J. Gumperz and Dell Hymes. New York, Holt, Rinehart and Winston. 407-434.

Carden, Guy. 1970. A note on conflicting idiolects. Linguistic Inquiry 1. 281-90.

Carden, Guy. 1972. Dialect variation and abstract syntax. In: Some new directions in linguistics. Edited by Roger W. Shuy. Washington, D. C., Georgetown University Press. 1-34.

Carden, Guy. 1973. Disambiguation, favored readings, and variable rules. In: New ways of analyzing variation in English. Edited by Charles-James N. Bailey and Roger W. Shuy. Washington, D. C., Georgetown University Press. 171-182.

Casson, Ronald. 1973. Equivalence rule analysis of American kinship terminology. Anthropological Linguistics 15. 189-202.

Chomsky, Noam A. 1965. Aspects of the theory of syntax. Cambridge, Mass., The M. I. T. Press.

D'Andrade, Roy G. 1970. Structure and syntax in the semantic analysis of kinship terminologies. In: Cognition: A multiple view. Edited by P. Garvin. New York, Sparton Books. 87-144.

Kay, Paul. 1973a. On the form of dictionary entries: English kinship semantics. In: Toward tomorrow's linguistics. Edited by Roger W. Shuy and Charles-James N. Bailey. Washington, D. C., Georgetown University Press. 120-138.

Kay, Paul. 1973b. The generative analysis of kinship semantics: A reanalysis of the Seneca data. Working Papers in Linguistics. University of Hawaii. 5. 79-95.

Labov, William. 1966. The social stratification of English in New York City. Washington, D. C., Center for Applied Linguistics.

Lounsbury, Floyd. 1956. Semantic analysis of the Pawnee kinship usage. Lg. 32. 138-154.

McCawley, James D. 1970. Where do noun phrases come from? In: Readings in English transformational grammar. Edited by R. A. Jacobs and P. S. Rosenbaum. Waltham, Mass., Ginn-Blaisdell. 168-187.

McCawley James D. To appear. Syntactic and logical arguments for semantic structures. Proceedings of the Fifth International Seminar on Theoretical Linguistics. Tokyo, TEC Corp.

Postal, Paul M. 1971. Cross-over phenomena. New York, Holt, Rinehart and Winston.

Randall, Robert. n.d. The semantic systems analysis of kinship terminologies: Some conjectures about psychology and symbol change. Ms.

Schneider, David M. 1968. American kinship: A cultural account. Englewood Cliffs, N.J., Prentice-Hall.

Stampe, David. 1972. A dissertation on natural phonology. Unpublished Ph.D. dissertation. University of Chicago.

Talmy, Leonard. 1972. Semantic structure in English and Atsugewi. Unpublished Ph.D. dissertation. University of California, Berkeley.